D0194810

THE BLOODY SHIRT

OTHER BOOKS BY STEPHEN BUDIANSKY

diansky, Stephen.
e bloody shirt :
rror after Appomattox
08.
3052136832224
                03/20/08

THE BLOODY SHIRT

Terror After Appomattox

STEPHEN BUDIANSKY

VIKING

VIKING
Published by the Penguin Group
Penguin Group (USA) Inc., 375 Hudson Street, New York, New York 10014, U.S.A. • Penguin
Group (Canada), 90 Eglinton Avenue East, Suite 700, Toronto, Ontario, Canada M4P 2Y3
(a division of Pearson Penguin Canada Inc.) • Penguin Books Ltd, 80 Strand, London WC2R
0RL, England • Penguin Ireland, 25 St. Stephen's Green, Dublin 2, Ireland (a division of Pen-
guin Books Ltd) • Penguin Books Australia Ltd, 250 Camberwell Road, Camberwell, Victoria
3124, Australia (a division of Pearson Australia Group Pty Ltd) • Penguin Books India Pvt
Ltd, 11 Community Centre, Panchsheel Park, New Delhi - 110 017, India • Penguin Group
(NZ), 67 Apollo Drive, Rosedale, North Shore 0632, New Zealand (a division of Pearson New
Zealand Ltd) • Penguin Books (South Africa) (Pty) Ltd, 24 Sturdee Avenue, Rosebank, Johan-
nesburg 2196, South Africa

Penguin Books Ltd, Registered Offices: 80 Strand, London WC2R 0RL, England

First published in 2008 by Viking Penguin, a member of Penguin Group (USA) Inc.

1 3 5 7 9 10 8 6 4 2

Copyright © Stephen Budiansky, 2008
All rights reserved

PHOTOGRAPH CREDITS: Insert, page 2 (left), 4 (right), 5 (center): Library of Congress. Page 1
(top): Harvard University Archives, page 1 (bottom) and page 5 (top and bottom): South Caroliniana Library, University of South Carolina, page 2 (right): Sophia Smith Collections, Smith
College, page 3 (right and left): Bentley Historical Library, University of Michigan), page 4
(right): Winthrop University Archives.
Pages 12, 17: Library of Congress. Page 265: South Caroliniana Library, University of South
Carolina.

ISBN 978-670-01840-6
Printed in the United States of America
Designed by Nancy Resnick

Without limiting the rights under copyright reserved above, no part of this publication may be
reproduced, stored in or introduced into a retrieval system, or transmitted, in any form or by any
means (electronic, mechanical, photocopying, recording or otherwise), without the prior written
permission of both the copyright owner and the above publisher of this book.

The scanning, uploading, and distribution of this book via the Internet or via any other means
without the permission of the publisher is illegal and punishable by law. Please purchase only
authorized electronic editions and do not participate in or encourage electronic piracy of copy-
rightable materials. Your support of the author's rights is appreciated.

For Lewis Lord

Contents

THE BLOODY SHIRT

Prologue

The title of this book refers to a small footnote to the brutal war of terrorist violence that was waged in the American South in the years immediately following the Civil War.

The terror began almost as soon as the Civil War ended in 1865; it lasted until 1876, when the last of the governments of the Southern states freely elected through universal manhood suffrage was toppled in a well-orchestrated campaign of violence, fraud, and intimidation—thereby putting an end to Reconstruction, erasing the freedmen's newly won political rights, and securing white conservative home rule to the South for a hundred years to come.

In some ways the small incident in question was no different from thousands of others like it that took place in those years. At ten o'clock on the night of March 9, 1871, a band of 120 men on horseback, disguised, heavily armed, even their horses cloaked in white sheets to conceal any identifiable markings, surrounded the house of one George R. Ross deep in the river-cut country southeast of the town of Aberdeen in Monroe County, Mississippi. Allen P. Huggins, a Northern man who had settled in Mississippi after the war, was staying the night there, and he was awakened by a loud voice calling upon Ross to bring out "the man who was in the house."

Huggins looked out the window and, by the bright moonlight, saw the porch crowded with men in white hoods and robes. They told him that unless he came out to receive their "warning," they would burn the place down.

Ross—"a good, respectable Democrat"—pleaded with Huggins to do as they asked and spare his frightened wife and children. So after securing a promise that "not a hair of your head shall be injured," Huggins agreed to go down to the gate to hear what the men had come to tell him. It was just this. The men—whom Huggins would later describe as "gentlemanly fellows, men of cultivation, well

educated, a much different class of men than I ever supposed I would
meet in a Ku-Klux gang"—did not like his "radical ways," they said.
As superintendent of schools for the county, Huggins had instituted
public schooling, was trying to "educate the negroes," they said. They
had stood it just as long as they were going to. Now he had ten days to
leave—leave the county, leave the state altogether—or be killed.

Huggins replied that he would go when he was good and ready
to go.

So the men marched him down the road, and when they reached a
small hill a quarter of a mile away, one of them came toward him
from where the horses were being held, and in his hand was a stout
stirrup leather. And without any further ceremony, he began beating
Huggins with the stirrup, with all his might.

Then the men took turns, each eager to get his licks in. "They said
they all wanted to get a chance at me," Huggins recalled afterward,
"that I was stubborn, and just such a man as they liked to pound."
Counting aloud each stroke, they stopped after twenty-five and again
asked him if he would leave and again he refused; and so after fifty,
and so after seventy-five, until he was left senseless, more dead than
alive. When he came to, the men trained their pistols on him and repeated their warning, that if any of them laid eyes upon him in ten
days' time, he was a dead man.

And the sequel was this—or at least this was the story everyone in
Monroe County believed, and in time everyone in Mississippi and
the whole South had heard it, too: that a U.S. Army lieutenant who
was stationed nearby recovered the bloody nightshirt that Huggins
had worn that night, and he carried it to Washington, D.C., where he
presented it to Congressman Benjamin F. Butler, and in a fiery speech
on the floor of the United States Congress a few weeks later in which
he denounced Southern outrages and called for passage of a bill to
give the federal government the power to break the Ku Klux terror,
Butler had literally waved this bloodstained token of a Northern
man's suffering at the hand of the Ku Klux. And so was born the
memorable phrase, "waving the bloody shirt."

Waving the bloody shirt: it would become the standard retort, the
standard expression of dismissive Southern contempt whenever a

Northern politician mentioned any of the thousands upon thousands of murders, whippings, mutilations, and rapes that were perpetrated against freedmen and freedwomen and white Republicans in the South in those years. The phrase was used over and over during the Reconstruction era. It was a staple of the furious and sarcastic editorials that filled Southern newspapers in those days, of the indignant orations by Southern white political leaders who protested that no people had suffered more, been humiliated more, been punished more than they had. The phrase has since entered the American political lexicon as a synonym for any rabble-rousing demagoguery, any below-the-belt appeal aimed at stirring old enmities.

That the Southerners who uttered this phrase were so unconcerned about the obvious implications it carried for their own criminality, however, seems remarkable, for whoever was waving the shirt, there was unavoidably, or so one would think, the matter of just whose blood it was, and how it had gotten there. That white Southerners would unabashedly trace the origin of this metaphor to a real incident involving an unprovoked attack of savage barbarity carried out by their own most respectable members of Southern white society makes it all the more astonishing.

Most astonishing of all was the fact that the whole business about Allen Huggins's bloody shirt being carried to Washington and waved on the House floor by Benjamin Butler was a fiction.

The story about Huggins being whipped by the Ku Klux was true enough. Huggins was whipped on that bright moonlit night so ferociously that he could barely walk for a week or two afterward, so ferociously that in a burning anger that overcame any fear of his own death he traveled to Washington to testify before Congress and then returned to Monroe County with a deputy U.S. marshal's badge and a determination to arrest every man he could lay his hands on who had been a part of the reign of Ku Klux murder and terror in those parts. And Benjamin Butler—"Beast Butler," as he was invariably called in the Southern press, the man who had committed the unpardonable insult against Southern womanhood as the Union occupation commander in New Orleans during the war with his order that the next Southern woman who insulted his troops on the street would be "regarded and held liable to be treated as a woman of the town plying her avocation"—this nemesis of the South, now a Republican congressman from Massachusetts, did indeed make a long, impassioned speech about the Ku Klux outrages on the House floor that April, and did tell the story of Huggins's brutal beating in the course of it.

But nowhere in the *Congressional Globe*'s transcripts of every word that was uttered on the House floor is there any allusion to a bloody shirt; nowhere in the press accounts of the leading papers of the time is there any mention of a crazed congressman waving a bloodstained garment, on the floor or off; nowhere in any reports of Huggins's appearances before Congress does such a story appear. That part never happened.

This was not the first time Southerners had invented the fiction that Northerners were given to making fetishes of bloodstained tokens of their victimhood at Southern hands. The same story had cropped up fifteen years earlier in connection with another Massachusetts politician equally reviled in the South, Senator Charles Sumner.

Once again the beating was a fact, the alleged Northern reaction to it a fantasy. Furious at the insult to Southern honor Sumner had committed in a speech attacking slavery and the morality of the slave owner, South Carolina congressman Preston Brooks had approached Sumner in the Senate chamber, stood over his desk, and beat him on the head thirty times with his gold-headed cane until Sumner crumpled to the floor in a pool of his own blood.

And sure enough, Southerners were soon saying that Sumner's bloody coat had become a revered "holy relic" in Yankee and abolitionist circles. Sumner, they said, had carried his own blood-encrusted garment to England to show the Duchess of Argyle, when she invited him to dinner; had placed it in the hands of an awestruck John Brown, before his fateful raid on Harper's Ferry; had put it on public display in Exeter Hall. "All the abject whines of Mr. Sumner, for being well whipped," wrote one Southerner in 1856, a few months after the event, "all the exhibitions of his bloody shirt to stale Boston virgins who, in vexation of having failed to secure a man, would now wed a Sumner, have proved futile." Years later, years after the Civil

War, scornful stories about Northerners exhibiting Sumner's bloody shirt were still being circulated in the South. Not a scrap of it was true.

A footnote, but a telling one. To white conservative Southerners, the outrage was never the acts they committed, only the effrontery of having those acts held against them. The outrage was never the manly inflicting of well-deserved punishment on poltroons, only the craven and sniveling whines of the recipients of their wrath. And the outrage was never the violent defense of "honor" by the aristocrat, only the vulgar rabble-rousing by his social inferior. "The only article the North can retain for herself is that white feather which she has won in every skirmish," declared one Southerner, speaking of the Sumner-Brooks affair. Only a coward would revel in a token of his own defeat.

The bloody shirt perfectly captured the inversion of truth that would characterize the distorted memories of Reconstruction the nation would hold for generations after. The way it made a victim of the bully and a bully of the victim, turned the very act of Southern white violence into wounded Southern innocence, turned the very blood of their African American victims into an affront against Southern white decency; the way it suggested that the real story was not the atrocities white Southerners committed but only the attempt by their political enemies to make political hay out of those atrocities. The merest hint that a partisan motive lay behind the telling of these tales was enough to satisfy most white Southerners that the events never happened, or were exaggerated, or even that they had been conspiratorially engineered by the victims themselves to gain sympathy or political advantage.

If it was incomprehensible to many Northerners, it made perfect sense to those same white Southerners who, on more than one occasion, blamed the "cowardly negroes" for their unmanliness in having permitted themselves to be massacred by bands of armed white men: it only showed, they argued in complete earnest, that black men lacked the Anglo-Saxon virtues indispensable to free men who would exercise the lofty privilege of self-government. Any people who allowed their vote to be taken from them at gunpoint didn't deserve to keep it. (Of course, when African Americans did fight back, the fury of their white assailants knew no bounds.)

One white South Carolinian, of an old aristocratic family, uttered the truth in 1877. From the safety of anonymity, this voice in the wilderness spoke plainly:

> The most horrible tales of negro murders that have ever appeared in radical sheets at the North would pale before the relation of incidents known to every white man in the South. The intimidation of the negroes is a stern and awful fact. Yet what do Southerners say about it? It is the bloody shirt, the lying inventions of unscrupulous politicians, the last gasp of carpet-baggery and radical deviltry. So bitterly do Southerners hate to have the truth come out that it is at the risk of his life that any man dares to speak it. When a political crime is committed, they palliate it, smooth over everything, charge the blame on the murdered victims.

A generation later, a few elder statesmen of the South uttered the truth too. "We had to shoot negroes to get relief from the galling tyranny to which we had been subjected," baldly declared South Carolina's "Pitchfork Ben" Tillman, former governor, current United States senator. He was speaking in 1909 at a reunion of aging "Red Shirts" and white rifle club members who had roamed the state as young men in '76, sixteen-shooter Winchester rifles at their sides and a couple of huge navy pistols stuck in their belts; assassinating African American legislators and town constables, seizing ballot boxes, firing potshots at field hands as a general warning they'd better behave themselves. "It had been the settled purpose of the leading white men," Tillman went on, to "teach the negroes a lesson; as it was generally believed that nothing but bloodshed and a good deal of it could answer the purpose of redeeming the state from negro and carpet bag rule."

Another generation on, in the 1920s, one conservative Southern white historian dared break ranks with the lockstep judgment of his peers and let a bit more of the truth slip out: the 1876 election that had "redeemed" South Carolina, he wrote, "was little more than a ratification of the seizure of power by the rifle clubs in the previous months."

Such gasps of truth were as rare in the South as polar bears, and as out of place. So thoroughly did Southern mythmaking bury the bald facts, turn the blame on the victims, pass off a terrorist coup d'état as an affair of honor, a restoration—a "redemption"—of the South by its "natural leaders," that even today, even after a half century of relentless revision by historians determined to bring out what had been repressed, the truth remains furtive, a sly and scared animal skulking through thickets of deception.

A bald fact: Generations would hear how the South suffered "tyranny" under Reconstruction. Conveniently forgotten was the way that word was universally defined by white Southerners at the time: as a synonym for letting black men vote at all. A "remonstrance" issued by South Carolina's Democratic Central Committee in 1868, personally signed by the leading native white political figures of the state, declared that there was no greater outrage, no greater despotism, than the provision for universal male suffrage just enacted in the state's new constitution. There was but one possible consequence: "A superior race is put under the rule of an inferior race." They offered a stark warning: "We do not mean to threaten resistance by arms. But the white people of our State will never quietly submit to negro rule. This is a duty we owe to the proud Caucasian race, whose sovereignty on earth God has ordained."

"No free people, ever," declared a speaker at a convention of the state's white establishment a few years later, had been subjected to the "domination of their own slaves," and the applause was thunderous. "This is a white man's government" was the phrase echoed over and over in the prints of the Democratic press and the orations of politicians denouncing the "tyranny" to which the "oppressed" South was being subjected.

A bald fact: more than three thousand freedmen and their white Republican allies were murdered in the campaign of terrorist violence that overthrew the only representatively elected governments the

Southern states would know for a hundred years to come. Among the
dead were more than sixty state senators, judges, legislators, sheriffs,
constables, mayors, county commissioners, and other officeholders
whose only crime was to have been elected. They were lynched by
bands of disguised men who dragged them from cabins by night, or
were fired on from ambushes on lonely roadsides, or lured into a bar-
room by a false friend and on a prearranged signal shot so many times
that the corpse was nothing but shreds, or pulled off a train in broad
daylight by a body of heavily armed men resembling nothing so much
as a Confederate cavalry company and forced to kneel in the stubble
of an October field and shot in the head over and over again, at point-
blank.

So saturated is our collective memory with *Gone With the Wind*
stock characters of thieving carpetbaggers, ignorant Negroes, and low
scalawags that it comes as a shock not so much to discover that there
were men and women of courage, idealism, rectitude, and vision who
risked everything to try to build a new society of equality and justice
on the ruins of the Civil War, who fought to give lasting meaning to
the sacrifices of that terrible struggle, who gave their fortunes, ca-
reers, happiness, and lives to make real the simple and long-delayed
American promise that all men were created equal—it comes as a
shock not so much to be confronted by their idealism and courage and
uprightness as by the realization that they were convinced, up to the
very last, that they would succeed. Confident in the rightness of their
cause, backed by the military might of the United States government,
secure in the ringing declarations, now the supreme law of the land
embodied in the Thirteenth, Fourteenth, and Fifteenth amendments
of the Constitution, that not only was slavery dead but that equality
and the right to vote were the patrimony now of all Americans, they
could not imagine that their nation could win such a terrible war and
lose the ensuing peace.

Lose, the nation undeniably did. In 1879, an exhausted Albion
Tourgée, an Ohio-born man who as a state judge in North Carolina
had fearlessly defended the rights of the common man, colored and
white; who had defied Ku Klux threats and the sneers of the conservative bar when he impaneled African Americans on juries and fined

lawyers for saying "nigger" in his courtroom, gave a rueful and weary interview to the *New York Tribune:*

> In all except the actual results of the physical struggle, I consider the South to have been the real victors in the war. I am filled with admiration and amazement at the masterly way in which they have brought about these results. The way in which they have neutralized the results of the war and reversed the verdict of Appomattox is the grandest thing in American politics.

Amazement: because such an outcome was *not* inevitable or foreordained; because, in the end, Reconstruction did not fail, but was overthrown, with impunity and audacity, in one of the bloodiest, darkest, and still least known chapters of American history.

This book tells the stories of a few of the people who lived through that chapter. It does not purport to be anything like a complete history of Reconstruction. It does not pretend to explore, much less analyze, all the political and economic nuances that came to bear on the events of this exceedingly complex period in our nation's history. It does aim to challenge the palliative stereotypes, the exculpatory myths, and the outright bald-faced lies that still characterize far too much of what passes for common knowledge of this era.

As much as possible I have tried to tell the stories of these people through their own words—through the letters they wrote to friends and lovers, the reports they dutifully filed, the testimony they gave, the remembered conversations they set down in their diaries and memoirs—and through other contemporary sources such as newspapers, pamphlets, and speeches that give voice to the mood and spirit of the times. For helping me find these original sources I am deeply indebted to the women and men who staff the archives of this great nation; their unfailing professionalism, courtesy, eagerness to assist, and love of history and the truth remains an inspiration to us all. I would like to thank in particular the staffs of the South Caroliniana Library, the South Carolina Department of Archives and History, the Mississippi Department of Archives and History, the Sophia

Smith Collection at Smith College, the Duke University Special Collections Library, the National Archives, the University of Virginia Special Collections Library, and the South Carolina State Library.

My research of the papers of Adelbert and Blanche Butler Ames at Smith College was supported by the Caroline D. Bain scholar-in-residence fellowship, for which I would like to formally express my sincere gratitude here. I would also like to express my special thanks to an extraordinary local historian, Peter Hughes, who showed me around the lost site of Hamburg, South Carolina, and could not have been more generous with his time and expertise.

In the letters I have quoted I have frequently made excisions for conciseness and clarity. In doing so I have been extremely careful never to alter the original meaning, but have also refrained from burdening the printed page with ellipsis marks that are more appropriate to a scholarly journal than to a work of popular history. I have provided full references to the originals for anyone who wishes to consult them. I know some will object to this practice, but I was guided in part by the words of Carl Sandburg, who, in the introduction to his still wonderful biography of Abraham Lincoln, said he still sometimes regretted including all those three dots.

The quoted dialogue that appears is all taken directly from contemporary sources; I have not attempted any reconstructions myself.

In the milieu of the 1860s and 1870s that I have attempted to bring to life in the following pages, "black" could be as offensive a term as "nigger," and "African American" was a term as yet unknown. "Negro" and "colored" were the standard and respectful terms then, and though they may sound quaint or even patronizing to our ears today, I have chosen to employ them as being true to the spirit of the day.

I

"I THOUGHT THE SOUTH WANTED
IT TO END THERE"

Charleston after the war.

1

Piles of shattered glass lay thick on the streets of ruined Charleston; grass and even small shrubs grew unmolested in its untraveled thoroughfares.

To walk the lower half of the town was to walk a city of the dead. The grand houses along Meeting Street stood deserted, as they had for the better part of two years. Their owners had fled, first from the Yankee shells and mortars, then from the coming of the Yankees themselves.

Vandals and neglect had done what bombardment alone never could. Gardens gave themselves up to thickets of vines so rank and impenetrable that they might, said one Charleston lady, have guarded Sleeping Beauty's castle. Chimneys and archways lay tumbled into mounds of brick; columns leaned or reposed on their sides; piazzas sagged or gave way altogether. The floors of once elegant drawing rooms and dining chambers were awash in seas of plaster, lath, and the splinters of ornately carved and molded wood that once adorned mantelpieces and door frames.

The tall spire of St. Michael's Church, painted black to make it harder for the Union gunners out beyond the harbor to use as an aiming point, presided funereally over the whole desolated lower city. The congregations of Charleston's high-steepled churches had braved the bombardment for a while. But when shells began shattering headstones in the churchyards hard by, then actually passing through chancels and smashing organs in one church after another, the faithful made arrangements to pray for God's protection of the Southern Confederacy prudently out of range of the Union artillery.

It was the fires, though, that had done the worst. The fire of 1861, at the very end of the first year of the war, had turned into a maelstrom, and blocks upon blocks were burned to the foundations. Here and there a noble flight of stone steps remained, incongruously mounting from

the street to nowhere, or an ornamental iron paling stood ceremoniously enclosing nothing but a mound of rubble. Elsewhere, the city
seemed simply to have vanished. The two great halls where the Ordi-
nance of Secession had first been voted upon, and then signed, had
gone up in the flames, and were no more.

The cause of the fire was probably accident rather than malice. But
war and flight, and vandalism and neglect, had made rebuilding
impossible, and so every bit of damage remained frozen in place and
time, a cumulative tally of the afflictions of wartime.

Then the steady rain of Union shells the last year and a half of the
war, and bands of incendiary-minded boys playing in the ruins of
shadowy warehouses, had set fire upon further fire. It fell to the city's
ten companies of free colored firemen to save what was left of the
town, night after night.

But no human agency was equal to the final catastrophe as the city
fell to its besiegers. The last Confederate defenders of the city, as they
fled on a February night in the last tumultuous months of the war, put
the torch to the Ashley River bridge and the railroad depot, set ablaze
bales of cotton that had been stacked in the main squares, blew up
guns and powder to keep them from falling into enemy hands. Soon a
fire cut across the entire peninsula on which the great city of Charleston lay.

The first Union soldiers to arrive the next morning were the Twenty-
first U.S. Colored Troops, most of them former slaves. Their commander formally demanded and received the surrender of the city from
the mayor; the troops marched up ruined Meeting Street banners flying,
then labored for days putting out the blazes. The white Charleston-
ians, whose property they toiled to save, sullenly looked on.

A month later, there amid the ashes of the Confederacy's birthplace,
amid the shards of broken glass heaped upon the streets so fine and
deep that they looked like piles of diamonds discarded by some mad
and profligate potentate, amid the wreckage of a genteel civilization of
leisurely meals and lingering after-dinner cigars and pleasant evening
drives and vivacious conversation and lazy afternoons on sun-dappled
piazzas—a civilization based on that seemingly inescapable law of hu-

man affairs that "the most exquisite happiness shall be founded on the intensest misery of others," in the later rueful acknowledgment of one of the most privileged and self-critically honest of South Carolina aristocrats—it was there, amid the sneers and gloom of the vanquished who more typically lacked any such self-knowledge, that the most extraordinary celebration Charleston would ever see took place.

The war was not yet over. In just two weeks towns across the North would ring out with celebrations of Lee's surrender at Appomattox, but for now such a swift closure to five years of brutal fighting was an end not even to be hoped for. In three weeks those same towns would be draped in black in stunned mourning of Lincoln's death, an end not even imaginable.

But in Charleston on the rainy Tuesday noontide of March 21, 1865, a celebration of patriotic joy in the victory already gained, and of faith in the unknowable future, was getting under way on the glass-strewn, grass-filled streets of that ruined city.

Although they had had but two days to plan for it, four thousand colored men, women, and children—some just freed from the bondage of chattel slavery, some members of Charleston's almost aristocratic population of light-skinned free Negroes (some of them actually slave owners themselves), others wearing the blue uniform of the United States Army—crowded into Citadel Square.

At two o'clock the procession began. Two colored marshals on horseback led the way, wearing rosettes of red, white, and blue. Behind them came the Twenty-first Regiment, turned out in almost full force, marching smartly in step to the music of its regimental band. As the American flag passed by, the crowds of colored spectators lining the streets broke into cheers of wild enthusiasm, waving hats and handkerchiefs. Carriages bearing the Union generals in command of the occupation troops had to be halted frequently to receive the applause of the spectators.

Behind the soldiers came a company of schoolboys bearing a banner with the legend WE KNOW NO MASTERS BUT OURSELVES. Then a "car of Liberty," drawn by black horses, strewn with banners and streamers, on which were seated thirteen pretty young colored girls, each dressed in white, each representing one of the original thirteen states. Then eighteen hundred colored schoolboys and schoolgirls, their white teachers walking with them, the children carrying mottoes saluting the "heroes of the war" and declaring WE KNOW NO CASTE OR COLOR.

The free colored men of Charleston were represented by company upon company of tradesmen bearing the emblems of their trades: butchers with their knives, tailors with their shears, coopers with hoops; blacksmiths, wheelwrights, carpenters, sawyers, sailors, painters, barbers, newspaper carriers, firemen in their red shirts.

But most daring of all were the floats mocking, scorning, deriding slavery, and fairly gloating over the justice that its demise had come about from a war begun right there in Charleston with the firing on Fort Sumter almost exactly four years to the day, intended to ensure its perpetuation. First a mule pulled a cart on which a small boy energetically rang a bell and a sign declared A NUMBER OF NEGROES FOR SALE. A man playing the part of a slave auctioneer kept up a realistic patter, hawking the two women seated on a block next to him and their children standing by, cajoling the crowd for extravagant bids—in Confederate dollars—as he assured all hearers what excellent cooks or seamstresses or field hands they would make. A long rope trailed behind, to which more men and women were tied.

But this was followed by a hearse bearing a coffin: the coffin of slavery, suitably inscribed:

SLAVERY IS DEAD
WHO OWNS HIM? NO ONE
SUMTER DUG HIS GRAVE ON THE 13TH OF APRIL, 1861

Mourners dressed in deep black followed mock solemnly on foot.

The entire procession, three miles long, wound its way through all the main streets of the lower part of town, from the Citadel on south. "Throughout the march they observed good order," noted the *New York Times* correspondent who was on hand, "and showed by their joyful countenances that they thoroughly appreciated the improved change" of their condition. "Charleston never before witnessed such a

The graves of 257 Union prisoners at Charleston's Washington Race Course.

spectacle as that presented on Tuesday," he continued. "Of course, the innovation was by no means pleasing to the older residents, but they had sense enough to keep their thoughts to themselves. The only expression of dislike I heard uttered proceeded from a knot of young ladies standing on a balcony, who declared the whole affair was 'shameful,' 'disgraceful.'"

A month later an even larger outpouring of Charleston's colored population gathered for a more solemn ceremony. During the last year of the war the Confederate command in Charleston had used the Washington Race Course and Jockey Club, a horse-racing track just beyond the city's limits, as a prison for captured Union soldiers. They had dropped like flies there. Where the planter aristocracy had once gathered to watch their fine thoroughbreds run, the Union prisoners languished without shelter from sun or weather, malnourished, more than half-starved, disease-wracked. The wooden headboards that marked where the bodies had been dumped, coffinless, in shallow mass graves dug in a pasture behind the judge's stand, bore nothing but numbers. On the first was written "No. 1"; on the last, "No. 257."

In the center of the race course the ditches the prisoners had hacked out to try to divert the rainwater from their beds of bare earth were still visible. Tracks of grazing horses and cattle crisscrossed the red-clay mounds of the graves. Silently, the colored people nearby had watched the suffering and death of the Northern prisoners; quietly now, in the month of April 1865, twenty-eight men from one of Charleston's Negro churches began erecting a ten-foot-high fence around the burial place, clearing away the weeds, tidying the gravesites into neat rows. When they were done they whitewashed the fence boards and painted in black letters over the gateway arch MARTYRS OF THE RACE COURSE.

On the morning of May 1—May Day—ten thousand men, women, and children made the pilgrimage to the burial ground. Though they could scarcely know or imagine it, their act of homage was soon to be imitated across the country, the annual May ritual of decorating soldiers' graves that would come to be called Decoration Day, Memorial Day.

Carrying bouquets of roses, three thousand colored schoolchildren sang "John Brown's Body" as they marched from the race course in-field to the gate of the graveyard, then silently placed their flowers on the graves. They then went to the fields nearby and sang "America," "The Star-Spangled Banner," and "Rally 'Round the Flag." The women and men followed solemnly with more flowers, until the en-tire burying ground was a solid carpet of blossoms, not a speck of bare earth to be seen.

2

In September of that year of hope and of the future, 103 leading col-ored men of Charleston met. They drafted a petition, affixed their names to it, and delivered it to the leading white men of South Caro-lina's ancien regime, meeting then in convention assembled at Co-lumbia, entrusted with the task of drafting a new constitution that would guide their defeated state from secession to reunion, from slav-ery to whatever would come after.

"We are well aware that to some members of your honorable body," the colored petitioners cautiously began, "it may seem little short of presumption in us, thus to knock at the door of your Convention, with the request that, in its deliberations, we shall be recognized as a component part of the State."

But those "who give us credit for thinking at all," they hastened to continue, cannot deny that the fundamental "interests and affections" of the free colored man were no different from those of the free white man. Both were inseparably woven into the welfare of the state. Both alike shared a stake in its future prosperity. Apart from "the abstract justice of the thing itself," the "perfect equality of all men *before the Law*" was practical common ground on which both could stand re-gardless of any seeming antagonisms that might exist between the two classes of men.

And so 103 colored men of Charleston respectfully asked that "no clause shall be inserted" into the new constitution "which will debar any man from exercising the rights or privileges of citizenship because of the color of his skin."

Walking a tightrope between humility and pride, they continued:

> We know the deplorable ignorance of the majority of our people; we also are sensible of the deficiencies of those among us who have acquired some degree of education; and we ask not at this time that the ignorant shall be admitted to the exercises of a privilege which they might use to the injury of the State.

> But we do ask that if the ignorant white man is allowed to vote, that the ignorant colored man shall be allowed to vote also. We would be unmanly and uncandid did we not avow our intense joy at the course of events, which struck from our limbs the chains of slavery, but we would be equally unmanly and uncandid did we not express our sorrow that freedom for us and our race is accompanied by the ruin of thousands of those for whom, notwithstanding the bitterness of the past, and of the present, we cherish feelings of respect and affection. And we can assure your honorable body that such recognition of our manhood, as this petition asks for, is all that is needed to convince the colored people of this State, that the white men of the State are prepared to do them justice.

> Let us also assure your honorable body that nothing short of this, our respectful demand, will satisfy our people.

> If our prayer is not granted, there will doubtless be the same quiet and seeming patient submission to wrong that there has been in the past. We can bide our time. The day for which we watched & prayed came when we least expected it; the day of our complete enfranchisement will also come; and in that faith we will work and wait.

> We fully understand what prejudices & preconceived opinions must be overcome before our prayers can be granted; but we try to believe that the people of South

Carolina are capable of rising superior to the prejudices of habit and education; and buoyed up by this hope we respectfully ask that our prayer may be granted and we will ever pray.

They might have been calling across a sea for all their voices were heard.

"It is understood," reported the *Charleston Daily Courier* a few days later, and one could almost hear the sniff, "that a number of negroes in Charleston city have prepared a memorial, which they have requested to be presented to the Convention by a delegate from that place, in which they claim it to be the duty of the State to extend to them equal political rights and privileges. We trust for the future safety and welfare of the State that the document will not be placed on the records of the proceedings. It cannot but be the earnest desire of all members that the matter be ignored *in toto* during the session." The next day the convention voted that the petition from the colored citizens of Charleston be "laid on the table" without being read.

It was a cozy, comfortable club of familiars who met in Columbia.

The delegates to the convention included twelve men who had served as delegates to South Carolina's secession convention in 1860. Among them were the secession convention's president and the man who had introduced the motion for secession. Several ex-Confederate generals, an ex-Confederate senator, and South Carolina's first Confederate governor were present too.

So was the state's provisional governor, Benjamin F. Perry; he was a prewar Unionist who had opposed secession for fear it would endanger slavery, but then had rallied to the Confederate cause and served in South Carolina's Confederate legislature. Expecting stern terms from the federal government, Perry had been pleasantly surprised when President Johnson gave him the appointment as provisional governor and made clear he intended to leave the job of organizing the new state governments entirely in the hands of what white Southerners liked to call "the natural ruling element" of their society; the president asked Perry just to "write occasionally" and let him know how he was "getting on in reconstructing the state."

The new governor's first official act was to issue a proclamation reappointing all Confederate officials to the positions they had held in the state government at the time of the surrender.

In his opening address to the convention Perry made quick work of the freedmen. It was the delegates' unavoidable duty, he instructed them, "however painful it may be," to adopt a declaration affirming that slavery will never again exist within the borders of the state. "African slavery, which was a cherished institution of South Carolina from our earliest colonial history," he said, "is gone, dead forever," abolished by the war-making powers of the United States military authorities; it was likely that three quarters of the states would soon ratify the Thirteenth Amendment, thereby making abolition the supreme law of the land; it was a necessary condition for South Carolina's readmission to the Union that their state include a like declaration in their state's new constitution. "Until this is done, we shall be kept under military rule, and the negroes will be protected as 'freedmen' by the whole military force of the United States."

But to be no longer a slave in no way made the Negro a citizen, Perry hastened to add. The radicals in the North, who were already saying that there should be no distinction between voters on account of color, "forget that this is a white man's government, intended for white men only," Perry said. To speak of extending political equality to the Negro was nothing but "folly and madness."

A few months later it had become "folly, injustice, and madness."

"The African has been, in all ages, a savage or a slave," Perry declared. "God created him inferior to the white man in form, color, and intellect, and no legislation or culture can make him his equal. You might as well expect to make the fox the equal of the lion in courage and strength, or the ass the equal of the horse in symmetry and fleetness. His color is black; his head covered with wool instead of hair, his form and features will not compare with the Caucasian race, and it is in vain to think of elevating him to the dignity of the white man.

"God has created a difference between the two races, and nothing can make him equal."

The voices of the freedmen might have been calling across a sea as wide as the one their forebears were carried over.

3

Two letters from South Carolina that turbulent first year of peace: the one from a prominent landowner, the other from a Union general, a hundred miles and a world apart.

Aiken Oct 14th '65

Dear Sir:

With great diffidence and some hesitation I venture to enclose you certain propositions relative to the negro-discipline and negro-labor questions, which have occurred to me, and impressed me as essential to the preservation of our labor system, and, indeed, of our social system. As one of the Commission appointed to suggest such laws as are advisable for the regulation and for the protection of the negro, I venture to submit these propositions to your consideration.

I suppose it will be conceded, even by those who have least sympathy for the negro, and who in the past have had least confidence in the wisdom of the institution of slavery, and have been most doubtful of the benefits it has conferred, that the sudden entire overthrow of that system which has taken place is unwise, injurious, and dangerous to our whole system, pecuniary and social. To those who are of this way of thinking (and I scarcely think there are many in the State of any other way of thinking, except Mr. Benjamin F. Perry of Greenville), it must follow as a natural sequence, it appears to me, that, sudden and abrupt abolition having taken place by the force of arms, it should be to the utmost extent practicable be limited, controlled, and surrounded with such safeguards, as will make the change as slight as possible both to the white man and to the negro, the planter and the workman, the capitalist and the laborer. In other words, that the general interest both of the white man and of the negro requires that he should be kept as near to his former condition as Law can keep him and that he should be kept as near to the condition of slavery as possible, and as far from the condition of the white man as is practicable.

If you agree with me in these premises, I trust we shall not differ much in the conclusion—namely, as to what Laws are necessary to effect this end.

I know that there are those who look to getting rid of the negro entirely, and of resorting to white labor. I regard this idea as the mere infatuation of men who are at their wits' end. For in all of the cotton states all of the <u>good</u> lands are so malarious in the fall of the year as to render it impracticable for white men to labor under our suns. We must face the question—negroes must be made to work, or else cotton and rice must cease to be raised for export.

Your obt sevt
Edmund Rhett

Enclosure—

1st   An Act prohibiting all <u>Freedmen,</u> or persons of African descent made free by Act of the Convention in September last, from ever holding, or owning <u>Real Estate</u> in South Carolina, or their posterity after them. An act of this sort is essential in order to uproot the idea which has now run the negroes crazy all over this state—namely that they are all to have 40 acre lots of their own. Let the idea of their ever owning land pervade amongst them, and they will never work for the white man, or upon any land but their own. The Act is essential because it will at once cut off all competition between the white and the black man. The black man must then forever labor upon the capital of the white man, and the white man must take care of him, or else he will soon have no labor. I regard it as the most vital Law that can be made for our future prospering.

2nd   a stringent Act against vagrancy on the part of the Freedmen of African descent. A Law requiring each negro, in each district to have a recorded domicile which it shall be unlawful for him to leave without due notice given to some appointed magistrate; or without twelve months notice of the fact, and the place to which he intends to move; or some other restriction as to the method of his movements. Also requiring him to show that he is in the lawful employ of some white man. For the violation of such restrictions as these, or such other restrictions as may be deemed expedient, let the vagrant negro be taken up and put to hard labor upon public works in chain gangs, such as the repairing and building high roads, and the paving and cleaning of streets, for not less than 60 days at one time; and then to be returned to his locality.

The object of this Law would be to give fixedness to this population and to prevent their eternal wanderings and floating about the state from one point to another, lazy, lawless, thieving and vagrandizing.

3rd   An Act to enforce the fulfillment of contracts between the employer and the employee of freedmen—an Act by which the negro will be held both as a vagrant and a criminal should he leave the service of his employer until the term of the contract is fulfilled—by which he may be seized and put to hard labor for vagrancy, and 2) also be made to pay the planter the value of his wages for all the time of his contract not yet expired. The Law should be as stringent as words can make it to force the negro to work, and as penal as humanity would permit.

4th   an act to regulate discipline. It is essential that there should be some system of discipline on larger plantations. Both under the apprentice system, and under the coolie system, some corporal punishment is found necessary on the part of the employer. It strikes me that, considering the prejudice prevalent against whipping, the negro should be put on the footing of an enlisted soldier; that only such punishment as is customary in the Army towards white men, should be allowed towards the negro by the employer; that the employer should have the same power given to him as is given by the Articles of War to the commander of a garrison exclusive of the court martial. These powers it would be safe to give, and some must be given. It cannot be said to be cruel, for every white man in the Army of the United States lives under it.

Here, under these four propositions, we have the negro, first, put upon the footing of a denizen. He can own no Real Estate—the soil is out of his reach. Then we have him located, and prevented from vagrandizing. Then we compel him to keep his contracts. Then we control him, and keep him under good discipline. Under these Laws, he must labor faithfully according to the laws of demand and supply, or else he must leave the state.

I do not conceive it impracticable to pass such Laws. Of course this is no time to do it. The question should not be broached until we are back in the Union. If it is now broached, it will only strengthen the Black Republican Party, and render the admission of the State difficult. After we are admitted, I believe there will be little difficulty. The Administration will support us.

———•———

Charleston, S.C.
April 4th, 1866

Lieutenant

In obedience to verbal instruction from the Major General Comdg Dept. I submit the following report of what I consider to be the condition of affairs in the Western Military Dist. of this state. Since the early part of last Sept. I have commanded that Military Dist. with my Hd. Qs. at Columbia. During this period of time I have had ample opportunities for studying the public sentiment. The passion and prejudices of the various communities have been displayed in most unequivocal manner not only by word but by deeds. Provisional Gov. Perry reinstated all the civil officers of the state without distinction. The men who held these offices during the rebellion were generally the most radical. By this stroke of the pen the political machinery of the state was put into the hands of the most objectionable persons to our Government. As a consequence the moderate and well wishing became powerless. . . .

I could record here many acts done by this people which would make more clear what I am now discussing, and perhaps cause a conviction which every day of the last several months has strengthened in me.

I will however refer for a moment to the treatment our uniform has received since I came here, five of my men have been killed; a number wounded and many fired upon. Before I came an officer and a small number of men were killed. With one exception (which when the facts appear is no exception) no effort has been made by the citizens to bring the offenders to justice, or assist the military authorities. On the other hand guerillas and outlaws receive the kindest attention from the residents.

My reports as to the condition of the freed people contain all I would say in the subject. The outrages upon them which have been reported speak more effectually than anything else possibly can. As with my soldiers who have been killed and wounded no effort is made by citizens to protect the freedman or punish those who trespass upon his rights or assist us in punishing them. The condition of the freedman is simply this, so long as he is subordinate after the manner of a slave and not of a freedman, and does as well he is safe from violence; but when he attempts to depart from his old discipline and assert a single privilege he meets opposition, and in localities is punished with death. This results from the fact that many especially the ignorant can see in the negro only the slave.

It is my opinion that the time has not yet arrived when a northern man can live in the western part of this state in security should the troops be withdrawn. Even though U.S. forces are here it will be seen by the action of the people of Edgefield that a northern man cannot live there.

From various sources I have gathered facts which force me to the conclusion that my command is the most turbulent and disloyal of any east of the Mississippi River.

    I have the honor to be
        Very Respectfully
           Your obdt. servt.
            A. Ames
            Bvt. Maj. Genl. Comdg. Military Dist.
            Western S.C.

4

As a journalist, John Richard Dennett had written nothing to speak of before, and would write nothing to speak of again. But he had an eye like a camera's lens for detail and an ear like a musician's for the nuances and inflections of human speech. To these qualities were added an open mind and an honest curiosity, a law student's tenacity, and a young man's endurance.

In June of 1865, he boarded a New York steamer bound for Richmond, Virginia. Twenty-six years old, born in Canada, educated at Harvard College, Dennett had been "selected for his work with some care" by the editors of a newly launched magazine, *The Nation*. Northerners had only the vaguest sense of the true condition of the defeated South, or the mood of its people. Dennett was to travel the Southern states for eight months and find out what things were like. "His letters will appear every week," explained *The Nation*'s editors, "and he is charged with the duty of simply reporting what he sees and hears, leaving the public as far as possible to draw its own inferences." Dennett's reports were titled "The South As It Is."

From City Point, Virginia, where the James River abruptly narrows, a small river boat carried him to Richmond past the hulks of sunken ships and ruined bridges.

In Richmond he found cannonballs littering the streets and half the city subsisting on rations furnished by the United States authorities. During the war, shortages of staples had sent prices galloping. Now the shops were full of merchandise, flour, and meat, prices were down, but no one had money to buy.

A Northern Christian aid society, flying one of the few United States flags to be seen in the city, set up a tent in Capitol Square and handed out tickets for soup and flour. It also distributed garden seeds and tools to farmers whom the war had ruined. Their individual tales of woe were recorded in the account books of the society in the laconic detached prose of the professional charity giver. "G—— M—— has a wife and nine children; owns and cultivates six acres of land; has now a borrowed horse and plough, and no farming implements of his own." "W—— C—— owns a hundred acres, and cultivates forty-five; borrows a horse; all the implements on his place destroyed by General Butler's army; and he has nothing left but his farm." "Mrs. M—— C—— owns a hundred and fifty acres of land, has twenty-five under cultivation; hires a horse and cart from Negroes; has no implements left that can be used; has not a dollar."

A ruined railway carried the traveler no faster than a man could walk from south of Richmond to Lynchburg. The two passenger cars were decorated with painted Confederate flags and covered with the yellow-red mud of the land. Window frames were boarded up over long-vanished panes, a few tufts of horsehair and red plush offered the only reminders of seat cushions.

Every few hours the train would halt where a lonely country road crossed the line, a few passengers would get on or off, and a dozen or more Negroes, a few men in Confederate gray, and a few white women would appear hawking food and cigars to the travelers. Apples and peaches, ten cents a dozen. "A right good snack," cornbread and a leg of fowl, or a piece of bread, three fried eggs, and a slice of ham, bound up in a compact parcel, for a quarter. There were few takers. A crippled Negro man offered cider from a jug with a cornstalk stopper, his customers drinking from an old tinned-salmon can.

Where the railroad crossed a creek over a high, twelve-hundred-foot-long trestle, the passengers got out; the far end had been destroyed by Lee's men as they retreated before Sheridan's army. For a dollar, a wagon carried a traveler and his trunk over a low bridge of logs to a train waiting for them on the other end to continue the journey. In the open wagon in which Dennett rode an old man from North Carolina sat silently upon a coffin of rough boards holding the body of his son. Two wounded Confederate soldiers shared his grim seat.

At the connecting train the passengers waited two hours in the heat of a fierce afternoon sun. At last the conductor turned to the engineer and said, "Well, Oscar, reckon we'd better go." And the train began its slow crawl onward.

It was a rough, often unreal journey. In southern Virginia, Dennett rode horseback through forested tracks for hours, encountering no one. Fearful he had lost his way, he stopped to study a signpost and found it covered with penciled notes left by traversing armies and more recent passersby: "B.C., Captain Wofford's Georgians will go by way of the Court-House"; "Captain Williams—Charlotte Battery—we will go through Pittsylvania C.H."; "Jack, go the road with the pine branch"; "W.H.B., Raleigh, N.C., gone along April 5, 1865."

In the Unionist strongholds of North Carolina's poor hill country he came upon a white woman and a little girl gathering sticks and rotten wood by the roadside and stopped to inquire of his way, and he jotted down in his notebook afterward their wondering reaction to this apparition from a world beyond their ken.

"Mister, whar be ye frum?" the woman asked, looking hard at him.

"I'm from the North."

"The North! Be you a—one o' them—what they call Yankees? Don't be offended, gentleman, that's what they calls 'em; be you a Yankee?"

"I suppose I must be."

"Excuse me, gentleman, but I must look at you, fur I heerd so much about the Yankees and I niver seed one yit. Lord! Lord! A ra'al Yankee! Maria, he looks most like our folks, don't he? He sartin do. Well, I must praise the Yankees if they looks like you. Maria, don't they look right nice?"

He made a point of traveling to cities and country towns, plantations and backwoods, paths beaten and unbeaten. In the country he put up for the night in taverns that were little more than farmers' houses that took in travelers once in a while, angular farm women or broken-down former slaves waiting at table, sometimes putting out nothing but a plate of cornbread and a jug of buttermilk for supper. At some houses to which he had been directed he would ride up, tie up his horse, wait for hours for a sign of life or recognition.

A man dozed in the afternoon sun at the hall door of one, an empty pipe in his mouth, an old upturned hat by his feet that had obviously been used as a spittoon, mumbling something. "Never heed, old man's been drinking apple brandy," said his wife. "Walk into the parlor." Dinner that night was accompanied by the drone of an unintelligible song from the hallway.

At a log cabin he had called at to try to buy some feed for his horse, he found a pipe-smoking widow, spinning cotton at a wheel, who insisted he must be a preacher or a doctor, for no one else she had ever seen traveled with saddlebags like his. One of the half-dozen small and noisy children playing on the floor amused herself by putting the saddlebags on her back and crawling across the floor declaring she was "the preacher's hoss."

In Greensboro he was outrageously overcharged, six dollars and a quarter a day, for a mean hotel room, meager board, and, for his horse, the use of a small bare yard that lacked so much as the shade of a tree for shelter from sun and rain. The night it rained a deluge came through the roof boards into his room and soaked his bed through.

In South Carolina he rode through endless pine barrens on a stagecoach whose driver muttered imprecations at every "Damned Yankee wagon" he met, giving them as little of the road as possible, fixing each oncoming teamster with a long stare, duly returned.

By the side of the railway late one misty December moonlit night, where his train halted for a layover and the passengers bedded down as best they could for a few uncomfortable hours of sleep, he had wandered restlessly about and come upon a makeshift Negro camp nearby. Bags of corn and groundnuts tied up in sheets lay amid a jumble of salvaged possessions. Small fires burned in front of huts covered with canvas or rusty sheets of iron taken from the wrecks of locomotives Sherman's men had left behind. An old colored woman sat by one of the fires.

"You're sitting up late."

"Who for watch de tings, mawssa, ef we sleep? Who for watch my leel corn and grun-nut? Tell er, mawssa, 'bleeged to sit up late, 'less dey be gone 'fore day, clean."

"You've got a good deal of corn, have you?"

"Got not but tree peck. Dat's my sheer when dey sheered. Dunno ef I has tree peck."

"Is that what you've got to keep you next year?"

"Dat leel bit o' corn keep me! Can't. Not ef I was to eat it by grains."

On a steamboat to New Orleans, a handsome young mulatto man, fashionably dressed, fluent in French and English, deftly tended the bar for a steady stream of elegant Southern gentlemen customers through the afternoon and evening. Much of the talk was of the opportunities to be had in Mexico.

At a boardinghouse in Alabama the lady who sat next to him each night at the dinner table threatened her child that the Yankees would get him if he didn't behave.

In Louisiana he decided to walk the hundred miles from New Orleans to Baton Rouge, sent his valise and overcoat on by express, asked after the road, and was met by incredulous stares. No one went by land, they told him, they took the boat. And finally they directed him to the levee of the Mississippi River.

He walked mile after monotonous mile on the raised bank, an endless green ribbon beside the mile-wide yellow stream, the spring of sodden grass and clover beneath his feet, the glimpse of spreading live oaks and large white houses on the bank beyond.

He spent a night among the Creoles, who made a bed for him on two benches in the billiard room of their village coffeehouse, and fell asleep to the sound of his landlord's voice reading aloud to his wife from *Les Trois Mousquetaires*.

At lunch the next day, still among the Creoles, at a shop where he stopped to buy bread and cheese, he was an object of sympathy and curiosity as he had been nowhere else in his travels in the South. A half-dozen men clustered around him, asking questions through the one who knew English and acted as interpreter. Perhaps he was out of his work, and was seeking for a place? Perhaps he was a schoolmaster? Perhaps there was something wrong? Oh no, not that he was not all right. But a man, traveling on foot, by himself. Was there no trouble, no sweetheart?

And everywhere he went he listened, and recorded, and gently probed.

At the very start of his journey, on a steamer to Norfolk, he had sat on deck and struck up a conversation with a "Mr. K——," a Virginia planter.

Mr. K—— farmed fifteen hundred acres in Amelia County, about forty miles from Richmond; that country had mostly been spared the ravages of the war; farm equipment and labor was available; the wheat crop was already gathered and had done well; the oats were coming along and promising to be well above average. The tobacco should have gone in in February, but things were too uncertain then; corn should have gone in in April, but everyone was paying too much attention to Lee's evacuation of Richmond. Still, it should be a good year.

But his 115 slaves had mostly left him. "When the city was evacuated, of course, they heard that they were free. Well, sir, out of more than a hundred servants that were on my place on the first of April, I haven't six left," the planter complained. "They went, and I have been working my crop with Negroes that I have hired, and I suppose somebody else has hired mine."

"The Negro, I sincerely hope, may disappoint my expectations," he continued. "But if he does not, he is doomed to undergo extinction. Less than a hundred years of freedom will see the race practically exterminated. The Negro will not work more than enough to supply his bare necessities. There isn't a county in Virginia where we haven't had some hundreds of free Negroes, and they have always been perfectly worthless and lived in wretchedness. But the Negro will always need the care of someone superior to him, and unless in one form or another it is extended to him, the race will first become pauper and then disappear."

As they sat and talked they had been watching another steamer draw alongside their boat; it was now but a few yards away, and the two boats raced side by side for a few miles, now one pulling ahead, now the other. Acquaintances on the two boats hailed one another and exchanged morning greetings. At last their boat pulled clear, putting rods of clear water between them. "Fare you well chile," a deckhand shouted across in a parting razz, "we can't always be with you."

The two men sat and talked of this and that, and at last Dennett asked the planter if he did not believe that North and South would soon come together again with the old friendly feeling and be one people again.

The conversation had become so pleasant that Dennett was taken aback by the bitterness of the reply that followed.

"No, sir, never.

"The people of the South feel that they have been most unjustly, most tyrannically oppressed by the North. All our rights have been trampled upon. We knew that we had a perfect right to go and leave you. We could no longer give to the general Government the consent of the governed, and the general Government could therefore no longer have any just powers over us. But aside from that, our right to secede was perfect. Mr. Calhoun demonstrated that. And even Mr. Webster allows that one party to a compact having violated it, the other is released from all obligations. Now, the North has repeatedly violated the constitutional guaranties of slavery. Yes, sir, we had a most perfect right to secede, and we have been slaughtered by the thousands for attempting to exercise it. And yet it is the fashion to call us traitors! Now the people of the South are not going to stand for that. They are subjugated, conquered, and in their collective capacity they must submit to whatever may be inflicted upon them. But individually, between man and man, they are not going to endure the infamous charge of having committed treason." Mr. K—— allowed that he had been shocked that General Lee had applied for a pardon; it had lessened his opinion of the man that he should so tarnish a just cause by such a seeming admission of wrong.

Mr. K—— then asked Dennett if the intelligent and religious people of the North did not expect that God would visit a terrible retribution upon them for the unjust war they had waged and the calamities they had visited upon the South. Dennett replied that on the contrary Northerners believed they had done much "for the cause of humanity and true democracy."

He saw that his answer genuinely perplexed and surprised his traveling companion. "Possible!" the planter replied. "The people here look for some heavy visitation of Divine Providence upon you. But God will judge."

5

From every white Southerner he talked to, the journalist heard the same opinion: the Negroes were doomed to extinction. Planters and yeomen, secessionists and Unionists, wealthy and poor all agreed on that much.

The white loungers in every city hotel, Dennett noted, the loiterers at the depot, the idlers who gathered at every country store or tavern chewed their tobacco, struck a leisurely pose, sipped their apple brandy, peered out at the muddy road, and declared that the Negro was lazy, indolent, ill adapted for freedom, sure to die out.

In his weekly letters to *The Nation* Dennett nearly always refrained from offering comments or opinions, but this contradiction irked him. "In the country parts of Virginia I have seen at one time and another hundreds of white men," he observed, "and I doubt if I have seen in all more than ten men engaged in labor of any sort." A traveling companion he met on the railway, going up the line for a load of timber, allowed that his company "can't get white men enough," even though he was paying hands eighteen dollars a month plus board, fifty dollars for trained carpenters. "They're too damned proud to work. Rather loaf around Richmond and Petersburg."

And then most of the whites admitted that the Negroes in their neighborhood were doing "tolerably well," performing all the manual farm labor that needed doing. Dennett looked at the lists of "destitute rations" handed out by the United States authorities in two Virginia counties for the month of June; in Bedford County relief was furnished to 961 persons, 13 of them colored; in Campbell County 530 persons, 12 colored.

But still the Negroes were sure to die out, from a combination of their own laziness and the government's refusal to allow their employers to punish them for it.

On one twelve-hundred-acre farm Dennett listened while the

owner, a wealthy former slaveholder, railed against the new system of labor. He had been an exceptionally kindly master. His overseer, Mr. W——, would affirm the truth of this assertion. Had he ever once given an order to whip a single one of his niggers?

"I believe you never did, colonel."

"I wish still to treat my people in the same way," the owner continued, "but they are fast making it impossible for me to do so. There are always some bad men in every hundred, and now the bad niggers spoil the rest. Since mine were freed, they have become lazy, stubborn, and impudent. They know that they have escaped from all government; that we cannot chastise them. And they are not like white people. I begin to believe that they are without gratitude. Mine appear to have forgotten all the kindness and lenity with which they have been treated by me and my family."

He went on some time in this vein, complaining with especial bitterness that "the Government has taken away all the coercive power from us; a Negro does what he likes, and I cannot inflict adequate punishment."

How much does he pay his people, the colonel was asked.

"No money wages. If you give money to a nigger he goes and spends it for whiskey, and I have no intention of making the country any more unsafe to live in than it is at present. Besides, sir, and Mr. W—— will tell you the same, they are not worth it; a white man will do the work of three niggers, and one slave did more than three of these freedmen."

Again the overseer supplied the requested confirmation. "So, sure, anyhow they ha'n't done a third part what they might this year."

"I called my people together when your army first came here," the planter continued, "after General Lee's defeat, and told them I should not pay wages. 'You are free,' I said, 'to go where you please, but if you choose to stay here you may; you shall work for me as you have heretofore, and I will give you the same treatment you have always had, the same quantity and quality of food, and the same amount of clothing.'"

But now he would be vexed no longer; he was leasing the farm out to his overseer and be done with it.

"Having tried the new labor system, with the essential feature of it left out," Dennett observed, allowing himself another of his small measures of wry comment, "he of course finds it a failure."

But nothing, Dennett found, seemed to so confirm the Southern whites in their opinion that the free Negro was shiftless, bound for extinction, than the sight of colored people wandering the roads.

Traveling in South Carolina in December, he passed many parties of colored men, women, and children, young and old, many in rags, footsore, obviously hungry. "These were sights that seemed to fill every white Southerner with anger," Dennett wrote, invariably triggering imprecations about "lazy niggers." On the stagecoach the man next to him had erupted, "See those damned niggers! They think of nothing but crowding into Columbia. What do they want there?"

The Northern journalist asked them. An old, half-naked colored man in Columbia, one of those he had seen from the stagecoach on the road the day before, told him he was hoping to return to Georgetown, on the Carolina coast, where he had lived before the war. The Confederate authorities had ordered slaves moved away from the low districts for fear the Union army would invade. The old man told Dennett he wanted to get back because he hoped to get a job on a rice plantation; rice was the work he knew; he didn't know cotton very well. The man who had hired him this year had turned him loose with no wages, just some bushels of corn he and his family had carried away on their backs.

Many others Dennett stopped to talk with had much the same tale to tell. On a country road in late August, a sixty-year-old colored man slowly driving a cart loaded with sweet potatoes, peaches, and chickens, pulled by a thin and heavily galled horse, showed him his contract with his master. He had just been turned out, along with several other families. He had tended the house garden; one of his sons had been a ploughman, and another almost a full hand; his wife was the family's cook. The man pulled a folded paper out of his pocketbook and Dennett took down a copy into his notebook:

Under an agreement between me and James, a man formerly my property, I am to deliver him ten barrels of corn, at my residence, when shucked from the present crop, in full of all claims against me for wages this year. The same is to be delivered to any one he may sell said corn to, provided the terms of said agreement are complied with. Said payment is in full of his wages, his wife's and children's, who live with me at this time. Said agreement was made the 19th of August, 1865. (Signed) J. M. W.

The man had been working under no set terms until mid-August, when his former master had decided how much corn he would pay his workers, and then had presented them their contracts along with a notice to quit the plantation. At two dollars a barrel, as corn was then selling for, he had earned all of about twenty dollars for his family's work for the year.

"You mark me, thar'll be a heap o' trouble when the end o' the year comes and the niggers' times out that they's hired for," prophesied a poor white Southern man whom Dennett had passed half an hour with, reading to him a handbill listing horses and mules the government was selling off. "They'll be awfully defrauded. I can see it goin' on right under my own observation. I know houses whar they keep a nigger till his month's most out, then they make a muss with him, and kick him out without any wages. Poor men like me has got to pay for it. Of course, if they don't pay, the niggers can't keep themselves, and it'll come on us. They'll be cheated all kinds o' ways. Don't I know it? You mark me, a heap o' them niggers'll die like rotten sheep."

Some of the colored wanderers Dennett stopped and talked with had sadder tales to tell. A colored man on a road in Virginia had come from Georgia on foot hoping to find the wife he had not seen for years, since they had been sold apart, while still in slavery. In Louisiana he met many more colored men and women who had made equally long treks south in search of parents or children.

Never in all of his travels, Dennett said, did he meet up with one Negro who thought "that freedom meant exemption from work." Many asked him, with meaningful and hopeful looks, if he thought they might be able to rent a piece of land of their own for the coming year and work it for themselves.

On a solitary forest road in North Carolina one dark October evening he walked his horse alongside a freedman he had overtaken and
listened to him talk. "He knew I was a Yankee by my speech, he said.
There was a heap of difference between a Southern man and a Yankee, and he could tell one from the other very easy. He couldn't help
laughin' to remember what he used to think about Yankees—how
they had horns, some on 'em, and on'y one eye. That's what the rebels
told him. He hadn't felt sure which side would whip while the fightin'
was goin' on; kept hearin' that the rebels was whippin' studdy, drivin'
the Yankees back every battle he didn't know how many miles, so that
he didn't know what to think. He pretty much give up. But he used to
pray, and he knowed if the good time didn't come in his day it was
sure to come sometime; that he knew, for the Scriptures said, 'In the
latter days all mankind, the small and the great, shall eat his bread in
the sweat of his brow'; so the white folks would have to work as well
as the black ones. But by-and-bye Sherman came, and his army covered the face of the earth. Great God, what a company!"

6

And then there was the ever present violence, always simmering
below the surface, ever ready to erupt in a furious boil.

In his travels, Dennett often called on the harassed and over-
worked army officers who served as assistant superintendents of the
Freedmen's Bureau throughout the South. Most seemed decent men,
overwhelmed by the impossibility of their job, trying their best to
adjudicate endless labor disputes, to give the freedmen the hearing
they were still denied in the state courts. Their offices were always
jammed with supplicants. Their reports bulged with complaints and
frustration. Their subordinates varied from the sympathetic to the
indifferent to the corrupt, and included more than a few who contemptuously sided with the local whites, some who even pitched in on
occasion to give an "impudent nigger" a good thrashing.

There was a raw and familiar edge to the outrages that the freedmen lined up to complain about. The simple syllogism of violence that slaveholders were not about to forget in day or a year: impudence left unchecked led to defiance, they said, and defiance to insurrection, and so to Nat Turner and Denmark Vesey.

The violence the freedmen reported had all the angry and personal instinctiveness of the slaveholder defied. An employer knocked down the freedman who worked for him; the man complained; his employer was called in to give his side of the case. Yes, he struck the Negro; the Negro was insolent—he had called him "Mister Smith" instead of "Master." In North Carolina, Dennett made a digest of recent cases brought to the assistant superintendent at Salisbury:

> By colored man, John: that G. S. whipped his wife's sister because she left him, and forced her to go back and work for him.

> By colored man, Anderson: that his master whipped him because he went off the plantation to see his cousin, and threatens to whip him again when he comes back from making his complaint.

> By colored woman, Martha: That J. J. Parker overtook her while on her way to the office of the Superintendent of Freedmen, put one end of a rope around her neck, tied the other round the neck of his mule, and so dragged her more than two miles. Showed marks of rope.

> By colored man, Julius: That he had been sick of a fever two months, and had not yet recovered, when his master came to his cabin and beat him severely because he was not at work.

> By colored man, Elias: That some citizens took his gun away from him and told him no nigger had a right to carry a gun.

By colored man, Levi: That W. F. L. has whipped him
severely with a buggy trace. Shows his back all raw.

But there was a shadow larger than slavery's looming behind some
of the strange warnings and sadistic revenge that Dennett heard
about.

A lean, hard-faced white man stripping leaves from the cane in a
sorghum field stopped to pass the time of day and told how he had
gathered up some of the boys and run a nigger out of the place. Mister
Nigger had come to work for him but had quit after a week, and he
wasn't about to let the niggers walk over him like that, no sir; so he had
gathered up the boys and found him six miles down the road, staying
with some free niggers, and told him that if he was in the neighborhood after the next day they'd shoot him wherever they found him.

The Freedmen's Bureau report for the month of October that Dennett perused in South Carolina told of similar threats carried out. In
the Clarendon district, six former slaves left their plantation; the overseer pursued them with a pack of hounds and caught them. He shot
one attempting to escape and hung the other five by the roadside.

In Louisiana, an Englishman who had lived there for thirty-five
years rented land to freedmen. He received a warning:

> We have been informed that you are 'lowing niggers to
> squat about your land; or, in other words, you are renting
> niggers land. One of our committee told you that you
> would be burnt out, but you would not pay attention to
> him. Now, sir, your gin-house is burnt for renting niggers
> land. If this is not sufficient warning we will burn every-
> thing on your place. If that don't break it up, we will break
> your neck. If that don't break it up, we will shoot the nig-
> gers. Beware, sir, before it is too late, or you will be waited
> on by A COMMITTEE.

While he was in South Carolina, Dennett accompanied the chief
officer of the Freedmen's Bureau for the area, General Ely, to Edgefield Court-House.

The Edgefield district was a prosperous area of large plantations; it had escaped the ravages of war; the soil was light loam and level ground, good for cotton, unlike the sand and red earth of so much of the region; the old wealthy families were wealthy still and carrying on much as before.

Word of the general's coming had spread throughout the district. By three in the morning crowds of freedmen had already congregated in the village square before the courthouse. The general planned to address the freedmen, encourage them to make contracts for their labor with the planters for the coming year, caution them that the government had no land to give away to them, urge upon them thrift, honesty, industry, and chastity. But before his speech he sat in the midst of a crowd eager to tell their troubles.

A thirty-year-old mulatto man waited patiently for his turn. Then he told his story. He lived ten miles from the courthouse; he made and sold brandy for his trade. The white people around there had been saying that the Negroes had guns. Last Saturday fourteen local men, accompanied by a Yankee soldier, came to his house. They demanded his gun. He had no gun, he told them. They insisted he did. Finally one of the men said, "I'll get it out of him." He left for a few minutes and came back with a chain. Then the men hung him; hung him "till I lost my sense, and when I come to, they asked me, 'would I give up my gun, now?' And I told them, 'Gentlemen, I *got* no gun.'" And so they hung him until he again passed out, and again demanded his gun when he came to, and then a third time.

And still not getting satisfaction, they stripped him naked and gave him a merciless beating. The marks of the beating, and of the chain on his neck, were starkly visible as he stood before the general and the crowd in the courthouse square, quietly telling his story. "I told them the truth," he insisted, "for I hadn't got any arms. These here is all the arms I has got. And yet they put me to death three times. And I don't expect they're agoin' to let me live now I made this complain' to you, general; but they may kill me for good as soon as they choose."

And then the man began to cry. "Which I hasn't got anything in the world but myself, for I hasn't got any family, nor any parents, nor any land, nor any money, and I know I is not to be any worse off in the grave than I is now."

Two other cases of hangings were reported.

The general's speech was something of an anticlimax. It began to rain, and a drunken white man at the edge of the crowd shouted curses at the Yankees through it all, until he was finally hauled off to jail.

It was on the road to Charleston that Dennett came across the remains of a more macabre piece of violence. Riding all day through a heavy mist and sodden trees, he was hospitably taken in for the night at the house of a planter. Although, the planter said, his wife's uncle and aunt had just arrived and he had only one spare chamber, it was his rule never to turn a away a stranger. He would be glad to accommodate the traveler in the parlor, in a bed before the fire.

At supper, Dennett listened while talk turned to the inevitable question of the Negro.

"I'm told the nigger soldiers in Georgetown have been getting very independent latterly," the uncle declared. "But the Yankee officers, they say, make short work of it with 'em. I hear that one or two of 'em were shot down last week, and tumbled into the river, man and gun."

"Who did it?"

"Their own officers, the Yankees. That's a case of nigger shooting that won't be trumpeted all over Lincolndom, I expect."

"I wish they'd shoot 'em all," declared his wife. "I'm glad when I hear o' one of 'em got out of the way. If I could get up tomorrow morning and hear that every nigger in the country was dead, I'd just jump up and down."

"I don't want 'em to go quite as fast as soon as that. They'll go fast enough for me if they last a few years longer."

"You want to get a little more out of 'em first, don't you uncle? So do I; but I don't know how it's to be done."

His host, Dennett learned next morning, owned sixty-five hundred acres. They were sitting on the piazza waiting for breakfast; Dennett asked about the two human skulls he saw sitting in the corner. Was there a story connected with them?

"Yes, sir, they belonged to damned robbers who got their deserts at my hands one morning in May last," the planter said. "Some of our colored friends in Georgetown" had been emboldened by Union raiding expeditions toward the end of the war, and had begun to plunder plantation houses.

A band of Negro troops, or camp followers, had come into this district. "I got some of my neighbors together; we armed ourselves and pursued. I knew the country perfectly, and I wanted to get them where there was no bog or swamp for them to take to. When I had them in the right spot, we closed in at a canter. They showed fight, sir, but 'twas no use. Seven of them fell, five of the seven killed on the spot. That fellow, you see, never knew what hurt him." And the planter handed over one of the skulls, pointing to a neat pistol bullet hole in the center.

How had he prepared the skulls? Dennett asked. Had he boiled them to remove the flesh?

"No, sir. We let them lie where they fell, and the weather prepared them. I didn't bring them in till August."

In April of 1866, the weary and by now thoroughly disillusioned traveler was riding the train through Connecticut on his way home.

Gazing out the window, he mentioned to his seatmate his relief at seeing a countryside once again filled with schools, churches, neat villages, trim fences; such a contrast to the swamps and sandy levels, the wretched railways and worse roads, the slovenly plantations and the hovels of their laborers that had been his constant scenery for the past eight months.

The man next to him, a merchant from Rhode Island, asked his opinion of the loyalty of the South.

Dennett replied that he had made a point of talking to people of all classes all across the South; he had seldom found one who thought his state had done anything wrong by seceding. It was not a wrong thing that had been done, only an inexpedient thing, in their view. To be sure, Southerners acknowledged, they had been overmastered; but only by a Northern army that, as everyone knew, was full of mercenaries straight from Europe. "The people," Dennett told the man, "were sorry for nothing but their ill-success."

In one of his last letters to *The Nation* he told of the long talk he had had with a man from Ohio he had met in Baton Rouge. This man had come south to search for the remains of friends who had been killed in a steamboat explosion. He had traveled for weeks in Mississippi and Louisiana—the bodies, it was believed, might have come ashore anywhere between Vicksburg and the Gulf. He was an intelligent man, and his sad task had brought him into contact with men from many different walks of life, and he had made a point of finding out as much as he could about the opinions and feelings of the people of the South—and the experience had stunned him.

"You must understand," the man said, "that in 1860 I was a strong Douglas man. I didn't like Lincoln, and the abolitionists I hated; but, of course, I was Union. As the war went on I began to believe in Lincoln, and, by the time the Emancipation Proclamation was issued, I had been educated up to it and endorsed it. As a war measure, I mean; that was how Mr. Lincoln regarded it, and so did I. Well, since the war ended I've been a conservative; I've considered Stevens and Sumner dangerous men, who didn't understand the South, wanted to humble it and so on, and were standing in the way of peace. I believed what we used to hear, that the North didn't understand the South. I believe it yet, but in a very different sense.

"This journey has been the greatest that I have ever experienced. I came out with the kindest feelings for these people down here; I wanted to see it made easy; we had whipped them, and I wanted it to rest there. I thought the South wanted it to end there. But I was tremendously mistaken. They hate us and despise us and all belonging to us. They call us cut-throats, liars, thieves, vandals, cowards, and the very scum of the earth. They actually believe it. They won't even allow that we won our own battles. 'We were overpowered by numbers,' they say; 'of course we couldn't fight all Europe.' They've said that to me more than fifty times within the last few weeks. And they say that they are the gentlemen; we are amalgamationists, mudsills, vandals, and so forth. And I've heard and seen more brag, and lying, and profanity, and cruelty, down here, than I ever saw or heard before in all my life. The only people I find that a Northern man can make a friend of, the only ones that like the Government and believe in it, are the Negroes. I'm convinced they can vote just as intelligently as the poor whites. A Southerner would knock me down if I said that to him; but it's true.

"I tell you I'm going home to be a radical. Fight the devil with fire. I've learned to hate Southerners as I find them, and they can hate me if they want to. Every man that's seen what I've seen ought to let it be known. 'The North don't understand the South,' you know, and I'm going to help our people see two or three things: that the chivalry hate us and despise us; that a 'nigger' they don't consider human; that whatever harm they can do us without getting another whipping, they've got the will to do, and mean to do, too. I wish every county in the North would send out two men, who have the confidence of their fellow-citizens, and make them travel through the South and report the true condition of things. They couldn't make a true report without changing every honest administration man into a radical. I knew what I was when I came out, but I couldn't resist the evidence of my own senses."

For his part, Dennett had spent eight months reporting on the true condition of things and was doubtful that the truth could make any difference now. It was already too late, he feared; the moment had already been lost. The prophecies he ventured to offer in his final letter were all gloomy ones. If treason had been made odious the moment the war had ended, if the native Unionists of the South had been immediately supported with all the might of the government, then the men in the middle to be found in every community might have been emboldened to rally to their side, Dennett suggested. But instead, the Southern whites had coalesced around the same rebel spirits who had led them into secession; and what those men had once considered worth fighting for they were determined to fight for yet. "For some time to come," Dennett predicted, "the South will be a unit on all questions of Federal politics." There was little doubt whose side the colored people would be on if they got the vote; they knew who their friends were. But white Southerners would use every means in their power to prevent Negro suffrage from ever coming about; and to neutralize it if it did come about in spite of their best efforts to forestall that evil day.

"I think that the Negroes unprotected by the military authority of the general Government would hardly be able to cast votes enough to alter the elections of any one Southern county," Dennett wrote in his final letter.

"Let the Negro vote," warned the Virginia lumber merchant who had shared a train seat with Dennett near the start of his journey, "and the Southern people will have to be kept down by a standing army."

II

"THE WAR STILL EXISTS"

7

Prince Rivers had been a coachman, a man of natural dignity that slavery could never rob him of, even as it appropriated his person.

He had learned to read and write while a slave, and would in time sign his name with a flourish, P. R. Rivers. Once he had driven General Beauregard from Beaufort to Charleston. Then when Union troops seized Port Royal Island the first year of the war his owner had fled from Beaufort with his property. When his owner stopped to visit relatives at Edgefield, Rivers had promptly saddled his master's best horse and rode a hundred miles, straight through the Confederate lines, right back to Port Royal, and enlisted in the Union army. Wanted posters flapping on the roadside between Charleston and the coast soon after offered two thousand dollars reward for his capture.

By New Year's Day of 1863, the day the Emancipation Proclamation went into effect, Rivers, thirty-nine years old, was the sergeant of Company A, First South Carolina Volunteers. It was the first colored regiment in the United States Army, later to be called the Thirty-third United States Colored Troops.

The regiment's colonel, the Boston abolitionist and theologian Thomas Wentworth Higginson, chose Rivers to head the color guard and make a speech that day. The proclamation was read and the colors presented; the program called for Higginson to speak next, but out of the crowd came an old wavering colored man's voice, instantly joined by more and more of the assembled colored soldiers and visitors, singing words that suddenly had new meaning:

> My country 'tis of thee,
> Sweet land of liberty,
> Of thee I sing!

The white dignitaries on the platform looked at one another, unsure what to do about this departure from the printed program, but Higginson motioned them to silence. On and on the voices of freedmen and freedwomen wound through verse after verse, and when it was done tears were everywhere.

Not long after that Rivers was both color sergeant and provost sergeant of the entire regiment, in charge of keeping the camp in order, tenacious and unflinching when it came to rounding up deserters. Higginson later bitterly regretted that he had not pressed to have Rivers made an officer, for, as he reported, "There is not a white officer in this regiment who has more administrative ability, or more absolute authority over the men. They do not love him, but his mere presence has controlling power over them."

Higginson went on to describe a man not only of ability but of that indefinable magnetism that is the natural birthright of preachers, politicians, and lotharios. "He writes well enough to prepare for me a daily report of his duties in the camp; if his education reached a higher point, I see no reason why he should not command the Army of the Potomac. He is jet-black, or rather, I should say, *wine-black;* his complexion, like that of others of my darkest men, having a sort of rich, clear depth, without a trace of sootiness, and to my eye very handsome. His features are tolerably regular, and full of command, and his figure superior to that of any of our white officers,—being six feet high, perfectly proportioned, and of apparently inexhaustible strength and activity. His gait is like a panther's; I never saw such a tread. No anti-slavery novel has described a man of such marked ability. If there should ever be a black monarchy in South Carolina, he will be its king."

The Thirty-third U.S. Colored Troops joined the occupation of Charleston to fight the fires and restore order; was sent to Edgefield county in June after the surrender, to the towns of Hamburg and Aiken; and was finally mustered out of service almost a year after the war's end, in February of 1866.

"The hour is at hand when we must separate forever, but nothing can ever take from us the pride we feel," their commander had said that day in his farewell address. "The flag of our fathers, restored to its rightful significance, now floats over every foot of our territory, from Maine to California, and beholds only freemen! The prejudices which formerly existed against you are well nigh rooted out."

With those optimistic words ringing in his ears, it was to Edgefield county, and the town of Hamburg, that Rivers returned to seek his fortune in freedom.

Edgefield was a place so violent jokes had grown up about it. You could tell a *real* high-toned Edgefield gentleman, people in South Carolina said, because he was the one with *four* huge navy-sized revolvers stuck in his belt.

On a street over in Augusta a mad dog needed to be shot; a policeman called out to the crowd that had gathered, "Is there a man from Edgefield here?"

Edgefield had a reputation as one of the roughest counties in the state, conceded a local judge, with numerous cases of "murder or manslaughter, growing out of personal quarrels." A man playing at cards would say he had made a ten-dollar bet; another would reply that it was only five; the first man would call the second a damned liar; the second would return the insult; the first would pull out a pistol and shoot him dead. If they absolutely had to, juries would send a man who murdered another in such a defense of his honor to jail for six months, or maybe a year, or two. Then proper Edgefield society would welcome him back to its fold. Boys learned the lesson of defending their honor early. A wealthy Edgefield planter, Benjamin Tillman, Sr., sending his son off to school, wrote the lad's schoolmaster to expect some "collisions" with the other boys; his son's "*disposition* is such not to *submit* to imposition or insult by any."

Edgefield also had a reputation as a bastion of the most unregenerate slaveholders in the entire state, the entire South even. That same Edgefield schoolmaster, back in 1851, had penned one of the most furious defenses of Southern slavery against the "false philanthropy and mawkish sentimentalism of the abolitionists." He was a clergyman as well as a schoolmaster, and he knew what God thought. He published in Hamburg a pamphlet proving that "the association of the white and black races in the relation of master and slave is the appointed order of God, as set forth in the Bible, and constitutes the best social condition of both races, and the only principle of true republicanism." It wasn't true, as some Northerners had said, that only a few Southerners entertained "the extravagant opinion" that slavery was a positive blessing (as opposed to, say, a necessary burden at best). On the contrary, the reverend asserted, such views were not only widely held throughout the South, but "they are the veritable opinions entertained on the same subject by the God of the universe." He challenged any Northerner "to point us to a single precept or word uttered by Jesus Christ, or his Apostles, prohibitory of slavery, or even passing the first intimation of censure against the institution."

Hamburg was in the remote southeast corner of the county, hard by the Savannah River, and in its heyday before the Civil War it was a rough, wide-open town, full of cotton warehouses and rail yards, places to buy whiskey, and the slave dealers who were not welcomed in more respectable places. They did a brisk business; the Charleston newspapers often carried their advertisements.

> ONE HUNDRED AND TWENTY NEGROES FOR SALE—The subscriber has *just arrived from Petersburg, Virginia,* with one hundred and twenty *likely young negroes* of both sexes and every description, which he now offers for sale on the most reasonable terms. The lot now on hand consists of plough-boys, several likely and well-qualified house servants of both sexes, *several women with children, small girls* suitable for nurses, and SEVERAL SMALL BOYS WITHOUT THEIR MOTHERS. Planters and *traders* are earnestly requested to give the subscriber a call previously to making purchases *elsewhere,* as he is enabled to sell as cheap or cheaper than can be sold by *any other person in the trade.* BENJAMIN DAVIS *Hamburg, S.C., September 28, 1838.*

Hamburg had been founded by a half-mad German, Henry Shultz, full of dreams of fortune and revenge. He had come to Augusta, Georgia, from his native Hamburg, Germany, speaking no English and taking work as a boatman; within a few years he had floated bills to finance the building of a toll bridge across the Savannah River. Then he lost it all when the backers all suddenly demanded repayment simultaneously, and the bridge ended up being seized and knocked down to the city of Augusta itself. "This taking Augusta will repent to the end of time," he swore, "for I shall be able with permission of the Great Ruler to teach that once great city a lesson ever to be remembered how to tamper with common sense and the hard earnings of an honest man."

He set his new town smack across the river in South Carolina, named it after his birthplace across the seas, and for a while gave Augusta a run for its money, drawing away the cotton trade first by water and then by rail. In the process Shultz made and lost several more fortunes, fought endless court battles to reclaim his bridge, tried unsuccessfully to commit suicide when a key ruling went against him, and was convicted of manslaughter and sent to jail for six months for ordering a man whipped in an effort to get him to confess to a theft, and then the man had died on him a week later.

Hamburg lay on low ground, little better than a marsh to begin with, right by the river. It was at the mercy of periodic floods. It was never a pretty town, but Shultz had laid it out with broad streets, 100 to 150 feet wide, attracted not one but two railroads, established a successful bank. Sixty thousand bales of cotton a year went through the town in its prime; its population grew to fifteen hundred. Still, it was gritty and dreary; none of the luxury and society of planters in Charleston coming to town and sipping iced punch; Hamburg was rough and ugly and commercial in the worst sense of that word. A merchant who spent some time there in 1851 wrote a fed-up letter to a friend saying he was getting out of there, "one of the dullest places on earth." Being in Hamburg, he said, reminded him of wandering through "a country Grave Yard with leaning tomb Stones filled with bad epitaphs."

And then the railroads that had for a time been Hamburg's salvation did it in; planters who had trundled their cotton in great piled wagonloads to sell in Hamburg now could find closer outlets all along the rail line; the completion of a canal into Augusta and the extension of the South Carolina Rail Road right into Augusta over a new railroad bridge added to Hamburg's literal and figurative status as a town passed by. Shultz died in 1851, broke again. By the time of the Civil War, Hamburg was practically a ghost town. A traveler who rode through in 1862 called it "the most lonely, desolate looking place I had ever seen." Sherman's army came through in February 1865, tore up the train tracks, and didn't find much of anything else worth destroying.

But a lonely and desolate place was an opportunity for freedmen looking for a new life. Edgefield county's population was 60 percent colored, but Hamburg's was soon 75 percent; within a few years of the war's end its population swelled to eleven hundred. Throughout 1865 and 1866 there were reports of paid killers operating with near impunity elsewhere in Edgefield, especially in the rich plantation districts over at the other end of the county toward Edgefield Court-House, the village that served as the county seat. "It is almost a daily occurrence for black men to be hunted down with dogs and shot like wild beasts," a freedman from Edgefield told a government agent in the autumn of 1865. The colored people called them "bushwhackers"; an army board of inquiry sent to examine the situation amply confirmed the tales. A band of a hundred men, led by a former Confederate officer, marauded at will through Edgefield county, whipping or killing Negroes who dared to leave the employ of their former masters.

In April of 1866 Brevet Major General Adelbert Ames was ordered to send a full company of cavalry to hunt them down; before then, the entire occupation presence of the United States Army in Edgefield consisted of a squad of infantry—one sergeant and six men. A preliminary attempt to reinforce the unit produced nothing but a scoffing warning from the locals to the commander. It would take more than "14 or 15 Yanks to rule the District," he was told. A trooper who wandered into Edgefield Court-House from camp a few days later was drawn into an altercation, a menacing crowd formed, and when he drew his revolver and ordered the mob to fall back, the soldier was promptly shot dead by a man on horseback who galloped off.

But Hamburg offered the freedmen a strength in numbers and a safety in remoteness; Hamburg was a haven, at least a relative haven, a haven by comparison. Within a few years the town was home to hundreds of colored families who had broken free of the life of contracted farm workers, a life scarcely distinguishable from slavery. Among their numbers were schoolteachers, railroad employees, blacksmiths; a successful cotton broker, a printer, a clerk of the court; shoemakers, painters, carpenters; a constable. They bought lots and furnished homes. There were several who made considerable investments in farms and other real estate in South Carolina, and in states beyond.

If Prince Rivers was not yet South Carolina's king, as his colonel had once predicted he might someday be, he was Hamburg's prince. When colored men received the right to vote for delegates to the new constitutional conventions that Congress had ordered the Southern states to convene, Rivers was selected as a register of voters, and then elected as a delegate. That same year of miracles, 1868, he was elected to the state legislature and became a trial justice, or magistrate, for Hamburg. He handled the routine matters of small crime and small claims, writing his orders in a smooth flowing hand. Robert Hatcher, Jr., claimed he had cut fifteen cords of wood and eighty-eight cross-ties, had hauled ten cords of wood and pulled fodder for twelve days and picked pease for two days for one George Sharpton and was owed $40.30, which he had not been paid. Henry Powell, convicted of petty larceny and failing to pay the damages of twelve dollars and the costs of the court, sent to jail for thirty days. A. J. Griffin to appear upon complaint of Rebecca Lacy that she had good reason to fear bodily injury, binds them to peace recognizance of two hundred dollars for one year.

He had done his job for a year when one hundred citizens of Hamburg affixed their names to a petition to the governor.

> We the undersigned citizens of Edgefield County, residing in and near the town of Hamburg, having heard that an effort is being made by certain persons, to obtain the removal of Prince R Rivers Esqr from the office of Magistrate, protest against such removal for the following reasons. While we are not disposed to argue that Prince R Rivers is the very best man that might have been appointed

to fill the important office of Magistrate, we are con-
strained to believe him better qualified, everything considered than any of those who seek from personal considerations
his removal. His official conduct has been marked by an
impartial fairness that has not failed to command the respect and admiration of our most respectable citizens tho
politically opposed to Rivers, and hence we desire to keep in
office the man who has shown himself able to rise against
existing prejudices, and to administer justice under the law
with such an even hand as to draw down upon his shoulders
the accumulative wrath of those less scrupulous, tho perhaps
more learned in the law, than himself.

So Rivers kept his job.

The town's charter, which had been revoked in 1868 when Hamburg was but still emerging from its ghost-town days, was restored
in 1871 by an act of the legislature, and Hamburg again became a
self-governing polity with its own intendant, or mayor, and a council of four wardens, with the authority to manage its own elections,
to establish a market-house, and to enact bylaws respecting streets,
roads, and business therein, and to regulate its police system thereof,
and to promote health, order, and good government; and to collect
license fees for the sale of spirituous liquors and for keeping taverns
and billiard tables and on all drays and carts; and to arrest and commit to jail persons guilty of disorderly conduct to the annoyance of
its citizens.

In due order Prince Rivers was elected intendant of Hamburg, to
add to his other considerable duties.

8

Cuttings from the South Carolina and Georgia press from the years 1868 to 1872.

[THE EDGEFIELD ADVERTISER]

Sketches of the Delegates to the Great Ringed-Streaked-and-Striped Convention

THE EDGEFIELD DELEGATION.

R. B. Elliot—negro—is regarded by the white people of Edgefield as the "head centre" of the delegation from their district to the Club House assembly. He hails from Massachusetts, where he claims to have been a lawyer. He did not appear in the district to which he honors by misrepresenting until the summer of 1867. He made sundry speeches, swaggered insolently and talked largely, with the hope of provoking the attention of the white people; and failing in this, subsided into the dusky crowd of freedmen, and has not since been heard of above the surface. In the zenith of his importance and glory, he took unto himself a wife, in the person of an abandoned mulatto woman, of notorious habits and character, repudiated even by the negroes. To consummate his matrimonial happiness, he borrowed from his friends and admirers various sums of money, which he has failed to replace.

Prince Rivers (coloured), formerly a coachman of Mr. Henry M. Stuart of Beaufort, who was a refugee in Edgefield during the war, is the next most promising fellow among them. He is a fine specimen of a full-blooded negro, and was remarkable, when a slave, as being a good boatman and an accomplished whip. When he made his first appearance upon his coach-box you were at a loss which to admire most—the polish of his horses, the polish of his manners, the polish of his skin, or the resplendent polish of his shirt collars. Prince has a taste for letters, and he learned to read and write. This latter accomplishment brought him to grief on one occasion. Then he exercised his genius in writing passes for some sable damsels, omitting at the same time to put his own signature to the document.

During the war Prince became dissatisfied. Like young Norval "he had heard of wars and longed to follow to the field." He accordingly *borrowed* his master's horse and left for the coast. He passed through the Confederate lines and joined the United States army.

Prince was sent to Edgefield as a register, which paved the way for him as a delegate to the convention. What kind of Solon he will make is doubtful. He has shown his wisdom so far by holding his tongue. Will he have the wit to continue to do so? He is frightfully black, ignorant and impudent—talks like a low country "gulla nigger." He has been devoting himself, since his discharge from the army, entirely to politics, and is a very consequential member of the Union league, appears to be a bird of passage, here, there and everywhere, except in his proper sphere, with curry-comb and horsebrush, or on the box of some genteel carriage.

John Bonum—is a Charleston negro, as black as the ace of spades.

John Wooley, is a white man, from Graniteville, of whom nothing can be learned, except that in his own neighborhood he bears the reputation of being a very low and utterly good-for-nothing individual. As far as the unlawful assembly is concerned, he is altogether insignificant.

[PAMPHLET.]

THE RESPECTFUL REMONSTRANCE,

ON BEHALF OF

THE WHITE PEOPLE OF SOUTH CAROLINA,

AGAINST THE CONSTITUTION OF THE LATE CONVENTION OF THAT STATE, NOW SUBMITTED TO CONGRESS FOR RATIFICATION

... That Constitution was the work of Northern adventurers, Southern renegades and ignorant negroes. Not one per centum of the white population of the State approves it, and not two per centum of the negroes who voted for its adoption know any more than a dog, horse, or cat, what his act of voting implied. That Constitution enfranchises every male negro over the age of twenty-one. The negro being in a large numerical majority, as compared with the whites, the effect is that the new Constitution establishes in this State negro supremacy, with all its train of countless evils. A superior race—a portion, Senators and Representatives, of the same proud race to which it is your pride to belong—is put under the rule of an inferior race—the abject slaves of yesterday, the flushed freedmen of to-day. And think you there can be any just, lasting reconstruction on this basis? We do not mean to threaten resistance by arms. But the white people of our State will never quietly submit to negro rule. We may have to pass under the yoke you have authorized, but we will keep up this contest until we have regained the heritage of political control handed down to us by an honored ancestry. This is a duty we owe to the land that is ours, to the graves that it contains, and to the race of which you and we are alike members—the proud Caucasian race, whose sovereignty on earth God has ordained. . . .

Democratic party State Central Executive Committee

Another Poland.

South Carolina is Polandized—aye, worse than that, *Africanized!*

That gallant, heroic little State, with its State pride, pride of race, and pride of lineage, *is no more!*

The South Carolina which the white race that settled and has inhabited her, giving her an existence and history extending over more than two centuries, has passed from control of that race, and has been made an Africanized province of the New Nation, which the Puritans of New England have been laboring for more than half a century to establish in place of the beautiful and beneficent structure of Constitutional government, founded by a common ancestry, and adapted, above all other systems ever devised by men, to make a people great, free, prosperous and happy.

But all this has passed away, and the political power in South Carolina has been placed in the hands of the negroes, who outnumber, by many thousands, the white population. And not only South Carolina, whose fate is sealed for the present, but all her sister States of the South, are doomed to similar Africanization.

But, thank God, wherever, and whatever extent, they may succeed in doing their devil's work, it will not stand, it cannot last. The people are rising against them, and the signs and evidence are unmistakable, that this is to be a white man's Government and a white man's country!

We say to the suffering, down-trodden, maligned and maltreated men and women of the South, be patient, be hopeful, be brave!

The hour of redemption is at hand for both you and me, and only for a little time shall this execrable Jacobin rule, this abhorrent reign of negro barbarism, live to curse our common country!

. . . [Prince Rivers is] so black that charcoal would make a snowy mark on his august phiz. Be that as it may he occupies an important position in Hamburg, where he feels his importance, grinning and guffawing like a Brazilian ape, as he dispenses law to the "poor white trash" and the aristocratic "colored people" who come before the ebony Murat of the Carolina forces. This autocrat's first step towards bringing what may be serious trouble is that of posting a sign on the Hamburg bridge to the effect that any Augusta sow which wandered into his dominion would be taken up and released only on payment of $5. This was in retaliation of the action of the Augusta council to charge toll to all pedestrians, most of whom are impecunious black vagabonds.

DISTINGUISHED OFFICIAL VISITOR—Prince Rivers, the sable Mayor of Hamburg, came to the city yesterday afternoon, to hold a conference with his Honor, Mayor Estes, touching the taxation of the Carolina end of the City Bridge by the corporation of Hamburg. While awaiting the arrival of Mayor Estes at the City Hall, he beguiled the time with an inspection of the Council Chamber, and other features of interest in the interior of the building, but is not reported as expressing any purpose to purchase our temple of justice for the Hamburg government. He was civilly entertained and chaperoned among the mysteries of the inner chambers of the building by the courteous Keeper of the Hall, who seemed to take an especial pleasure in exhibiting to the "Black Prince" the *modus operandi* of a white man's government. The distinguished visitor failed to see Mayor Estes, however, and retired to his kingdom across the river in good order.

[THE EDGEFIELD ADVERTISER]

Poor old Hamburg! At an election held the 2nd instant, for municipal officers of that ancient burg, Prince Rivers (Negro) was elected intendant; and Louis Schiller, A. T. Attaway, A. Nurnberger and Joe Thomas, wardens. Poor old God-forsaken Hamburg!—once the flourishing cotton mart of Western Carolina, now the abode of the most consummate Radical thieves, plunderers and curs of low degree, than ever cursed any other spot on the broad face of this green earth of ours. The few decent people who are residents—and there are very few—have our warmest commiseration; and we would urge them to gather up their households and hie away to the neighboring hills and there pray fervently for a spring freshet. A freshet 40 feet high is now the only hope for the redemption of Hamburg. Brethren, let's pray!

9

Adelbert Ames was born on the coast of Maine, the son of a sea captain.

As a boy he sailed the world, saw the islands of the Pacific and the East, the famous ports of Europe and Africa.

He learned to use a sextant and to sketch in watercolors. He kept company he later disapproved of. The gangs of boys who ran around the limekilns of Rockland were as bad as the crews of a Yankee trading clipper. "A seaport town like that is not a good place for the education and improvement of youth," he wrote of his old home from the perspective of a very serious thirty-one-year-old man. "I realize every day the injury done me by my limekiln and sailor companions. One might as well think of handling pitch without being soiled as to give a boy the liberty of that city and expect him to grow to manhood and not be unfavorably influenced." Sometimes when he was a boy his mother managed to keep him home by promising to sing to him, and then she would sing the whole evening through.

The rough company of his youth seemed to have sobered him, whatever his later regrets; Ames went to West Point and emerged, in the words of one admirer, "about as close an approximation to Sir Galahad as was likely to be found in the Union army." He rarely smoked, drank little, eschewed debauchery, hardly even swore. At Bull Run, commanding an artillery battery, he was shot through the thigh almost as soon as the battle began but refused to leave the field. Unable to mount his horse, he had his men lift him on and off a caisson every time they changed position. He continued to direct their fire until he finally collapsed from loss of blood.

He recovered and was sent north, to whip a new regiment into shape. The Twentieth Maine Volunteer Infantry proved to be a rag-tag band of farmers with no uniforms, no arms, and a casual attitude toward orders. Every command from an officer was treated as a proposition to be discussed and debated, town meeting fashion. This situation did make Ames swear, repeatedly.

"This is a hell of a regiment!" he said, and began drilling them without mercy. "Col. A. will take the men out to drill & he will d'm them up hill and down," one hapless sergeant wrote home. "I swear they will shoot him the first battle we are in." For the sergeant's part, he would be content if Ames were put in the state's prison or promoted to brigadier general—anything to get him off his back.

They didn't shoot him their first battle. At Fredericksburg, Ames coolly led his men right through a withering Confederate cannonade, and they followed, with a discipline they didn't know they had. Their tall, thin colonel was the only regiment commander in the brigade who had stepped to the front of his men when ordered forward. Walking over the dead of the regiment pinned down in front of him, Ames sought out its commander and quietly told him, "I will move over your line and relieve your men."

He commanded a division at Gettysburg and led a daring and successful amphibious assault against Fort Fisher in the final months of the war, when it guarded the Confederacy's last remaining port of Wilmington, North Carolina. "He seemed to have a life that was under some mystic protection," his aide-de-camp would wondrously recall of those war years. "Every one who rode with him in battle soon discovered that Ames never hesitated to take desperate chances under fire. Although he never permitted anything to stand in his way, and never asked men to go where he would not go himself, still his manner was always cool, calm, and gentlemanly. Under the heaviest fire, when men and officers were being stricken down around him, he would sit on his horse and quietly give his orders, which were invariably communicated in the most polite way, and generally in the form of a request. I often thought when I saw him under fire that if one of his legs had been carried away by a round shot he would merely turn to some officer or soldier near by and quietly say, 'Will you kindly assist me from my horse'!"

On occupation duty in South Carolina after the war he fretted over whether to stay in the army. He thought of a career in the law, he thought of joining his parents in Northfield, Minnesota, where they had bought a flour-mill business; his uncle, disagreeing, advised him not to give up the "*position* and *pay* of an officer."

But though he had been brevetted a major general in both the volunteer service and the regular army for gallantry in action, his permanent rank was still only that of a captain, and he thought his chances for even so much as a colonelcy in the postwar army were "very shadowy." He wrote his parents, "I will take anything they choose to give me while I am debating in my own mind what I shall do, and nothing will bind me after that time if I decide to try civil life." Overall he thought President Johnson's hands-off policies toward the South more right than those of the radicals in Congress, was skeptical of Negro suffrage, but his letters home that first autumn of peace betrayed more of a shock at the attitudes he encountered in the South than the formality of his official dispatches admitted:

> The climate is finer here than I ever imagined it could be in our country. We have had frost occasionally but few days have been uncomfortably cold. I can hardly realize it is near the first of December.

I am still at my duties, which consist in little more than aiding the agents of the Treasury Department and the Freedmen's Bureau and in trying white men for killing negroes, of which work we have more than we can well do.

In fact, the guard house is full of such persons. They think about as much of taking the life of a Freedman as I would that of a dog. Those we try are receiving severe punishment in the form of imprisonment for years in our seacoast fortifications—and I am in hopes that in course of time the pious people of this State will be convinced that according to our law it is, if not a sin, at least a crime to kill what they term a—"nigger."

When we go there will be no security for them and they will be in a much worse condition than when slaves—for then they were worth from five to ten hundred dollars and were objects of care—now they are not worth the ground in which they are buried one would think by the treatment they receive at the hands of those who have associated with them all their lives. If left to the tender mercies of the State I pity them—for that matter I pity them anyhow.

I am continuing my studies in law—even if I never practice it, it will be most beneficial to me. I do little else than pore over my books—all of which are of a substantial character. Society here is closed to us officers of the army, and I am of necessity forced to turn to books.

I am anxious to go North myself, but must or will wait till my services are no longer needed here—instead of resigning as I am sometimes half a mind to do.

He was granted a year's leave of absence; he traveled to Europe. He studiously applied himself to German and French; he kept a journal in which he studiously noted his disappointments. In London he went to hear Charles Dickens read from *Pickwick Papers* and came away feeling that "a good comedian would have done Charles Dickens better than Charles Dickens could do himself." The spectacle of a midnight masked ball at the opera house during the Christmas season in London slightly shocked him; all the women were "low." A Yale student he met in Paris complained that that city was inferior to the United States: "A short visit to one of the places of low life fill him with bitterness because it is not bad enough—even New Haven can equal it."

Ames found the high life of Paris just as bitter, for his part; the more he saw of high society the more he found it to be full of "hollowness." He went to art galleries, saw the *Barber of Seville,* was constantly busy and mostly miserable. In Luxembourg, in the picture gallery at the palace, he ran into an old friend from Maine he hadn't seen for years; his friend was now living abroad, eking out a living as a landscape painter, married to a woman he loved, not yet successful or famous, but "seems happy and contented."

"I, on the other hand, have accomplished much—but to what end?" Ames lamented with the self-pity of a man who feared that at age thirty his best years were already passed:

> Instead of having that which gives peace and contentment, I am adrift, seeking for what God only knows. I do not. Thus far life has been with me one severe struggle and now that a time of rest is upon me, I am lost to find my position.
>
> Heretofore, I have had something to look forward to—to my West Point life—to my graduation and an existence free from the trammels of school life—to the war—my advancement and its successful issue. Then, to the day of my departure for Europe and the world there. All this has been accomplished, but I have found the beautiful objects at a distance, plain and valueless in my own hands.
>
> I trust the future, though—I can do no more—perhaps in doing this, I do too much.

While still abroad he received news that he allowed to decide his future for the while: he had been promoted to the permanent rank of lieutenant colonel in the regular army.

Upon his return home in 1867 he was assigned to travel through Mississippi inspecting the posts of the Fourth Military District: fourteen hundred bored and restless troops sprinkled across the state, a hundred here, fifty there; a token of federal authority more than a real fighting force, among them but a single company of cavalry to cover a territory three hundred miles long and two hundred miles wide.

He also found time to visit Washington the following spring, 1868. There he spent so much time seated by the twenty-one-year-old Blanche Butler in the Senate gallery that the pair attracted the notice of a newspaper sketch artist.

She was the daughter of General Benjamin Butler, now a congressman from Massachusetts, the most active of the House managers pressing the case for impeachment in the trial of Andrew Johnson then taking place—the culmination of Republican furor at the betrayal they felt in Johnson's making common cause with the ex-Confederates he had once sworn to purge from the new order of the defeated South.

General Butler had been Ames's commander during an abortive first attempt to take Fort Fisher, and it was largely through the incompetence of Butler's planning and generalship that Ames's men had fought valiantly to within seventy-five yards of the fort only to be forced to fall back. Butler was unmistakably a politician; he was large, jowly, and bald; he was not a pretty man to look at it whatever one thought of his politics.

If looks were any guide, Blanche Butler might as well have come from Mars as be the daughter of "Beast" Butler. She was tall and slim, with long auburn curls falling below her shoulders and a face whose simple unaffected beauty defied the whims of fashion, sensuous and gentle, broad full lips, and eyes that carried a glint of intelligent amusement. She was already known as one of Washington's great beauties; she had no shortage of admirers; it would be two years before Ames saw or heard from her again.

Back in Mississippi that summer, Ames was appointed by the commander of the Fourth Military District to assume the duties of provisional governor of the state, pending ratification of the new state constitution and the holding of elections.

The current occupant of the office was Benjamin G. Humphreys, an
ex-Confederate brigadier general whom the white voters of the state
had elected in 1865. In that year Humphreys had urged on the legislature the need to adopt at once a stringent code to regulate the freedmen.
"Under the pressure of federal bayonets, urged on by the misdirected
sympathies of the world, the people of Mississippi have abolished the
institution of slavery," he told the legislators. "The Negro is free, whether
we like it or not. To be free, however, does not make him a citizen, or
entitle him to political or social equality with the white race."

The new law passed at Humphreys's urging accordingly reenacted in
toto the penal laws that had applied to slaves and applied them to the
freedmen; it ordered the "apprenticing" of Negro children to their former owners; it declared as vagrants any Negroes without an employment contract for the year and directed the local sheriff to auction off
their labor; it authorized any white citizen to arrest a freedman who quit
his service before the expiration of his term; it forbade Negroes from
renting or owning land or possessing arms; it established a white militia
to guard against black insurrections. In December 1867 Humphreys
issued a proclamation warning of just such an impending insurrection.
A subsequent investigation could not find on what evidence Humphreys
had reached this conclusion. Enough was enough, and, with the authority of Congress, Humphreys was removed by military order.

General Ames sent a polite message to his predecessor, allowing that
he might continue to occupy the governor's mansion for the meanwhile,
and asking when he might call upon him "for the purpose of making
such arrangements as may be necessary to carry into effect the order."

After a week Humphreys replied that he considered his removal a
"usurpation of the civil government of Mississippi—unwarranted by
and in violation of the Constitution of the United States. I must therefore, in view of my duty to the constitutional rights of the people of
Mississippi, refuse to vacate the office of Governor, or surrender the
archives and public property of the State, until a legally qualified successor under the constitution of the State of Mississippi is appointed."

Ames sent a few soldiers to the take possession of the governor's
office in the statehouse. He sent the ousted governor a tougher letter
than his first one.

July 6th, 1868

Sir:

Soon after my arrival here as Provisional Governor, I notified you that you might continue to occupy the Governor's mansion. Since then I have had cause to change my mind in the matter.

You will oblige me by vacating the mansion at as early a day as convenient.

Very respectfully, your obedient servant,
A. Ames, Provisional Governor

Humphreys replied that "the Governor's mansion was built by the taxpayers of Mississippi for the use and occupancy of their constitutional Governors and their families. They elected me to that office in 1865, and I, with my family, have been in peaceable, quiet, and legal possession ever since. In view of the expressed desire of the just and lawful owners that this property remain in the continuous possession of their own chosen custodian, I must respectfully decline to oblige yourself."

Ames tried tact.

July 9th 1868

Sir:

I have been informed (it is possible my information is incorrect) that you do not find it convenient to vacate the Governor's mansion.

I presume it is because of the difficulty in finding other fit residence. It is my wish to put you to as little personal inconvenience as possible. Under the above supposition, I have no objection to your occupying a part of the house. Next Monday, by which time you can make the necessary arrangements, I, with others, will take possession of a part of the house. So long as we may remain joint tenants, great care shall be taken not to inconvenience your family.

Very respectfully yours, etc.
A. Ames, Provisional Governor

Humphreys replied that "it will be disagreeable to share the apartments of the Governor's mansion with other permanent tenants."

Finally, Ames shot forth a brusque rejoinder. "You entirely ignore the reconstruction acts of Congress, and the action taken by those empowered to act under them. I recognize no other authority." He sent his aide to deliver an order, accompanied by a touch of sarcasm, and a squad of soldiers:

July 13, 1868

Sir:

General Ames, the Provisional Governor of this State, has called upon me, as the officer in command of this post, to gain possession of one-half of the mansion now occupied by you.

I send Lieutenant Bache, with a guard of men, to see that General Ames' request is carried out. Lieutenant Bache will hand you this letter.

I do not desire to use force if I can help it, but he will be instructed to do so if necessary. I wish to avoid all unpleasantness to yourself and family, but if you desire, for political purposes, to have a military "pantomime," I have also instructed Lieutenant Bache to carry it out with all the appearances of a reality, without actual indignity.

I am, sir, very respectfully, your obedient servant.

James Biddle

Captain and Lieut.-Col. U.S.A. commanding post

The "pantomime" was accordingly carried out. Humphreys and his family marched out between a file of soldiers, the *Vicksburg Times* declaring THE FIRST ACT OF OUR NEW DESPOT—SHOULDER-STRAPS IN THE EXECUTIVE MANSION.

Ames responded in turn by making clear that he didn't give a fig for public opinion; he was a soldier with a job to do and clear orders to do it.

At the direction of Congress, he dismissed all ex-Confederate officials still holding state and local offices—which covered just about all of them—and appointed hundreds of new county supervisors, mayors, judges, sheriffs, and constables in their stead. Among them were the first colored men in the state's history to hold public office, albeit minor ones, mainly constables and justices of the peace. When President Grant came into office in the spring of 1869, he appointed Ames to command the Fourth Military District in addition to continuing his duties as provisional governor, and Ames at once issued a military order making colored men competent jurors and reducing the poll tax.

The fourteen hundred U.S. troops on duty in the state when Ames assumed the governorship in June 1868 had dwindled to three hundred by October of 1869; he noted in his official report that fall that their employment "has been confined almost exclusively to expeditions into the country for the purpose of arresting lawless characters who had been guilty of murder or other serious offenses." They had their hands full in that task, however; for the "prevailing sentiment in many sections of the State," Ames bluntly reported, was a refusal to accept the new realities that the war had established. Whites who dared to differ from the old-line attitudes were driven from their homes; freedmen organizing to vote were beaten or killed; the killers were invariably shielded by their neighbors. "Civil officers are unequal to the task of bringing such violators of the law to justice. The assistance of troops is demanded." None of which prevented the white press from screaming about "military despotism" and "bayonet rule."

When Ames named military officers, typically a lieutenant or captain, to serve as inspectors of registration for each county, the white press screamed again, charging that he was seeking to carry the upcoming elections by force. To the adjutant general, Ames reported scornfully, "Three hundred and twenty two men, including the regimental band, non-commissioned staff, clerks and orderlies &c. &c. are all I have with which to force a state to vote against its will!"

To General Sherman, whom Grant had appointed general-in-chief, he added more seriously: "The contest is not between two established parties, as they are elsewhere, but between loyal men and a class of men who are disloyal." The same men who led the state to secession were now seeking to regain power through violence and intimidation. The murders taking place across the state were not "usual events of ordinary times," but "outrages mainly based on political enmity and hatred."

"The war still exists in a very important phase here."

10

In the fall of 1865, Albert T. Morgan went to Mississippi to seek his fortune. "Boys, you'll rue the day," his father told Albert and his brother. But they went anyway, as young men will. There were fortunes to be made in cotton, and when they got off the steamer at Vicksburg the town was full of others who had come down the Mississippi with the same idea. The hotels were full and land agents were busy with long lists of plantations for sale and plantations for rent.

Morgan and his brother knew something about planting and hard work. They were from that restless pioneer stock that had moved westward in the generation before the Civil War, drawn ever onward by opportunity. Their parents had gone from New Hampshire to New York, hacked one farm out of the dense wilderness there, then made the longer trek to Wisconsin and broke the virgin prairie.

At Gettysburg, Albert had taken a ball through the thigh that had shattered the bone and passed out through his buttock; he had returned to duty but was a wreck, with a sallow complexion, a shriveled, dragging leg, a collapsed abdomen held in place only by a truss, and a malaria-wracked frame that had dropped to 145 pounds.

"Physically, I had all my life been a coward," he later wrote, admitting he had run at the first battle of Bull Run, along with so many other green Union boys, and that even afterward he never could get himself in range of the enemy's guns except "through sheer force of will over my physical members, which were always stricken as with palsy just before a battle."

Still, he had exercised that force of will enough to have begun the war as an eighteen-year-old private straight from his first year at Oberlin College and ended commanding a regiment, a brevet lieutenant colonel, promoted twice for conspicuous gallantry.

And then the war had ended, and the newspapers were full of editorials extolling the South as the new frontier; the old exhortation "Go West, young man," Morgan would recall, had become "Go South, young man!"

In Vicksburg the natives seemed equally enthusiastic in their welcome of the "suitable Northern gentlemen of means" who had come to put their capital and energy into their war-stricken, impoverished land. The land agents were delighted to show them any property they might wish to see. The owners were eager to sell or let.

The first hint that all might not be so pleasant came when Morgan took a steamer up from Vicksburg to inspect a property his agent had recommended. He disembarked at a lonely river landing with but a few rough buildings in sight. In the rude lodgings which were all that were available, Morgan shared supper with fifteen rough-looking characters, most of them wearing Confederate gray and pistols at their waists.

They were there to attend the county court, which was being held in a barnlike building little better than the board shanty that served as the lodging house. The men glared at him when Morgan declined a drink of whiskey from one of the two large bottles that stood at either end of the table.

One demanded to know his name and his business. Morgan answered frankly.

"No Yankee radical could ever come into that county, make a crop, and get away with it," the man replied.

With no boat or other escape until morning, Morgan realized he would have to bluff it out. Rising to his feet, he declared that he was there on legitimate business as he had every right to be; if any of them possessed the "chivalry" so often claimed to be a peculiar part of the Southern character, they would never have behaved as they had done to an utter stranger in their midst.

He strode into the next room and heard the men whispering among themselves. The leader then came to apologize and suggested that he himself was thinking of renting his plantation; he would personally send his horse and boy for the traveler the next morning. In the morning, after the planter had gone, the landlady—a freedwoman—urgently advised Morgan to get on the boat and go; she had heard the men plotting to waylay him on the roadside and hang him to a tree. He left.

Back in Vicksburg he was assured that these were a few "irresponsible, worthless fellows" he had run into, and he ought not to heed anything they said or did.

Two days later his brother returned with a far better report from his own inspection trip: Tokeba plantation was just what they were looking for. Nine hundred acres of open land, right by a growing commercial center, Yazoo City. The owner, a Mrs. White, had been perfectly charming and hospitable; in light of the fact that the Morgans were proposing to lease the property for three years, and planned to settle permanently in the area, she was willing to reduce the rent from ten dollars an acre of open land to seven.

She would even throw in a cypress brake of several thousand trees, and allow them to use it for anything they wished, including the manufacture of commercial lumber for market. The next morning Albert's brother hurried north to purchase equipment for a sawmill while Albert took the steamer up the river to Yazoo City to complete the formalities on the lease of Tokeba.

His first day there, a fine Sunday morning in November, he ascended the hills that rose to the east of town and looked down on his new home. Two and half miles upriver the bluffs crowd close to the east bank of the Yazoo, and on the opposite bank lay Tokeba, an open spot in a vast forest of gum and cypress trees, bounded on the south by the cypress brake and on the north by a creek, Tokeba Bayou, which gave it its name. It was an Indian word, but it was pronounced locally as something like "took a bar," and that was what people said the name came from; it had once been a famous spot for bear hunting.

From the Yazoo River on west eighty miles to the Mississippi lay the flat alluvial plain, the great Delta of rich soils and untapped wealth.

Mrs. White and her husband the colonel wouldn't hear of Morgan staying at the hotel when he called on them at their home in town; he must be their guest "for the present." The next morning the colonel mounted an old gray horse and put Morgan on a smart, mouse-colored mule, and off they set for the plantation. An old bent-over colored man stood at the ferry waiting to pole them across.

"Good-morning, Bristol."

"Good-morning, marstah."

"This gentleman is Captain Morgan's brother, Bristol. We're going over to take a look at Tokeba this morning. How's aunt—" But the colonel never finished his question. "Hey, you black rascal! Don't go putting on the airs of a gentleman about me. D'ye hear? Mind that!"

What had the poor fellow done? Morgan wondered. For the life of him he hadn't noticed anything to criticize in the man's deportment.

But apparently the colonel had, for he continued his threats and invectives, then began to discourse for Morgan's benefit on the laziness, thievery, and general treachery of "the whole damned nigrah tribe," pronouncing "nigrah" with that proprietary snap Morgan would subsequently hear often coming from the lips of "the real Southern lady or gentleman."

The colonel's equanimity recovered some as they rode over the grounds: past the gin-house, past the family residence surrounded by stately China and magnolia trees, past the cypress brake filled with trees six or even eight feet wide, rising straight as an arrow eighty feet to the first limb. But the sight of the nearly deserted slave quarters, cabins enough for 125 hands, led to more bitter words from the colonel about the ingratitude of the slaves; only two of the cabins were still occupied, one by an old man looking after his mother, said to be near a hundred years old, the other by a much younger woman nursing a baby; the woman had lost a leg.

But then this led to a long anecdote, told with the enjoyment of fond recollection, about the time the colonel had run for state senate. He had run as an old-line Whig, back before the war, and had gone about canvassing the district on horseback with two mules following behind; on the one he had packed an ample supply of whiskey and tobacco, on the other "that gal, Sal, by God, sir"; back then she'd been

a "likely gal," hadn't yet lost her leg. Everywhere he went he offered
the voters to "choose their taste" from the "creature comforts" he
toted with him. "By God, sir, that did the business for me, and I was
the first Whig senator ever sent to the legislature from this county."

Aside from puzzlement over Morgan's continuing refusal to take a
drink with him—the colonel strongly advised a morning dram as essential to health in that climate, and an evening dram for proper di-
gestion, and a nightcap for sound and healthful sleep, and frequent
additional trips to the sideboard in between for good measure—he
seemed to be perfectly pleased with his wife's new tenant, and continued to make him welcome at his home in town. Every evening Morgan joined the family circle at dinner and sat in the parlor afterward,
conversing pleasantly with the young ladies of the family and the frequent visitors who joined them, all members of the best families of
the county. When the talk turned from time to time to the late war or
current politics, Morgan kept his views to himself. The Whites' social standing and his status as their "Yankee guest" meant, he found,
that he could go anywhere, "absolutely protected against insult."

That began to change soon enough.

Twice when seeking laborers to employ among the freedmen of
Yazoo City, Morgan was accompanied, not by his choice, by Colonel
White. On these occasions the colonel would alternate between addressing the freedmen as "hey, you, boy" and engaging in mocking,
elaborately facetious courtesies. "Mr. Julius Caesar," the colonel would
say, "how do you do today? How's your good lady?" Morgan realized
this was meant to be a hint to him "not to be nice in my manners of
addressing the freed people."

Soon Morgan's offers of fifteen dollars a month wages and his common civility to the freedmen he was seeking to engage began to attract
more pointed and less humorous comment from the white townspeople.
Some planter in town on similar business would watch silently as Morgan stood conversing with groups of freedmen, then back off and in a
stage whisper ask someone who he was, and then mutter, "I thought
so," scowl for a minute, then turn with a deprecatory jerk of the head or
wave of the hand.

Soon it became clear that there was trouble ahead if he continued trying to hire workers on the streets of Yazoo City, and so he went down to Vicksburg, where he heard a large group of freedmen were squatting at a former Union army camp on an island in the Mississippi River. There he found all the workers he needed; there he also, for the first time, learned the truth about Colonel and Mrs. White. Many of the freedmen there were the former slaves of Tokeba. They knew exactly who Morgan was; the "word was put out"; they had all heard Tokeba had been rented to the Yankees. They were happy to come back to Tokeba, and especially happy to work for the Yankees.

They also wanted to tell him some stories. Morgan sat up most of the night listening.

Simply, the Whites had been brutal slave owners, Mrs. White even more cruel and tyrannical than her husband, regularly meting out floggings, brandings, and starvings as punishment for minor infractions. "Did you see dat ole jail dar on Tok'ba?" asked one. No, he had not seen any jail. But he found it when he returned, the solid, windowless log structure the freedmen had described, where the colonel had once locked up several of his slaves and gone off to New Orleans, and several of them were dead when he returned, and no one had dared interfere in the meanwhile.

The colonel took the news that Morgan had hired back many of his ex-slaves queerly. He got more drunk than usual that night. The rest of the family acted hurt.

Soon after that Morgan sat through a dinner at which a number of "prominent gentlemen" of the town were present, and the talk turned entirely to how the South had been "overpowered" by "Lincoln's hirelings"; and to general indignation over the Freedmen's Bureau, the Civil Rights Bill, and other attempts by those who did not understand "the nigrah character" to substitute their judgment for that of the black man's former masters, "the only persons competent" to manage him.

Morgan again stuck to his policy of silence. But one of the prominent gentlemen insisted he offer his views. Morgan had stored up enough resentment over weeks of silence, and now the dam burst. He

told them he had been no "hireling"; that Grant was a great general
and Lincoln a great man; that the freedmen deserved all the rights of
citizenship.

Not long after that Morgan paid over the $3,150 due in advance
for one half of the first year's lease on Tokeba, and moved out to the
plantation.

A few days later Morgan's brother returned from Wisconsin, always the bearer of good news. He had engaged a lumberman and a
sawmill, and within weeks things were humming at Tokeba. New
hired men and new bought mules were busy breaking ground; the
anvil rang all day long in the blacksmith's shop, making and repairing plows and implements. And on a calm day the steady singing of
the sawmill could be heard on the streets of Yazoo City, two miles
away.

With the sounds of success rose more resentment.

Rumors now began to fly in earnest. Some were true, some were
untrue; some plainspoken, others hinting. Morgan was said to have
allowed his Negroes to call him "Colonel Morgan" rather than "master." He himself was said to have called his colored blacksmith's wife
"Mrs. Smith." Mrs. White had driven out to Tokeba the other day
and there was Morgan's brother right alongside "his nigrahs," working away at the mill, and when he came over to speak to the lady he
was in his shirtsleeves. Those were the true ones.

Morgan was supposed to have declared that "a nigrah wench was
as good as a white lady." This one had layers to it, layers that ran deep
through the unspoken manners of Southern society.

The plantation office was a small building within the yard of the
house, but separate from it, surrounded by its own bower of China
trees. It had been the colonel's "study." Morgan had been puzzled for
some time by the constant traffic of well-dressed and light-skinned
colored girls who always seemed to come by when he was out there.
They would pass by two or three times an evening, some of them, on
some pretext or another, making themselves quite conspicuous, always stopping in at the office at some point to make some inquiry.
Morgan would place a chair for his visitor, exchange some polite
words.

Finally one day one of them said, "Colonel, it 'peers to me you are a long time taking a hint!"

"She was a very comely person," Morgan later recalled, "and I have often wondered why I was so dull of comprehension." Be that as it may, it took him several more minutes of painfully naive questioning to figure out what she was getting at, at which point he turned bright red and awkwardly ended the interview, having made clear his deep moral disapproval of one of the oldest customs of the place.

A few days later he ran into Colonel White in town. Calling Morgan aside, face turning purple, hands shaking, he told Morgan he must publish a "card" in the local newspaper at once denying that he had ever said "a nigrah wench is as good as a white lady."

He had made every excuse he could for Morgan with his friends. But "our people," the colonel went on, "are very sensitive upon one question, and cannot tolerate in our midst any division of sentiment. We are bound to look upon any man as a public enemy, by God, sir, I care not who he is or whence he comes, who does not consent to this. The nigrah is an animal by God; and by God, sir, he must be kept in his place; and who knows better how to manage a horse or a steer than one who is familiar with his raising?" The ideas Morgan and his brother had been putting into the heads of the nigrahs was intolerable, sir. Why just this morning, his own serving girl Rose had come in to bring him his toddy and called him "Colonel White." By God, sir, she would not repeat the insult, the hussy.

Morgan later learned what everyone else in town knew: that Rose was the colonel's favorite concubine.

When the colonel stopped to draw his breath at last Morgan replied that he had no intention of interfering with the customs of others, but he and his brother had paid the rent for Tokeba according to their agreed contract; they were the legal owners for three years, were risking their own money in the venture, and only claimed the same right as any other men to manage their business as they saw fit without interference.

"Well, by God, sir, as you make your bed you must lie. I took you for a gentleman. You are only a scalawag."

Now the insults and confrontations became general. The brothers had sold a large consignment of lumber to a merchant in town on credit. Morgan went to ask for payment of the bill after some months had gone by. The man, a drugstore owner, an ex-Confederate captain, large, and powerfully built, asked him to call back in a week; he was a little short of funds at the moment. The two men parted and Morgan started down the street. He had gone but half a block when he heard his name called and hurried footsteps behind him. He turned and saw it was the captain, his face growing redder and redder as he approached. "What in the hell do you mean, you Yankee son of a bitch?" the man began as he came up next to him. "By God, sir, I'll have you to bear in mind that I pay my debts; I'm a gentleman, by God, sir, and if you don't know it, I'll teach you how to conduct yourself toward one, damn you."

Morgan was stunned; he was also at that moment recovering from an attack of malaria that had left him weak. The next thing he knew he had been knocked to the pavement by a roundhouse punch under his ear. His assailant then jumped on him and continued pummeling his head and face.

A crowd quickly gathered to cheer the captain on. "Fair play, here! Fair play! Kill the damn Yankee! Kill him, damn him!"

But even that was not the worst. In a symbolic act much appreciated by the Whites' ex-slaves, Morgan had had the old jail torn down and the logs reused to build a schoolhouse on Tokeba. A friend of their sister's, a young Northern woman, agreed to come and teach the thirty children of the freedmen who worked the farm and mill.

This made all their previous offenses against Southern mores pale by comparison. The "nigger school marm," who had the fault of being not only respectable but also young and pretty, was ostracized by the ladies of Yazoo City; it was an outrage, they loudly declared whenever they happened to catch sight of her, to subject a young lady "to the consequences of such a calling"; a "crime against her sex and her race."

From that point on, Morgan recalled, "it was simply an accident" if he or his brother returned from an errand in town without having been grossly insulted. White women would gather up their skirts and hasten to turn away on encountering them; at the post office white men would block the way to the window and jostle them when they tried to collect their mail.

On the streets the Morgans were commanded to get off the sidewalk and "walk in the street with the niggers and other cattle."

11

Their first year's crop had been a near failure, only sixty-eight bales of cotton, worth about fourteen thousand dollars, against the thirty-six thousand dollars they had so far sunk into Tokeba. The sawmill had kept them afloat, though, just about "coining money." Even the floods that had threatened the second year's planting of cotton had been a boon to the lumber business, allowing them to float out logs from parts of the cypress brake inaccessible before.

The summer of 1867 found the Morgans hopeful of turning the corner at last. Six hundred acres of cotton, as fine a stand as Tokeba had ever seen, glinted white with filling bolls. A half a million board feet of cypress lumber lay stacked by the mill, a million cut shingles; another million board feet of logs lay in the river, tied in cribs ready for the mill.

In early September the army worms came. In a week the six hundred acres of cotton looked like a fire had swept through it. The first installment on their second year's rent was due, and they paid the colonel twenty-four hundred dollars, which was all they had in ready cash, and got an extension on the remaining eight hundred.

At the end of the month the sheriff came. He bore a writ of attachment authorizing the seizure of all of their property.

The Whites' revenge had come. Colonel White, as agent-in-fact for his wife, had appeared before the magistrate and sworn that because he had reason to believe that the Morgans intended to remove their property out of the county "for the purpose of defrauding him" of his rent, he was entitled to seize and sell it at once—to cover not only the eight hundred dollars they actually owed at that moment but also the second installment of their rent for 1867, which was not due for another three months, and their entire rent for the coming year as well.

The Morgans could easily have raised the entire sum by selling their stock of lumber and continuing to operate the mill. The sheriff placed an armed guard over the mill and timber, and forbade them to touch it.

On the day of the sheriff's sale no one bid against the colonel. He bought the Morgans' $11,000 sawmill for $100. Horses and mules which were worth $130 apiece went for as little as $25. The logs in the river were left to break loose from their cribs and go to waste, along with most of the cut lumber.

Twenty thousand dollars' worth of property was knocked down for less than the rent the colonel claimed for his due; and so the Morgans lost everything and still owed. The sheriff triumphantly conveyed the seized stock across the ferry and down the main street of Yazoo City, and the townspeople came out to cheer. "Hurrah for Colonel White! We'll get rid of the damned Yankee sons of bitches now! Drive 'em out of the country!"

Morgan and his brother found shelter with friends; the town's Republican postmaster lent a hand, and one large plantation owner, a Unionist during the war, invited Morgan to make his home his own—as long as he kept the fact a secret.

To the colored people, the Morgans were still heroes. Riding his horse down the road from town one day Morgan saw an old colored man leading a little girl by the hand. The moment they saw him they darted into the bushes by the roadside.

Morgan called after the man, asking what was the matter.

"Nothin', marsa."

"Don't be afraid; what's the matter? Why do you leave the road?"

The old man came hesitantly forward, but his face brightened at once when Morgan told him his name and where he lived.

"You beez de Yankee con'l whar live on Marsa White's plantation?"

"Yes."

"You beez de ge'man de white folks were a talkin' right smart about?"

"Yes, I guess so."

"Well, den I reckon you is. Bless de Lord!"

The little girl's dress was stiff with blood. The story tumbled out. The previous night she had fallen asleep and been slow to get the door when her white employer had returned home nigh on midnight. He had beaten her severely; the old man, her father, had heard her screams and taken her away to his cabin.

The next morning the white man came to force the girl to return to her duties at the house. The old man's son tried to shut the door to their shack; when he did so, he was instantly shot dead with a blast from a double-barreled shotgun.

Morgan helped the man file charges and find a lawyer to prosecute. The defense admitted the killing but claimed it was justified; the defendant had feared the son was reaching for a gun. The colored man's attorney apologized profusely; he had taken the case only because "there are strangers in our midst, and my refusal to appear for this nigrah might be misconstrued to the injury of our people." He had "never appeared in a cause so repugnant to all his finer feelings."

The defendant offered to plead guilty to manslaughter; the judge had him post a bond as surety for his appearance; and that was the last the case was ever heard of in the Yazoo County court.

Now in the fall of 1867, when Morgan was broke and out of work, his colored friends rallied to him. He still owed money to his former employees, but they insisted they would not take a penny. And not long before the election for delegates to the state constitutional convention that November, a delegation of freedmen came to him beseeching him to run.

Morgan won by a vote of fifteen hundred to four hundred, stunning the native whites.

Selling a small quantity of refuse lumber that Colonel White had overlooked, Morgan scraped up a few dollars to buy himself a new suit and pay his share of the election expenses—$22.33 for printing ballots and hiring a horse.

In the stagecoach in Yazoo City waiting to leave for the journey to Jackson, he was again beset by taunts and insults. A crowd quickly gathered.

"Halloa, polecat!"

"Whar ye goin', polecat?"

"G'wain ter the nigger convention?"

There and back he was refused meals at eating houses and mocked and taunted; so were all the delegates. A Northern salesman traveling in the stage with Morgan, quick to sense an opportunity, filled his order book at every stop along the way by loudly denouncing the "radical black and tan convention" and offering to "whip the scalawag" himself. He assured his delighted customers that when he returned to New York he would be glad to be able to say that all the accounts printed in the papers of "outrages in the South upon Northern gentlemen are damned lies."

On his return to Yazoo City, Morgan found that his brother and another Northern friend had taken up quarters in what they facetiously called "the Yankee Stronghold"; but it wasn't much of a joke. The landlady they had first rented from in town had been threatened in a note signed "K.K.K." to get rid of "the den of Yankee vipers" or have the place burned down.

The local merchants had refused supplies; a colored woman who offered to bring them their meals was intercepted in the street and had the dishes knocked out of her hands; a colored shoemaker who had then offered to move in and have his family look after them found his trade boycotted.

Now the Yankees were holed up over a law office in a room with iron bars on the windows and a double bolt on the door and a small arsenal of carbines, shotguns, and pistols ready at hand. A dozen Negro men volunteered to stand guard outside every night. The denizens of the Yankee Stronghold passed the time studying law for admission to the bar.

On another return to Yazoo City there were new taunts for Morgan.

"Say, got any money left over from yer last investment?"

"G'wain back to Tokeba?"

"How's the sawmill business?"

"Got yer carpet-bag packed?"

On one political speaking trip to a staunchly Unionist county in the north of the state, Morgan was lectured by a white physician on the evils of a provision in the proposed new constitution. Section 22 of Article XII recognized as legally married any man and woman cohabiting as man and wife, and empowered the legislature to punish by law concubinage and adultery.

They sat on the gallery of a pleasant hotel, smoking cigars, looking out over the lights of the town below. The air was soft with the luxurious fragrance of flowers, and the doctor was wrought.

"Why, sir, that so-called constitution elevates every nigrah wench in this state to the equality of our own daughters. The monstrous thing! Ever since Washington's time—and he understood it—the world wide fame of the fair ladies of the South for beauty, for refinement, for chastity has been our proudest boast. This vile thing you call a constitution robs us of that too."

"My good sir, how do you make that out?"

"Possibly you all are ignorant of the effects of the work you all have been doing down there at Jackson. Everybody who has resided in the South long enough to get acquainted with our people and their ways must know that the nigrah women have always stood between our daughters and the superabundant sexual energy of our hot-blooded youth. And, by God sir, your so-called constitution tears down the restrictions that the foresight of our statesmen for more than a century has placed upon the nigrah race in our country. If you ratify it and it is forced on the people of the state, all the damned nigrah wenches will think themselves too good for their place, and our young men'll be driven back upon the white ladies, and we'll have prostitution like you all have it in the North, and as it is known in other countries." Morgan had to look carefully at the doctor, and the reaction of his audience of twenty local white men, to make sure he was not in jest. He was not.

But the colored people held true. In the fall of 1869 Morgan, still no politician, was elected to the state senate from Yazoo County.

In that same fall, he had been in Jackson on campaign business when a political ally invited him to visit a colored school. As they approached the building he heard the pupils singing "Your Mission," and then "John Brown's Body," then some song he didn't know but which began, "We are rising as a people." One voice rose above the others, and Morgan stopped transfixed, halting his friend, to listen.

Then they entered the school and the teacher came forward to greet them. "We are always glad to have such distinguished gentlemen visit our school; it encourages the children," she said with a smile. She was a light-skinned colored woman, barely older than many of her pupils and younger than some in fact; she looked no more than eighteen herself, with a young woman's figure, simply yet elegantly dressed, "with all the simple grace of an honest, blushing country girl, yet with all the dignity of a veritable queen," as Morgan would later tell the story over and over.

Or, more simply: "The first time I saw Carrie, I lost my head."

She was bright, attractive, and possessed of a remarkable command over her seventy students, who ranged over all grades and ages, from small children to grown men.

When school was dismissed he walked with her on her route home, and learned more about her. Her name was Carolyn Victoria Highgate. She was twenty years old, from Syracuse, New York. She and her widowed mother and three sisters had all come south to teach and help the freedmen, had been doing so since the end of the war. She also led a Sunday school and a temperance society.

He was head over heels in love. He promised to give up the filthy habit of smoking cigars, for her. A few months later, as one of his first acts as a state senator, he introduced a bill repealing the Mississippi state statute, still on the books, that criminalized interracial marriage. The newly elected Republican majority of the legislature easily passed it into law.

The gloom and anger of the Yazoo years began to lift. He wrote his new friend and political ally Adelbert Ames a sprawling, ecstatic, twelve-page letter full of hope for the better world they were making.

> Truly these are grand times!
> The gloomy, portentous clouds which threatened anarchy and confusion to the whole country have been dispelled by the sunlight of the new era. Am I extravagant? I don't think I am. I have perfect faith in the result.

Yes, they still faced opposition. But even that was an inspiration only to fight harder, to fix their goal more truly, "to work, work!

work!!"; "the storm clouds only remaining as the glass through which we are enabled to see without being blinded."

It *had* been a mistake, he felt, ever to try to conciliate their opponents; every attempt at appeasement had been taken as a confession of weakness; nothing should have been granted the rebels until they voluntarily embraced all of the conditions of pardon. "Have they done this even yet in Mississippi?"

> When I reflect what hardships and losses we have sustained during and since the war because we were Republicans: how we have been ostracized, insulted, mobbed, and outraged by the men who surrendered to us at Appomattox, and swore fealty to our Gov^{mt} only to show us subsequently how that oath was only meant by them to be a means to their release that they might be free to exhibit their hatred, contempt, and independence, not only of the people who had conquered, but of the Government that have <u>pardoned</u> them . . .

He left that sentence unfinished; he went on:

> The errors of slavery and secession die hard.
> It is no matter of wonder to me that the children of that civilization which warred against the new should fail to comprehend the times that are upon us.
> Well, they are passing away! After all—

> > This world is not so bad a world
> > As some would like to make it.
> > But whether good or whether bad,
> > Depends on how you take it.

> It may be that the overtaxed brainpower of the nation, in its efforts to mould the destiny of this great country in compliance with the idea of justice and humanity which must be nearest to God's shall also become wearied. Then will the world stand still!

The world cannot stand still.
The devil and democratic party combined cannot stay
the onward march of the new civilization.

Albert Morgan and Carolyn Highgate were married in Jackson on
August 3, 1870, a few weeks after the end of the legislative session.
The ceremony was performed by a fellow legislator, J. Aaron Moore,
a colored man who was a Methodist Episcopal minister. The couple
barely escaped being attacked by a mob that night.

There were a few other reminders that the new civilization had not
yet arrived in its fully completed form. The Mississippi newspapers
reveled for months, printing vulgar comments about the couple. On
their wedding trip north, on their way to Cleveland, the couple had
an embarrassing episode in Louisville and the Mississippi newspapers
reveled more:

[THE HINDS COUNTY GAZETTE]

THE COLORED PEOPLE—We must give the following which
is by far too good to be lost.
From the Louisville Courier-Journal.
"Quite a sensation was created on the Nashville train which
arrived in this city 1 p.m. yesterday by "Hon." Albert Morgan, a
white Radical Senator, and his bride, a lady of high color and
standing. Upon their arrival at the depot, they attempted to get
into a bus with the white people, but Mr. Jno. Critchlow, the
collector of the transfer company, compelled the honorable gent
to get into the bus with his African brethren. Morgan is on his
way to his old home in Cleveland to spend the honey-moon."
Morgan having declared by his conduct his equality with the
negro race, and the negroes every where having received him as
their equal, we do not see that he has any right to complain that
he was seated in the colored reserved car, or that the negroes
therein should object that he was forced in among them.

They spent the month of September in western New York visiting
Carrie's sister Edmonia, who had returned north after five exhausting

years of teaching in Virginia, Louisiana, and Mississippi; she had spent the past year raising money for new schools and giving lectures to abolitionist societies, admonishing her audiences that even with the end of slavery their work was but half done. A few weeks later the Morgans received word that Edmonia, twenty-six, was dead. A story in the Syracuse newspaper supplied squalid details. The body of Miss Edmonia Highgate, a mulatto, schoolteacher by profession, well known in the city, was found in a shabby boardinghouse. A postmortem examination revealed that she had been pregnant, and had died from the effects of treatment for abortion.

Morgan's subsequent investigation discovered that she had been secretly married to a white man named Vosburg, who had insisted on the arrangement to keep the truth from his family, on whom he was financially dependent. "The world will condemn *me* for an honorable choice and an honorable courtship and marriage than it will Vosburg for this cowardly murder with the world as accessory," Morgan wrote a friend.

"My darling wife is nearly crazy," he wrote in another letter that fall.

The Mississippi press reveled as never before. Morgan wrote a letter to the Republican newspaper, full of raw pain; he had taken no notice of the slurs and comments about his marriage; but the devil himself, he said, would have been "content to stop with slandering me" and not reach into the grave of his wife's dead sister.

Back in Yazoo City, a few days after their return to Mississippi that November, Morgan was out one day when two colored "ladies" called upon "Mrs. Senator Morgan" to pay their respects and welcome her to Yazoo. This was a bit of rich sarcasm. They were two gaudily made up tarts, bedecked in expensive silks, jewels, and bonnets, put up to it, as it later came out, by some of the white ladies of the town.

But, as Morgan related, his wife had lived in the South long enough to know how to deal with such a social emergency, and adroitly sidestepped the problem of having to ask her callers in by having two chairs placed outside on the porch and politely bidding the women to be seated. They left in a huff. Word came back that at least a few of the proper ladies of Yazoo City expressed a certain grudging admiration for Mrs. Morgan's handling of things; at least she wasn't a coward. "Life in the old land yet, wife," said Morgan to his bride.

12

Cuttings from the Mississippi press from the elections of 1868 and 1869.

[THE MISSISSIPPI PILOT]

MISSISSIPPI DEMOCRATIC PLATFORM

"Resolved, that the government of the United States, under the Constitution, is a government of *white men,* for the benefit of *white men;* that the negro has, rightfully, no lot or part therein, except the right of protection of person and property." Resolution adopted at Greensboro, Choctaw County

"Resolved, that the nefarious design of the Republican party in Congress to place the white men of the Southern States under the governmental control of their late slaves, and degrade the Caucasian race as the inferiors of the African negro; is a crime against the civilization of the age, which needs only to be mentioned to be scorned by all intelligent minds, and we therefore call upon the people of Mississippi to vindicate alike the superiority of their race over the negro, and their political power to maintain constitutional liberty." Platform of the Democratic White man's party of Mississippi

"And that we regard the Reconstruction Acts (so-called) of Congress as such, as usurpations, and unconstitutional, revolutionary, and void." Democratic Platform

"The discountenance of every Republican, in every relation of life, with a pledge to each other, and to the Club, that we will neither employ them, nor rent nor hire to them on any terms whatsoever. All persons refusing to join this Club shall be regarded and treated as enemies of the Club, and of society." Resolutions of the Democratic Club of Dry Grove, Hinds county, Miss.

—————

[THE VICKSBURG DAILY TIMES]

A GOOD RESOLUTION

The Democratic Club of Marion, Alabama, recently adopted unanimously the following resolution:

"*Resolved*, That the members of this club, in their social intercourse, will not recognize any man as a gentleman, or a friend to his country, who may accept any appointment to office under the reconstruction acts of the Congress of the United States."

This resolution is good, but does not go far enough. If our people will refuse to speak to, or hold any kind of intercourse with such scoundrels, much of their harm is gone forever. Would any sensible man exchange any kind of courtesies with the villains who burn his house or murder his family? We fancy not. And yet the despicable wretches who seek to place us under the domination of ignorant negroes— to force them upon us as our political and social equals— affect to be terribly shocked that the Southern people should look upon them with scorn and abhorrence. This is the only true policy. Between the white men of the South and the advocates of negro suffrage, there should be a deep ditch and a high wall, and these obstacles should be as fixed as fate, and as impassable as the gulf which separated Dives from Lazarus, when the former was in hell, suffering all its torments, and the latter was experiencing the beatitude of Heaven. They should be made to feel that they are despised outcasts, cut off from all human fellowship and sympathy, and no companionship save that of the ignorant and besotted negroes they are seeking to use for their own base and selfish purposes. If the white men of the South were to adopt this policy—if they will neither speak to, or be spoken to by them, the negroes even will soon despise and scorn them as much as we do. Let this be done and our word for it the country will soon be rid of their presence. For ourselves personally, no man who favors negro suffrage and domination can be permitted to speak to us, to touch our hand, or receive in any manner the most ordinary courtesy or civility from us. Between them and us there is not a murderer or thief in the world for whom we have not more respect than we have for the vagabonds who are seeking to impose negro rule upon the people of the South.

The most abandoned criminal, the most cowardly murderer, the most despicable highwayman, that ever expiated their crimes on the gallows, in the State prison, or the galleys, are honorable and princely gentlemen compared to such wretched sneaks.

[THE MERIDIAN MERCURY]

IT IS OVER

With a sigh of relief, thank God, we can announce that it is over, the election, the most disgusting, disgraceful and degrading thing ever devised by the malice of man. Thank God it is over! And pray His holy name to remove the sin-created and sin-creating thing, *negro suffrage,* the most abominable of abominations, the "sum of all villainies," to which the sin of slavery is as snowy white is to coal black; to remove it from the land, and sink the hell-deserving authors of it to everlasting perdition! Confound them; blast them, scorch them with His righteous anger, and sink them to the lower depths, deeper down than the sympathy of the Infernal Spirits that inhabit the blazing regions of Hell can ever reach.

To say that the Great Ruler will not listen to the prayer, if we pray fervently, and walk uprightly, and keep ourselves unspotted and free from all contamination with the accursed thing, and hate carpet-baggers and scalawaggers, and proudly scorn to debase ourselves, as they do, to say that He will not listen to such a prayer, is to impugn God's justice.

Then with the skull and bones of the "Lost Cause" before us, we will swear that, "This is a White Man's Government; and, trusting in our firm purpose, our good right arms and the God of Right, we will maintain it so!"

If we falter now, we shall be damned; and let us see to it, that he be damned who does falter. Out upon a recreant white man who turns his back upon his race to marshal and direct negroes who are howling like savages at the ballot-box in the work of degradation! Condemn him! Spit upon him!

Now that it is over, let there be a searching of hearts. It can scarcely be possible that those who have participated in the late struggle have been contaminated with negro suffrage, or can look upon it with the least degree of allowance. Those even who have been most active and successful in the canvass with the negroes, and who in their enthusiasm may have been led to invoke God's blessing on the "glorious colored Democracy," should have the sternest face set against the abomination of negro suffrage. They have seen the monster, seen it good, and should have learned to hate it with intensity. But, let there be an inward searching of hearts, and if there be any weakness, any faltering in the cause of white supremacy, a manly struggle will overcome it.

Could Salmon P. Chase have been in Meridian during the three days of our election, and seen what was to be seen, in his heart he must have been cured of his abominable notions of universal suffrage. Look back at the things we have passed through and be a white man.

In whatever we do to maintain the supremacy of our race, remember it will and should recoil upon us, and defeat our ends and aims, if we forget to be forbearing with the negro, and just and honorable in all our dealings with him; and yet, while we are all this, we must make him understand that we are the men we were when we held him in abject bondage, and make him feel that when forbearance ceases to be a virtue, he has aroused a power that will control or destroy him.

———•———

[THE YAZOO BANNER]

SONG.

AIR—*If you belong to Gideon's Band.*

Old Morgan came to the Southern land,
With a little carpet-bag in his hand.

CHORUS.

If you belong to the Ku Klux Klan,
Here's my heart and here's my hand,
If you belong to the Ku Klux Klan,
We are marching for a home.

Old Morgan thought he would get bigger,
By running a saw-mill with a nigger.
If you belong to the Ku Klux Klan, &c.

The crop it failed and the saw-mill busted,
And the nigger got very badly wusted.
If you belong to the Ku Klux Klan, &c.

And Morgan is a gay old rat,
And the boys they called him a "polecat."
If you belong to the Ku Klux Klan, &c.

But some close at his heels would tag,
And call this hero "scalawag."

13

Adelbert Ames's marriage took place just two weeks before Albert Morgan's. He was now Senator Ames, sent to Washington by the newly elected Mississippi legislature by a near unanimous vote. He resigned his commission in the army after signing his own credentials: "I, Adelbert Ames, Brevet Major-General United States Army, provisional governor of the State of Mississippi, do hereby certify that Adelbert Ames was elected United States Senator by the Legislature of this State on the 18th day of January, 1870."

In Washington he cooled his heels while Senate Democrats objected that he was not a bona fide resident of Mississippi and had no right to represent the inhabitants thereof. His daily route to and from the Capitol took him right past the Butler home at 15th and I streets; in fact, he could see the house from his lodgings in McPherson Square, and he frequently stopped in to consult the congressman.

He also renewed his acquaintance with the congressman's daughter. While the Senate slowly debated his fate, the pair resumed their accustomed habit of occupying seats in the gallery together. They went on rides and drives; he found himself increasingly tortured by the sight of the unabated stream of admirers whom he often found occupying the Butlers' yellow-satin-lined drawing room when he came to call. One was an extremely wealthy, and extremely persistent, New York financier.

From the Senate gallery Ames heard himself denounced as a "tyrant," a "military despot," an "autocrat" by the Democrats. They said his election was a "mockery" and a "farce." They said he had exploited his powers as a military commander to advance his selfish political ambitions. They said if he had a wife and family and had bought a house in Mississippi and settled them there it might be different. But he had not even migrated to the state voluntarily; he had been sent there under military orders. The Judiciary Committee reported a resolution declaring Adelbert Ames not eligible to be seated as the senator from Mississippi.

But his supporters were able to produce affidavits from a series of his acquaintances stating that Ames had repeatedly declared his intention of making Mississippi his permanent home; the constitution of the state itself declared as a legal inhabitant anyone who resided within its borders, regardless of how he got there; and then the state legislature sent to Washington a resolution reiterating its choice of a senator and urging his immediate admission. On April 1, Senator Sumner of Massachusetts rose to move that the word "not" be stricken from the committee's report, the amendment was adopted, and the motion passed on a roll-call vote of forty to twelve.

From Northfield his parents wrote him with their congratulations.

My Dear Son:

John got a paper that gives us the first knowledge that a seat had been given you in the Senate. We congratulate you on this great event, and hope you will be able to do your country good. Before you are great responsibilities. May God ever direct you in the right.

The papers say you are engaged to be married to Miss Butler. We suppose it is all a hoax, as had it been so you would have informed your parents before you had the public.

The rumor was only a few weeks premature.

Blanche Butler was twenty-three, Ames thirty-four. Beyond her looks and her usual stock of refined young lady's accomplishments—her family, though Episcopalians, had sent her to boarding school at the Academy of the Visitation, the Catholic convent in Georgetown, where she had learned French, piano, singing, painting, and drawing—she had an independence and liveliness of mind that stood out for one of her age, sex, and time. Her mother had been a famous Shakespearean actress. Blanche read and said things young ladies usually didn't.

She left on a trip with her family the day after their engagement, and from New York and Lowell sent her betrothed arch, loving letters in which she made it perfectly clear that she had no plans to be in awe of him. "I hope you are discontented too. I should be very intolerant of any happiness on your part, so if you do not miss me you must never let me know it." He sent her a ring, which she pronounced lovely but fragile; it was good their engagement was to be a short one, she said, for the ring would definitely fall apart were she to wear it for five or six years. "It is the style now to leave out the word 'obey' from the Marriage Service," she wrote as their wedding date approached. "I thought I had better write and ask if you have any objection—at the same time to inform you that I have not the least intention of making that promise."

She sent him a small locket with a miniature portrait of herself and a snip of her hair. He spent his time in Washington waiting restlessly for the Senate's adjournment in July, playing billiards, mooning about, fighting off recurring bouts of malaria, and pretending with less than complete success to dutifully attend to his new senatorial responsibilities. "I will close my first letter to you and go back to my seat to assume that dignified (?) indifferent air, just as though I have not been having a chat with my Love, so far away." He sent her a page protesting that he had no desire for her to "obey"; "if there be 'love' and 'honor' what need of the 'obey.'"

"Dear Blanche we must not expect to escape the sorrows and troubles and annoyances man is unavoidably subjected to," he wrote another time. "Your life has been a very happy one. Mine has been that of the ordinary mortal. But you know, Dear, we are the architects of our own happiness. Now, everything surpasses anything I ever dreamed of. If only we determine, and hold to our determination, to make each other happy—be charitable, careful, considerate towards each other. I love you, Darling."

Their wedding in Lowell was attended by six hundred people; a crowd of ten thousand gathered outside the church to cheer the couple. Back in Washington the bride's father built an addition to his house, a bedroom and office, for the newlyweds to occupy.

That fall the couple traveled to West Point, attended two dances, called on and were called upon by all the professors, went on to Minnesota to visit Ames's parents. Blanche found her sea captain father-in-law everything she could have wished; Captain Ames walked through the tall prairie grass with a sailor's roll, apologized for the rain that set in the first few days of their visit, glancing at her with a twinkle in the eye and offering, "Lonesome weather, isn't it?"

In November they headed south. Her mother had written to counsel that she must not travel to Mississippi until the frosts had put a halt to the yellow fever for the season; "there will be time enough, and you must not encounter a double danger—the fever and the rebels."

"I should be a little careful in Mississippi," she added in another letter. "Some of the people are very brutal. No one can tell what they might think to do."

For a few months the new wife kept a diary, noting in it her amused annoyance that her husband could get ready for bed so much quicker than she (and lie there, luxuriating with a book, while she must spend half an hour "puttering around" with her toilette—"Men always seem to have the advantage,—in dress, in law, in politics—everything. Will the time ever come when it will be equally easy for woman to exist?"), noting her jarred reaction to the climate, physical and social, of her new adopted home state. Everything was strange, from the food to the manners to the very look of land, and little of it was pleasing to her.

> My breakfast the next morning was prepared in the true Southern style. Lard and flour for bread—lard and ham for bacon—lard and beef for steak. Lard was the basis of everything. When I say that Holly Springs contained the best hotel we have yet met, or are likely to meet, some idea can be formed of the manner of living.

> The southern ladies still seem to think that it must be a great deprivation to the poor "Yanks" being debarred from their aristocratic and delightful society. So fixed indeed, are they in this opinion, that they actually use it as a threat. No woman with a spirit of a mouse would submit to such dictation. I suppose no New Englander can understand the weight such threats could have upon that set of people who are not the acknowledged leaders of society in these Mississippi towns. Social ostracism is their bête noir. They

would grovel, cringe, and deny their bosom friends rather than be subjected to it.

To me the only redeeming feature of the South is the climate. But that is not sufficient to cover its multitudinous disadvantages. The malarious atmosphere, with its baleful influence upon mind and body, the red clayey turfless soil, filled with watercourses and gullies, the slothful indolence of all its people, would be insurmountable reasons why I could never regard it with favor as a permanent place of residence. Yet we are to think of it speak of it as home for at least the next five years. In talking the matter over with Del last evening I told him that he must regard the first chill, or ague fit we may either of us feel, as a good reason for declining a renomination if it were tendered him. . . . Yet after a plantation has been bought, on which there will very likely be a house of some kind, what are we going to do? People will expect us to occupy it, certainly a portion of the year.

Only Natchez somewhat redeemed the South in her eyes, with its fine houses and tree-lined streets, its roadsides edged with grass sod rather than the bare ground she found everywhere else.

Still—no amusements, no libraries, no social intercourse, little goodwill, at least not from the native whites.

Staying with friends there, the couple were twice serenaded by colored well-wishers. She, the politician's daughter, was in many ways more wise and experienced about public expectations than he; one day as they were out for a ride she asked if he had a speech prepared if called upon to reply. He did not. She forced him to work one up and recite it to her to practice, which he did, his face blushing to the eyes in self-consciousness.

They were scarcely back in Washington, back for the opening of the new Congress in December, when Ames began to receive new bad tidings from his friends in Mississippi.

A. T. Morgan wrote to thank him for a subscription to the *Congressional Globe* that the senator had sent to his address in Yazoo City,

but to disabuse him of the idea that he had found it possible to maintain a house there, or leave his wife there, in his absence.

Feb. 18 1871

My dear friend,

From this circumstance I was tempted to believe that you
had concluded, or was of opinion, that "my family" was at Yazoo
permanently. I had not the good fortune to be so comfortably
fixed and had to keep my wife here with me, which fact relieves
me of anything like an "establishment" in Yazoo or indeed if this
does not comprise the establishment. I feel very contented with
things as they go. Tho they often cut very deep, the wounds no
longer leave scars. "Carpet baggers", white + colored, are
considerably below par just now and will, I fear, hardly be able
to reinstate themselves by the influence of their own merits on
the "public conscience." To reinstate them by other influences
would, I fear, constitute another chapter of blunders in the
history of Reconstruction. This much is certain. Ex Rebels are
thawing out of the "freeze" in which you left them and are
"sunning" themselves publicly. Colored people are getting
desperate. . . . They are now being subjected to all manner of
insults + injuries. To suppose they do not feel these things is to
suppose they are <u>not</u> human. They have no land nor can they get
it. They have no hotels nor can they build them. Nor have they
Rrs, steam boats, or other conveniences. The consequences of
treating them in every particular as a forever separate + distinct
race from the whites forces their best + purest men + women
into smoking cars, "on decks," +c. even though they pay their
way as whites do. The insults of this order of thing must be
terrible. In the public schools too—colored people see that first
rate teachers are employed to teach beginners of the "white"
schools, while third rate are employed for colored schools. That
"good" teachers (white) will not teach a colored school so long as
they can get a white one. The result is their schools must wait,
General! These people must have land, they must have
something which will make them independent of Rebel or

Yankee for the means to their civilization if they are to meet such obstacles at every step of their advance. The Dem papers are growing very bitter—talk about hanging +c.

Things are growing worse + worse every day. The only remedy in my judgement is to give land to these people thereby withdrawing them from the offices of the country and removing the terrorism + oppression of the whites. There will then be no need for carpet-baggers here to uphold the "union," as it will have been cemented by an act of justice to the former slaves. They will uphold it.

Please when you write tell me something to take me out of this gloom + despondency. I have made this very lengthy. I trust all is well with you and yours.

Very sincerely yours,
A. T. Morgan

A month later.

March 16th 1871

My Dear Sir,

If any effort should be made to drive me forcibly from the state, as was made on Mr Huggins the other day, in Monroe County, + as are almost daily made in this state, I shall avail myself of the right which belongs to me under the Constitution + laws of the country, and defend myself with such means as I may be able to command. And I assure you General these means will be found quite extensive when the issue is finally made up. Colored men everywhere—such men as Caldwell, whom you know, are getting out of patience with the failure of the Government to protect these people against violence + outrage. Every day women are being taken out, outraged + whipped, because they will respect themselves and their husbands. Men are being shot + hung, or otherwise mistreated, because they will not be slaves! These things are happening everywhere, we hear of them, we know of them and we see, with our own eyes, their cause and the effect produced,

and yet appeal to the law or the officers of the law is vain. It is
full time that our government should be made acquainted with
these things. True, the colored people are powerless to protect
themselves, as a people against the whites as a people in a conflict
they would surely go down, but, said a leading colored man to me
last night, "I propose to die a man, than to live the life of a dog."
I can see everywhere a growing determination on the part of the
colored people to assert their manhood in the face of the whole
world.

The colored people will be prepared to meet the mob when
they attempt to repeat the Meridian "affair." What a cold
blooded massacre that was! The colored people, <u>disarmed</u> by
the <u>Sheriff + his</u> posse were afterwards shot down + their
throats cut <u>by that same posse.</u> The old idea that black men had
no rights which a white man was bound to respect is growing
everywhere now more popular among the late rebels.

And I only wish you were our Governor instead of our
Senator. The Legislature is not likely to adjourn before May.
There is much to be done. Can you not give us the K K bill, the
national school law and Sumner civil rights bill? We <u>need</u> all
these + more to enable us to stem the storm that is already
upon us.

With highest regards
I am, General,

Hon A Ames   }   Yours Very Sincerely
Senate Chamber}   A. T. Morgan
Washington   }

A few days later Blanche Ames wrote her mother, "Gen'l Ames is
in great tribulation today—for he is to make his maiden speech this
afternoon."

The freshman senator survived the ordeal and began to relish the
fight, for two weeks later he took to the floor for an hour, scornfully
rebutting the charge of "carpetbagger," cataloguing the recent outrages
that had taken place in Mississippi that his friends had kept him
informed of by letter and telegram: thirty colored schoolhouses

burned in the last year, sixty-three murders committed by Ku Klux bands in just the previous three months.

> In 1869 I had to stand between peaceable and law-abiding citizens and this Ku Klux spirit, not perhaps so well organized and disciplined as now. Believing then, as I do now, that Democratic officials would not second my efforts to give needed protection, I displaced all such, together with those who could not take the oath prescribed by law. That those hostile to our government should know that colored men were not slaves but citizens, and for their advantage as a race and in recognition of their claims as loyal men, I gave them office; to secure their rights in the courts I put them in the jury-box, and relieved them so far as I could from the unjust and oppressive legislation of their late masters. A successful and a grateful party sent me here.

He spoke of seeing with his own eyes, as a district commander in charge of military tribunals, the scars and blood of the victims of violence: "I would not, I could not refuse to extend my protecting hand, the nation's protecting arm, in defense of those who, innocent of offense, with upturned faces, asked for life. If my action then was wrong, may I never know the right."

Democrats in the Senate replied that these events were not outrages but inevitability; what else do you expect, they asked, when you try to "force political equality" between the races? Forcing men, "against nature and the wisdom of Providence," they said, will always end in "ferocities and horrors."

That summer Blanche Ames and Carrie Morgan each gave birth to baby boys, the first of six children each would bear.

III

"THE HALF HAS NOT BEEN TOLD YOU"

14

Major Lewis Merrill had heard of the Ku Klux, and didn't believe a word of it.

A newspaper reporter once described Major Merrill. He had, the reporter wrote, "the head, face, and spectacles of a German professor, and the frame of an athlete." That also summed up the two sides of the character that lay beneath. Major Merrill could be tediously didactic; he could be boundlessly energetic.

He came from a family of Pennsylvania lawyers, had finished in the bottom half of his class at West Point, had an appetite for staff assignments and writing long punctilious reports; his enemies in the army said he was nothing but a "coffee-cooler." As a cadet at West Point he had been brought up before a court-martial, charged that "when corrected in the usual and proper manner by the Assistant Instructor at Cavalry drill on or about the 21st of May 1855, did lift up his sabre in a menacing manner at the Assistant Instructor, and did make use to him at the same time of the following strong language, 'Damn you get out of the way, or I'll hit you along the side of the head,' or words to that effect."

The accused conducted his own defense, submitted an eleven-page statement to the court, and in cross-examination succeeded in eliciting the facts that he was riding an unusually refractory horse that day, not his regular mount; that the assistant instructor, a fellow cadet, had attempted to halt Cadet Merrill's horse when it broke ranks at the gallop by riding alongside and waving his saber in front of the horse's head; that this was not the usual or customary manner to halt a horse and did not constitute a "correction"; and that the assistant instructor might not have heard correctly the words that Cadet Merrill had uttered.

Question by the accused. Was not your left side towards me at the time and are you not very hard of hearing on that side?

Answer. He was on my left; my hearing on that side is somewhat defective.

The court found Cadet Merrill guilty, but struck out the words "in the usual and proper manner" and the words "or I'll hit you along the side of the head" from the verdict, and sentenced him to take rank at the foot of his class. The secretary of war, Jefferson Davis, confirmed the verdict but remitted the sentence.

Merrill acquired a fair number of his enemies when he subsequently acted as judge advocate on courts-martial himself, prosecuting fellow officers for misconduct, of which there was no shortage in the cavalry. During the war he had been a tenacious antiguerrilla fighter. In Missouri he had raised his own volunteer cavalry regiment, "Merrill's Horse," and in time was breveted a brigadier general of volunteers. He was ordered to clear the rebel guerrillas out of northeast Missouri. The guerrillas operated behind Union lines, robbing, kidnapping, murdering pro-Union civilians, killing Union prisoners. He tried arresting Confederate sympathizers, fifteen hundred of them, and releasing them once they had sworn an oath of loyalty. "I cannot point to one single instance in which they have faithfully kept their promise," he reported.

So in September 1862 he convened a military commission and tried twenty-two rebel guerrillas who had committed particularly gruesome murders, all after having been arrested at least once before and released on their oath. They were convicted and sentenced to death. When a seventy-year-old pro-Union civilian was kidnapped from the area, notice was given that unless he were released unharmed, ten of the condemned men would be executed at once. The abducted man was murdered; the ten prisoners were shot by firing squads. The other twelve who had been convicted and sentenced to death were shot not long afterward. Merrill personally wrote out the orders detailing how the executions were to take place—the condemned men marched into a hollow square, each at the end of the file of the six-man squad that was to dispatch them—and turned down their last-minute scrawled pleas for mercy.

The men of the surrounding communities whom Merrill believed to be the secret leaders of the guerrilla bands—the "haven't done nothing" men, as he called them, who always managed to escape arrest and punishment themselves—were banished summarily from the region. That seemed to solve the troubles, and northeast Missouri became considerably more tranquil.

Sometime after that Lincoln summoned the cavalryman to the White House.

"I want to inquire about that shooting in Missouri," the president told him.

"I can give you a written report in a few minutes that will explain all," he replied.

"I don't want anything in writing, General. I want you to tell me the story."

So he did, adding when he was done, "I telegraphed you a number of times asking your approval of the order and asking you, Mr. President, to issue the order yourself, but I asked in vain; and as it was a necessity, I took responsibility. It was my duty, and I have never felt a twinge of conscience that suggested I did other than right to my trust."

Lincoln walked over to the young officer and laid a hand on his shoulder. "Remember, young man," the president told him, "there are some things which should be done which it would not do for superiors to order done."

In this kind of war Merrill learned to use spies and subterfuge as well as the more orthodox cavalry tactics he had learned as a cadet and a second lieutenant at West Point and Fort Riley. He learned to doubt supposed "deserters" coming into his own lines with tales to tell; he had the officers of his staff befriend a Confederate prisoner and get him drunk to get him talking.

After the war he commanded troops of cavalry on the Platte and served as judge advocate on several courts-martial. At one trial, which took place in New Mexico in November 1869, he prosecuted a hapless quartermaster named Lauffer, who was accused of disobeying the orders of his commanding officer by submitting an improper affidavit to account for the loss of a "public mule" he was responsible for. The mule had been loaned to a mail agent who got drunk and let it wander off. Lauffer wanted to file an affidavit from the mail agent to excuse the loss of the animal. The commander said the mule shouldn't have been loaned in the first place and insisted that the enlisted man who did so should be made to pay for it. Lauffer filed the affidavit anyway. At the trial the commander admitted he hadn't actually given Lauffer a direct order not to use the affidavit, and that there was no reason to actually disbelieve the mail agent's story. So Lauffer was acquitted.

A few months later, detailed to Fort Leavenworth, Merrill prosecuted a Major Augustus Armes, an unpleasant egomaniac of a cavalryman who was accused of "producing and publicly exhibiting at the mess-table, at Fort Harker, Kansas, several lewd, indecent, obscene, and lascivious pictures"; of "then and there giving said pictures to the Negro servant Ben, and ordering him to carry them to a Miss Shaw, and ask her what she thought of them"; and "when the said girl, after such public insult, resented it by slapping his face at the table, calling her a 'damned fool.'" Armes was convicted and dismissed from the service.

Not long after that Lauffer left the service too; although he had been acquitted in the mule incident, he was so manifestly incompetent that he knew he would not survive a board charged with weeding out unfit officers, and decided to resign before he was thrown out. Merrill thought that was the end of two petty irritations. In fact, his enemies would keep dragging up these two seeming innocuous cases for years afterward.

It was about this time that Merrill ran afoul of the field commander of the Seventh Cavalry, his commanding officer, one George Armstrong Custer. One time Custer granted Merrill a routine leave of absence. When Custer's commanding general expressed displeasure on learning that Merrill was away, Custer claimed to know nothing about it.

Another time, in the latter part of 1870, Merrill was called to give evidence before the fitness board about some other officers in the Seventh Cavalry. In defending them he reluctantly, and as circumspectly as he could, offered some criticisms of Lieutenant Colonel Custer's notions of discipline and an officer's duty. These got back to Custer.

Not long after that Merrill heard that Custer was energetically circulating a piece of malicious gossip to the effect that Merrill had taken a bribe from Lauffer to go easy on him when he had prosecuted him in New Mexico. Some money actually had changed hands between them, which looked bad on the surface, though the real explanation was perfectly innocent: Lauffer owed Merrill five hundred dollars from a poker game. He had paid two hundred, and toward the end of the year 1870 Merrill wrote asking for the rest, and Lauffer wrote back saying that he had since learned that "this was an illegal and improper" payment, and that in fact Merrill had better return the two hundred right away or he was going to go to the adjutant general with "a full explanation."

Merrill at first thought that by "illegal and improper" the man was referring to a technical regulation that prohibited disbursing officers from engaging in any game of chance played for money; he wrote back that it was nonetheless a debt of honor that Lauffer should acknowledge as an officer and a gentleman. Soon after, however, Merrill caught wind of the new story Lauffer was telling, that the two hundred dollars had been a bribe. He also learned of Custer's role in spreading the story.

Merrill at once wrote to the adjutant general demanding an immediate board of inquiry to investigate the accusation against him so that he might clear his name. When that was turned down he followed up with another ten pages of close legal argument and closer reasoning reiterating his right to protect his "official repute against malignant attack."

He also wrote a blistering letter to his superior officer telling him exactly what he thought of his conduct.

"A very small amount of common courtesy," Major Merrill informed Colonel Custer, "might have suggested to you that upon hearing so vile a slander against an officer of the same regiment with yourself, you should make it your business to see that he was informed of it, and had the opportunity to meet it. Certainly any thing approaching the feeling of honor which has at all times been the boast of the Military profession, would have prompted you to be certain that the Officer concerned had this knowledge before you, yourself, gave the story to the common gossip of the army, behind his back and without his knowledge. I am entirely sure that you never believed the slander, and I am very sure also that it never had the slightest credence or weight in any quarter except what your repetition of it among strangers to me, may have given it."

Having been turned down again on his request for a board of inquiry, on the grounds that nothing had yet been actually placed in the official record, Merrill now challenged Custer to bring formal charges against him himself so that he, Merrill, could publicly refute the slander. Custer did not reply.

It was while all of this was going on that Major Merrill received orders to proceed with Company K of the Seventh Cavalry, and to assume command of the post of Yorkville, South Carolina, and there to aid the civil authorities of the state and the United States if called upon by them for assistance in halting the outrages being committed by the Ku Klux against the colored population of the area. He was to be a policeman but without even the powers routinely commanded by a village constable: his orders limited his own authority chiefly to the exercise of "moral influence"; he could employ force only to protect from mob violence or illegal arrest victims of the Ku Klux who had actually taken shelter in his camp. He left behind the plains of Kansas and a regiment full of petty animosities and jealousies and headed east.

On the way to South Carolina he stopped in Louisville. There he went to call on the commander of the Department of the South, General Alfred H. Terry. He told the general that he knew little more about the Ku Klux than what he had read in the newspapers. Surely, he ventured to say, the stories in circulation were enormous exaggerations; the newspaper stories, at least, were incredible—tales of shadowy bands whipping and beating leading Republicans in strange nighttime ceremonies, of schoolhouses set ablaze, Republican officeholders forced to resign on threat of death, entire towns seized by a thousand disguised men taking up position in eerie silence and stringing up a dozen Negroes who had dared to enlist in the state militia.

Terry was a Yale-educated lawyer. He replied, "When you get to South Carolina you will find that the half has not been told you."

Yorkville lay eighty-three miles northwest of the capital of Columbia, up the mainline of the Charlotte, Columbia, and Augusta Rail Road to Chesterville, then twenty-three miles over the tiny Kings Mountain Rail Road to Yorkville.

The train between Chesterville and Yorkville ran there and back once a day, four days a week, Mondays, Tuesdays, Wednesdays, and Saturdays, a tiny puffing locomotive pulling a single freight car and a single passenger car, making ten miles an hour over wooden rails covered with thin straps of iron. Changing trains in Chesterville a passenger bound for Yorkville was at a loss to find either a printed timetable or anyone in town who could say for certain when the train would leave. If he asked hard enough someone might point out the conductor walking along the street, who would say, "about two o'clock, a little befuh o' a little aftah," and assure the traveler he had plenty of time to go have his dinner at the hotel; "the train'll wait fo' you."

Major Merrill and the cavalry got to Yorkville the last week of March of 1871.

A company of United States infantry had got there a month earlier. They had a strange story to tell about the day of their arrival. The company had gotten to Chesterville on a Saturday night at the end of February, having made arrangements with the railroad to send a special train over from Yorkville the next afternoon to carry them the last leg of their journey. The train never came on Sunday. When it came on Monday, the soldiers were told that the track had been torn up the day before, which was why the train was delayed.

When the troops got to Yorkville they learned that they had just missed a minor battle. At one o'clock that morning all hell had broken loose in town. The town had been awakened by shouts and gunfire. A band of a hundred men, many of them disguised, had set upon Rose's Hotel, a well-appointed establishment on Congress Street, right in the center of town. Edward Rose, whose family owned the hotel, was the county's treasurer, a white Republican. He kept his office and sleeping quarters there at the hotel. When the mob came in the front, Rose dove out a back window. The men then proceeded to ransack the office, steal some loose change, smash up the bar along with whatever whiskey they couldn't get down their throats or take with them, and generally express their frustration that Rose had gotten away, because they had come to hang him. They then continued on up the street searching for a colored county supervisor they didn't like either, but didn't find him at home, and some colored people in a field nearby started shooting back, so the mob skedaddled.

Rose turned up at the infantry camp the next night, and shortly after that slipped out of town wearing an army uniform and made it to Columbia and didn't stop going until he reached Canada.

The timing of the attack, coinciding with the delayed train, was certainly suspicious. Still, for the first few days after Company K's arrival, Major Merrill was ready to believe he was on a fool's errand.

In a grove of oaks by the train depot rows of white canvas tents rose in geometric order, troops of blue-coated troopers trotted through town or lounged on the balconies of Rose's Hotel, and all seemed quiet on the pretty tree-lined streets of Yorkville. It was a town of fifteen hundred people, a number of elegant Georgian and Greek Revival houses, several hotels of which Rose's was "the most palatial," a row of substantial stately church buildings, Presbyterian, Methodist, Baptist, Episcopal, the last boasting a square Gothic bell tower and a bell cast from five hundred Mexican silver pieces donated by a parishioner, a good selection of grocery stores, millinery and shoe shops, and specialty stores. There were doctors' and lawyers' offices, a sturdy brick jail on the west end of town, and an equally sturdy brick building housing the offices of the local newspaper, the *Yorkville Enquirer.*

Inside the hotel Major Merrill sat at a desk and busied himself with the endless minutiae and drudgery of running an army post. He wrote out his letters; his adjutant copied them into the bound volume he had duly requisitioned from headquarters for the purpose.

To the chief of commissary of subsistence for the Department of the South he had the honor to state that he received his communication and could explain why *two* bottles of pickles had been purchased per month for each of the two company messes. Although this appeared large, Major Merrill begged to state that it was an authorized purchase. The company had arrived with only a few days of subsistence and no files of instructions or orders and requisitions had to be made at once. He had done his best to cut down the lists of stores, and would endeavor to do so more in the matter of items referred to.

To the assistant adjutant general he had the honor to report that fresh beef was available on the open market but of inferior quality and

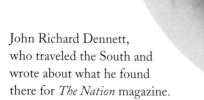

John Richard Dennett,
who traveled the South and
wrote about what he found
there for *The Nation* magazine.

Prince R. Rivers, who escaped
slavery, fought for the Union,
and became a South Carolina
legislator and trial justice.

Adelbert Ames, who won the Medal of Honor at Bull Run and lost the fight against white terrorists as the Republican governor of Mississippi.

Blanche Butler Ames, who was a famous Washington beauty, the daughter of a Shakespearean actress and a Massachusetts congressman.

Albert T. Morgan, who settled in Yazoo City, married an African American woman, and barely escaped with his life when white rifle clubs seized power.

Carolyn Highgate Morgan, who came to Mississippi from her native New
York State, with her mother and sisters, to teach in schools for the freedmen.

Lewis Merrill (top left, with other officers of the Seventh Cavalry), who fought the Ku Klux in South Carolina and White Leaguers in Louisiana.

James Longstreet, who was the most brilliant general of the Confederate army and became a pariah and scapegoat in the South when he supported the Republicans after the war.

(clockwise from top): Martin Witherspoon
Gary, Matthew C. Butler, and Benjamin
R. Tillman, who helped to plot and
instigate the Hamburg massacre.

at high price owing to a lack of competition. The fuel wood sold on the open market was mostly green or half-rotted windfalls, owing to the indolence of the local population. Some barrels of pork supplied by the depot in Columbia were bad.

It was proving exceedingly difficult to secure suitable living quarters for the officers. The hotel was being rented at a rate of twenty-five dollars per room per month, and that included use of the hotel's stables for the cavalry horses and some suitable outbuildings for the company kitchens and mess; but only one other house in town was available for rent and prices had been driven up by the loss of five houses in the town due to fires in the last year and a half and the failure to have yet replaced them. Rooms in private houses were extremely scarce and went for at least sixteen to twenty dollars a month even for the poorest accommodations. He had submitted an estimate of eighteen dollars per room only because this was the maximum permitted by regulation; yet it would not be able to cover the actual costs.

He had been able to rent space in the town jail for use by men under sentence by court-martial. He was unable to say whether the number of court-martial cases among the enlisted men was in excess of the usual for commands similarly circumstanced, but they were unduly frequent. Infractions included drunk on duty, reporting drunk and unfit for duty, disobeying orders, absent without leave, absent from guard duty, fighting. A private was reported to have said to another, before striking him, "You son of a bitch, I'll show you who is boss here." The abundant availability of cheap liquor at the town's many whiskey shops, with the impossibility of close supervision of the men while stationed in a village, was a constant temptation.

A few days after his arrival some of the leading citizens came to call on the major. They assured him they were opposed to violence. They pointed to an editorial in the *Enquirer:* Although the residents of the county were agreed that "there is no likelihood of any disturbances occurring at present," the editor of the local journal opined, nonetheless in a show of good faith they had called for a public meeting to adopt "such measures as might be deemed proper to maintain order and quiet." In that way "the exaggerated statements which are current abroad may be put to rest."

A subsequent number of the paper reported the resolutions of this meeting. It was a curious production. The statement included one sentence cautioning citizens that "force, if persisted in," will surely be suppressed "by the power of the Federal Government."

The rest of the document was a recital of the litany of wrongs that the white people of South Carolina had suffered. "Without intending to justify the acts of violence which have been committed in this county," the white citizens of York County asserted, "it is proper to set forth the fact that the negro radical government of this State is responsible for all the evils that are upon us."

First, the white people had offered the Negroes a chance: they had given them the chance in the last election to vote with them, against the radicals. "This reasonable offer was rejected; the black vote was massed against the white man."

What had ensued was inevitable. "Threatened by the bayonets of our former slaves, insultingly and defiantly marching by night and by day, in squads, and by companies, through the peaceful county and in the thronged streets; taxed until the last dollar is wrung from an oppressed and impoverished people; tormented to madness by a thousand acts of injustice and tyranny; retaliation must commence—it has commenced. The guilty perpetrators of crime and outrage have been overtaken and scourged. It was the result of their own aggression."

The centerpiece was a resolution which read, "*Resolved,* That the existing negro government of South Carolina is a reproach to the civilization of the age; a stain upon the manhood of an intelligent and gallant people who have so long and so patiently endured and submitted to be ruled by their former slaves. We are tired of it, and will exert every legitimate and constitutional means to effect a change."

When he had a free moment, the major went out for himself to have a look at the section of track that had been torn up the day of the infantry company's planned arrival, and he talked to the railroad's employees.

A mere two rails had been removed, and neatly. One of them, the conductor acknowledged, had been propped up so it would be clearly visible to the engine driver. On the Sunday that the troops were supposed to come the driver had set forth to Chesterville with only his locomotive, not bothering to see to it that a passenger car was attached, and had driven one mile until he came to the break, then returned to Yorkville and declared the track impassable.

Merrill observed that much greater damage could easily have been done along that particular stretch of track; the ties were rotten for some distance in either direction and might easily have been torn up. But the two missing rails hadn't even been damaged; in fact, they hadn't even been carried off but left right along the track. Any workman could have repaired the break in twenty minutes. This in fact happened on the following day, Monday.

In other words, it had been a mere pretext, carried out with the full connivance of the railroad's managers. In fact the whole town had been in on the plot, not excepting the very same leading citizens who had called on him to assure their goodwill and opposition to any disturbances of the peace.

15

Within a few weeks Merrill was reporting that even the pretense of calm had been dropped.

> Headquarters Post Yorkville S.C.
> May 4th 1871

Asst. Adjt. Genl.
    Dept. of South
Sir
    I have the honor to submit the following report, of the condition of affairs in this district since my arrival and up to the present time.
    On my arrival here March 26 I found the excitement at this place considerably less than it had been a short time previous. The presence of Capt. Christopher's company of Infantry had

tended to prevent lawlessness, and produced quiet by affording shelter to refugees from such violence, and by an apprehension on the part of the whites, that it would be called upon for use, if their lawlessness continued.

Upon my arrival I was kindly and courteously received by the principal citizens of the town, and subsequently, by the leading men of the county. They all assured me that the state of affairs in the county was bettering rapidly and that there was every prospect now for permanent quiet.

For nearly three weeks after my arrival, I heard of no instance of lawlessness occurring. At that time Ku Klux organizations began operations again, and have continued then ever since. The first one reported to me was of their visit to a man by the name of Brandt; they offered him no personal violence, and claimed to be searching for some state arms, supposed to be concealed in his house. On the following Saturday night, a band of some fifteen or eighteen of Ku Klux visited the plantation of a Dr Lowry, some seven miles from the town, in search of a negro man, who fled on their approach; failing to find him they seized his father, and whipped him severely, alleging as the reason that he had failed to bring up his son properly. One of these men was recognized by every negro who saw the party. He is a physician who has for years practiced among them and all of them knew him well. There was no room for doubt in the matter, could the negroes be induced to testify to the facts; but of some eight or ten who recognized him, and with whom I have conversed, there is only one who is willing to swear to the facts, and his evidence and recognition was the weakest of all. All the others, while freely telling me all they knew of the facts, and unhesitatingly identifying this particular man, refuse to appear and testify before a court. They say that if I could assure them of protection afterwards or could provide some way for them to get out of the county, they would willingly do it, but that while they have to live and work where they do, it would be more than their lives are worth to testify. This is a bad state of facts, but it is true they would not be safe a moment after they had given evidence against any of the Ku Klux.

I have had excellent relations thus far with the sheriff of this county, who is a good man, disposed to do his duty, but with the characteristic shiftlessness of the officials here generally, letting his chance slip or failing to follow up intelligently the trail of these fellows.

I have some hopes of being able to trap some of these scoundrels, and bringing them to punishment. The difficulties are numerous and I am not sanguine about the result, but see so much good to be accomplished by the punishment of even two or three that I shall spare no effort to accomplish it. The tracing and capturing these fellows would be the merest childs play, if I had the authority to go about it as I saw fit, but the necessity of keeping within the lawful limits of peace measures and civil processes hampers every action and complicates every plan.

I am well satisfied that the Ku Klux organization is much greater in numbers than is commonly supposed, and that a large number of the most respectable people in the county are more or less intimately connected with it. The debauched sentiment of the old slave-holding communities is not up to the mark of seeing any great offense in "whipping a negro for being a radical." The old sentiment is still rife, which prompts the settlement of a difference of opinion, by killing the man who dares to differ from them.

I do not very clearly see any way out of the difficulty, and the prospect of a peaceable future here is gloomy.

I was at first led to believe that the worst was past and so reported, but a fuller information leads me to fear that the fire is only smouldering. The negroes are conceded on all hands, to have gone to work with more energy and hope of success, this spring than ever before; but many plantations are now almost abandoned, and it is with difficulty that negroes are persuaded to remain on others. In many instances they have abandoned their crops and fled, and all are uneasy and restless, for fear they may be marked for victims of the next night's whipping.

I am not prepared to recommend yet, that any larger power should be given the military, unless it should be the complete military control of the county. The last is a measure of too much general consequence to permit me to judge of its propriety from the narrow view I get of the whole matter.

I am, Sir

Very Respectfully

Your Obdt Servt

Lewis Merrill

Major Seventh Cavalry

Commanding Post.

Methodically Major Merrill began accumulating a file of cases old and new; names, dates, locations, details were dutifully noted. Quietly he began spreading money around from a small secret service fund he had been entrusted to employ.

It was not long before his files contained documentation of four hundred whippings and six murders committed by the Ku Klux in York County since December. Several Negro schoolhouses and churches had also been burned. He knew with perfect certainty the names of eight or ten of the most prominent citizens who were involved. He knew of many more through circumstantial evidence that amounted to positive proof.

One of the most recent murders had occurred just a few weeks before he had arrived. The facts were not hard to find; everyone knew them; the coroner's jury alone purported to be mystified. No further investigation or arrests had occurred. But the major had no trouble finding witnesses and informants.

On the night of March 6, a party of seventy Ku Klux, led by a prominent physician of the area, had set out to find Jim Williams, the Negro captain of the local state militia company. They stopped at the house of a colored man, knocked him on the head with a pistol a few times until the blood was pouring down the man's face, and demanded he show them the way to Williams's house. "We are going on to kill Williams and are going to kill all these damn niggers that votes the radical ticket," they told him.

Arriving at Williams's place around two in the morning, a party of about ten of the men dragged him out of the house. His wife heard what sounded like strangling sounds. She opened the door to plead with the men not to hurt her husband. They told her to shut the door and take the children and go to bed.

Later that morning the members of the militia company followed the tracks left by the Ku Klux horsemen. They found the spot where the horses had been hitched while the smaller party had gone up to Williams's house. They found Williams's body hanging from a pine tree. On his breast a note had been pinned. It read, "Jim Williams on his big muster."

With no one willing to testify in this or any of the other cases, Merrill concluded, "it is idle to attempt arrests, unless the parties can be caught redhanded."

He already had informers, and set out to lay a trap; the plan was to dispatch part of the cavalry company to intercept a Ku Klux band during one of their planned nighttime forays; the sheriff agreed to accompany the troops and make the arrests. Just when all was ready the sheriff began making excuses, and begged off. Merrill almost decided to throw caution to the wind and make the attempt himself, sheriff or no sheriff, but then began to imagine how even a slight misstep by one of his soldiers might be used against him, even lead to civil charges being initiated against them, and so in the end he desisted. "It requires great patience and self control, to keep ones hands off these infamous cowards," he reported to his department headquarters, "when absolute knowledge exists, of who they are, and what they do, and what they propose to do."

He had another idea to step up the pressure. He called in one of the town's prominent lawyers, an ex-Confederate colonel, and told him he would like to have a meeting in his office with fifteen or twenty of the leading men, to see if "some means could be devised by which these disturbances would cease, and the necessity of military intervention or interference would be entirely avoided."

They came to his office at eleven o'clock on a Saturday morning in mid-May, and the major proceeded ever so politely to make it clear that he knew everything they were up to, everything that was going on. He described in minute detail recent Ku Klux raids, making it clear that they could do nothing without him learning of it, implying strongly that there were informers in their own ranks, and they could trust no one.

He expressed gentle amusement when one of the men asked for the names of the guilty parties so that they might see them brought to justice; the major said he was sure the names were as well known to them as they were to him; he could have them arrested himself within the hour if the authority were given him. Indeed, he expected daily to be receiving an order from the president suspending the writ of habeas corpus under the recent act of Congress that authorized the use of military authority to enforce the Fourteenth Amendment. This, he himself felt, would be unfortunate, he explained, because in such an event those arrested would be held for trial at the next session of the United States court in Columbia, Charleston, or Greenville, bail would surely be denied, some innocent men would inevitably be swept up with the guilty in the mass arrests, and the expense of procuring witnesses and counsel would be onerous, far more than the people of the area could afford.

The only alternative would be for the prominent men of the community no longer to keep silent in the face of unlawful acts, but rather publicly declare that such unlawful acts are wrong on principle, and must be unequivocally condemned.

His audience included two of the town's physicians, several lawyers, merchants, the former president of the railroad, the august editor of the *Yorkville Enquirer*. He was certain that at least two of the assembled were top leaders of the local Ku Klux organization.

The men held a second meeting, which Merrill made a point of not attending himself, leaving them to stew among themselves over what he had told them. Shortly thereafter several hundred citizens of York County signed their names to a published notice that duly appeared in the *Enquirer*. While not directly mentioning past events, the signers pledged themselves to "prevent further acts of violence" and to "aid and support the civil authorities in bringing offenders to justice."

Merrill reported to his commander that he had "no great faith in pledges of this kind." His intention had been a bit more subtle and devious. By embarrassing many men into signing the pledge "who have actually engaged in acts of violence," by publicly committing "the principal leaders of the Ku Klux order, against the continuance of these acts of disorder and violence," the notice would "breed a distrust of each other, among these fellows, which will be some check upon them."

But still the violence continued, and the cavalryman's files grew. A colored man had his house burnt down; a man was beaten with a ramrod; another colored man was given his choice of being killed or whipped 150 lashes, and chose the latter. A white man was hung to a tree and then cut down before he strangled but was then beaten severely; he came to town not long after that but refused to see Merrill, sending as reason he would surely be killed if were seen talking to him. Most of the colored men of the county were lying out in the woods and swamps every night in fear of a visit from the Ku Klux.

On a day at the end of May, Merrill sat at his writing desk in his private house and penned a confidential dispatch to his department headquarters. He placed it in a sealed envelope, put the envelope in the hands of one Colonel Seward, an army paymaster who was traveling on the train to Chester, and asked him to deliver it to the telegraph operator, there to be sent over the wires. The single copy of the dispatch that Merrill retained remained inside his desk at home until late in the day, when he gave it to his adjutant to enter into the office books.

That evening one of his Ku Klux informants came to see him under the cover of darkness. He told him that it was known around town not only that he had sent a telegram, but what the telegram said.

Merrill shrugged that off as mere inference from his having gone to the depot and having been seen sending papers on the train. But the next day he heard from others that the common knowledge of what he had written was disturbingly accurate: "Maj. Merrill had telegraphed for authority to arrest the Ku Klux, and had got no answer." That was indeed exactly what he had telegraphed to ask: whether he could carry out arrests on his own authority, with or without the cooperation of the reluctant county sheriff.

It took little more inquiry and plumbing of his sources to learn a few more suggestive facts. The driver of the train was definitely a Ku Klux member, the telegraph operator in Chester probably so. The time at which the contents of his telegram were known in Yorkville, and known in particular by the man Merrill by now knew for certain was the leader of the local Ku Klux, almost surely meant that word

had come back on the return train the evening of the same day he
sent it. And the only people who could have seen the original telegram at that point were Merrill himself, his adjutant—and the telegraph operator. The accuracy of the information the Ku Klux chief
subsequently passed on to others almost certainly implied that he
had obtained a verbatim written copy of the original. The railroad
driver had been seen conferring with the Ku Klux chief on his return; they were not men who in the normal course of business would
be thrown together.

Merrill's further probing revealed that a good many, if not all, of
the railroad and telegraph employees in the region were Ku Klux.

The man who had come to see Merrill and tip him off was now
being dogged and watched himself. He had already come under sus-
picion for betraying his fellows. Now he had been summoned to
appear before a council of the heads of five of the local Ku Klux orders
to explain why he had been seen in the grounds of Major Merrill's
private house late at night.

Merrill began sending his important wires in code, "Choctaw" he
called it. He had another informant, a colored man whom the Ku
Klux had ordered to accompany them on their raids, and who they
thought was utterly cowed, but who now came and told him of a
planned attack on his camp, which Merrill was able to deftly thwart
with a silent sentry here and a word to the wise about town there.

The men about town he spoke to on the matter were very curious to
know who the major's informant was, when he told them he knew all
about the plans to shoot up his camp and was quite prepared to meet it;
he replied that of course he could not say. He did say, however, that he
expected any day now the appointment of a United States commissioner empowered to make arrests, and when that happened all of the
men named as parties to the planned attack would be arrested on other
charges.

He also set paid watchers on every one of the "leading men" of
York County who spoke soothing words in public, and ordered murders and suborned perjury in private.

16

Slowly, through the chain of command, from Yorkville to the headquarters of the Department of the South in Louisville, to the adjutant general in Washington, a message made its way to the secretary of war.

Head Qrs Dept. South
Louisville Ky June 11 '71
Sir,
    I have the honor to forward enclosed copies of two (2) reports made by Major Lewis Merrill Seventh Cavalry, commanding the Post of Yorkville S.C. Yorkville is in what is probably the most disturbed district of that State, and these reports present, I think, a very clear and just view of the situation of affairs there, and of the difficulties which attend any attempt to bring to justice men who commit those crimes which are commonly known as Ku Klux outrage. Major Merrill is an officer of great intelligence, and I think that the utmost confidence may be placed in his representations.
    In connection with these reports, I beg leave to present views which have occurred to me in regard to the general subject of the suppression of the Ku Klux organization. This organization is spread over so very large an extent of country that it is manifestly impossible to deal with it efficiently throughout all the states in which it exists at one and the same time. The whole army of the United States would be insufficient to give protection throughout the South to all those who from time to time are in danger from the members of the Klan. Fortunately, it is not necessary, as I think, to attack the organization at every point. If in a single state it could be suppressed, and in that state <u>exemplary</u> <u>punishment</u> meeted out to some of the most prominent criminals, I think that a

fatal blow would be given everywhere, or that at any rate the task of suppression elsewhere would thereafter be an easy one.

Manifestly, however, military power alone is not sufficient to meet the emergency. Whatever may be the zeal and efficiency of the officers civil and military, one great difficulty is to be encountered and overcome before their efforts can result in good. Major Merrill reports that in his short experience in South Carolina, he has already met it. It is the great unwillingness of the people in general to give sworn information upon which arrests may be made, or to testify against members of the Klan before grand or petit juries, an unwillingness which arises from their fears of revenge.

> Alfred H Terry
> Brig General Com'g

On the sultry July streets of Yorkville there now appeared a Mephistopholean figure: dressed in black; tall, narrow; topped with a black stovepipe hat.

Everywhere he went he was followed by a band of hooting children, and scowled at, hissed at, and openly insulted by the knots of respectable white men about town that he passed on the streets. His name was A. S. Wallace; "Ass Wallace" they called after him.

He was a native of York County but rarely dared set foot there after being elected the Republican congressman from the district. Now he had come home with a congressional subcommittee investigating the Ku Klux outrages, and was going about his constituency locating the colored men and women who had been their victims and pleading with them to come forward and tell their stories.

Major Merrill's spies who had infiltrated the local Ku Klux reported that its leaders had held a meeting three days earlier, and had agreed to kill any of their members who revealed any of their secrets to the investigators.

The three subcommittee members arrived from Columbia and received a reception similar to Wallace's. The *Yorkville Enquirer* ran amusing little stories referring to them as the "sub-outrage committee."

Attorney Witherspoon was one of their early witnesses, the man who had arranged for the meeting of prominent men with Major Merrill back in May. He was asked about the loud insults directed at them in the streets, the men who would pass and say, as if referring in passing to a point of previous conversation but loudly, and pointedly intended for their ears, "Yankees," "damned Yankees," "Yankee sons of bitches."

The first expression, the attorney explained, was merely a perfectly neutral term that conveyed no reproach in the least.

So they would call me a "Yankee from Ohio"? helpfully offered the subcommittee's Democratic member, Mr. Van Trump of Ohio.

"Yes, sir; any one who is a stranger from the North."

And as for the other expressions? asked the chairman. How are we to understand them?

"You have heard the heated expression of some man who had swallowed bad whiskey."

One night at dinner at Rawlinson's Hotel, Major Merrill sat with Wallace and Representative Job Stevenson, one of the subcommittee members, and the members of the congressional staff who had accompanied them on their fact-finding travels. One of the regular boarders at the hotel was a local, an ex-Confederate major by the name of Mr. Barry. Barry came in just after the men had sat down and took a seat directly opposite from Wallace.

"Are you the Hon. Mr. Wallace?" he loudly demanded. No one answered. Barry picked up a pitcher of cream and started to hurl it at Wallace, but the hotel's owner, Mr. Rawlinson, tried to block the throw and the cream ended up mostly on Congressman Stevenson instead. Everyone jumped to their feet and reached for their pockets. The locals assumed they were going for pistols, but only handkerchiefs came out. The hotel owner hustled Barry out of the room, and Barry then sent his profuse apologies—to Mr. Stevenson. He then went about boasting of his accomplishment, apologizing that he had not been able to make it hot coffee as he had originally intended. The next morning Wallace was renamed "Buttermilk Wallace" by the wags of the town.

After dinner a band of colored musicians came to the hotel to serenade the visitors. A crowd of whites came to heckle the band. A scuffle broke out, a white constable shot a colored man who refused to get off the sidewalk, and Merrill quickly took command of the situation, asking the colored people to go home and persuading the white mayor to get the whites to do the same.

———•———

The *Yorkville Enquirer* reported news near and far. A bale of new cotton had been received in New Orleans from Texas. It was graded as middling, and sold for twenty-seven cents a pound. A Portland man sued his barber for cutting off his mustache; the barber said he did not see any mustache to speak of. Mr. Edmund Rhett, for a number of years associate editor of the *Mercury* newspaper, noted for its uncompromising stand in defense of Southern rights, had died in Charleston. It was so hot in Montgomery, Alabama, last week that one wag proposed building a fire in his stove to cool the atmosphere. The suboutrage committee in Yorkville was continuing its work.

The subcommittee stayed in town six days. Mr. Van Trump was conspicuous in addressing the colored men and women who testified by their first names, and cross-examining them as to whether they understood the meaning of an oath.

Major Merrill gave his testimony with all of his cavalryman's bluff directness. He went through his list of cases, and was asked by Mr. Stevenson for his general impressions.

Answer. I am now of opinion that I never conceived of such a state of social disorganization being possible in any civilized community as exists in this county now. Although quiet, it is now very little better than it has been previously. There appears to me to be a diseased state of public sentiment in regard to the administration of justice. In all my conversations with people, I have been met constantly with the palliative remark in regard to these outrages—conceding that they are wrong and all that—almost always the conversation has contained the substance of this remark, "But you cannot but acknowledge that they have done some good." It is that point in the conversation of the best men of the community here which has so startled me as to the demoralization of public opinion.

Question (Mr. Stevenson). If I understand you, then, you came here predisposed to doubt the extent and serious character of this Ku-Klux organization and its proceedings?

Answer. Let me put it stronger even than that. I was absolutely incredulous, not only of its extent, but of the possibility of such a state of facts as exists here.

But it was the testimony of Elias Hill that cast a hush over the room, that seemed to be a tale from a romance, or a latter-day story of Job. He was a crippled man, with legs so shriveled they were no bigger than a child's, an arm drawn up and perpetually frozen in rheumatic pain. He was carried into the hearing room and set up in a chair. He held in one hand a stick that allowed him, with great effort, to shift his position. But when he began to speak it was in a strong and melodious voice, the voice of a preacher.

He had been born a slave, right there in York County, in 1819. He had been crippled by disease at age seven, had never walked again after that. He was now fifty-two. His father had purchased his own freedom, and when he had saved enough to buy his wife's, too, her master insisted he take the boy as well, because he was useless to him.

The crippled boy learned to read and write, became a schoolteacher to the other colored children, for ten years now had been preaching, with a license to preach from the Baptist church. The colored people who lived nearby gathered at his home to hear his sermons, or carried him to their church two and a half miles away, gently placing him in a spring buggy, driving as carefully as they could, lifting him gently out. They cared for him, helped feed him, paid him what they could to teach their children, brought him a little extra work now and then writing their business letters for them.

On a night in May, a little after midnight, he had been awakened by the dogs barking and the sound of horses rapidly approaching his yard. His brother's house lay in the same yard, and he heard the door being broken down and almost immediately his sister-in-law screaming and the sound of lashes striking home. "Where's Elias?" demanded a voice. A few moments later his own door burst open. A man glee-fully shouted, "Here he is! Here he is! We've found him!" A rough hand threw aside the bedclothes and grabbed his withered arm and threw him on the ground outside. The men then pummeled him with their fists and a pistol butt, jerked his painfully atrophied legs, or-dered him to pull his shirt up and horsewhipped him eight cuts on his hip, and finally put a leather strap around his neck and said they were going to throw him in the river and drown him. They ransacked his house, demanding a letter he had had from Congressman Wallace. "You were writing something about the Ku-Klux, and haven't you been preaching and praying about the Ku-Klux?" one of the men said. They found the letter and burned it in front of him. Then another of the men said they wouldn't kill him if he put a card in the newspaper saying he was renouncing all Republicanism and wouldn't ever vote, and if he stopped taking the Republican newspaper from Charleston, and if he left off preaching.

Finally they let his sister-in-law carry him back to the house and lay him on his bed, giving her a couple of parting lashes with a leather strap as she did so.

Mr. Stevenson asked him about an article in the newspaper saying he was leaving for Liberia, along with seventy or eighty other families of colored people from his part of the county. Was it a fact that he was making such arrangements?

Answer. Yes, sir; that is the fact.

Question. And others are making arrangements to follow you?

Answer. Yes, sir; to go to the same place, whether because I am going or for some other cause I cannot tell; but we all ascribe the same cause for this movement; we do not believe it possible, from the past history and present aspect of affairs, for our people to live in this country peaceably, and educate and elevate their children to that degree which they desire. They do not believe it possible— neither do I.

Mr. Van Trump tried to cross-examine, and was gently and charitably made a fool of.

Question. You do not feel very kindly toward the white race?

Answer. I am afraid of them now.

Question. Frightened at them?

Answer. Yes, sir. I have good-will, love, and affection toward them, but I fear them.

Question. Is that because you are a Baptist, or why?

Answer. I know it is my duty as a human being to respect all the human race, and also the grace of God teaches me to say so.

Question. I ask you if the subject-matter of your sermons is the wrongs and cruelties inflicted by these white people?

Answer. No, sir; not at all. I was accused of that on the night when they beat me; but that is not the subject on which I preach; it is Scriptural salvation.

Question. When you are preaching, do you preach republicanism in your sermons?

Answer. No, sir; I preach the Gospel, repentance toward God, and faith in our Lord Jesus Christ.

In September, Major Merrill sat in the York County courtroom and listened to the judge's charge to the grand jury. The leading citizens of the county had all along insisted there was no need for the army; they could enforce the laws themselves; the county grand jury would investigate any alleged outrages and see that justice was done. But the judge had barely begun when it became apparent that the proceeding was to be "so broad a farce," as Merrill would later describe it, that it was distasteful even to be brought in contact with it. The judge informed the grand jurors that of course it was their duty to ask Major Merrill to testify before them and inquire on what he based his allegations of wrongdoing; no doubt the officer would be very happy to learn that he had been mistaken in his information.

That evening the judge called upon the major and tried to explain. He hemmed and hawed a bit, and finally said, "Do not you think it would be inexpedient to stir things up now by an investigation?"

The whole town was in on the joke, and decided to help it along. A large number of the prominent citizens of Yorkville signed a petition to the president of the United States declaring that no outrages had occurred in their county for the past month. Merrill's reports showed that there had been at least ten incidents, including one murder. "I made extensive inquiry among the signers of this paper as to the grounds on which they based a statement of the kind," Merrill subsequently reported, "and was invariably met with the answer that if any outrages had occurred they had not heard of them."

The *Yorkville Enquirer* ran a story asserting that a colored schoolhouse in Yorkville, destroyed for the fourth time in less than a year, had been torn down by rival factions of Negroes "each wishing to control the building." Upon confronting the newspaper editor and demanding to know on what basis he had printed this assertion, which flatly contradicted information he himself had, Merrill was told it was a "street rumor, and was obtained from parties whose name he [the editor] could not recall."

Around town people were gloating; this would be the comeuppance of Major Merrill, they were saying. The grand jury would make it look like the congressional subcommittee and the War Department had been "willfully deceived" in everything Merrill had reported.

Merrill called the bluff and turned over detailed information on over one hundred crimes. Two weeks later the jury issued its report, and the part that still had Merrill fuming with indignation months later had to do with a case in which four colored men and two women were brutally whipped. "Information was furnished the grand jury by Major Merrill to the effect that six persons had recently been whipped in the southeastern part of the county," the jury reported. "After careful examination of the facts we ascertained that no such outrage occurred in this county. The officer alluded to as making the report expressed himself as satisfied as to his mistake, and proffered to correct any erroneous report of the affair that may have emanated from him."

In fact, the whipping had happened, and exactly as Merrill described—only it had occurred just over the county line, in Chester County. Merrill noted with disgust that the jurymen had expended vastly more skill in concealing and evading the truth than would have been required to obtain it.

To cap it all, he learned from his informers that three of the county's trial justices and one third of the white jury members were Ku Klux members; two of the grand jury members had actually been accessories to Ku Klux murders.

In the midst of all this he heard from Colonel Custer. It appeared that Lauffer, the man who said he had paid Major Merrill a bribe at that court-martial back in New Mexico over the lost mule, was now suddenly unable, despite a "diligent search," to find a memorandum book in which he had made a record of the illicit transactions. That being the case, Lauffer felt he could not now "conscientiously" make an affidavit on the matter, as the adjutant general had asked him to. Again Merrill thought that was the end of the matter. Again he underestimated his enemies' tenacity.

The next month brought news at last that the president of the United States had issued a decree ordering the Ku Klux to disperse within five days and turn in all weapons, disguises, and paraphernalia of their organization; it was the last legal step required under the Enforcement Act passed by Congress earlier in the year; then the federal government could suspend the writ of habeas corpus and send the army to make arrests on its own authority.

Now an additional company of infantry and two companies of cavalry reinforcements arrived. So did the United States attorney general, Amos T. Akerman, a Georgia man who had fought with the Confederacy, organized the Republican party in his home state after the war, and personally had his life threatened for it. No one hooted him in the streets of Yorkville. He was an obscure man, with a purposeful look in his sharp eyes, clean shaven in this age of whiskers, a legal scholar with an iron belief in a stern God and the rule of law. Many of the Ku Klux leaders in the county fled the same day.

On October 17 a telegram arrived for Major Merrill from Washington, bearing notice that the president had suspended the writ of habeas corpus in nine counties of South Carolina, York County among them.

Two days later Merrill sent squadrons of cavalry galloping across York County to arrest eighty-two men, almost simultaneously and without incident. He made a point of sending them in broad daylight, arresting the prisoners in town or at their places of work; there were to be no midnight knocks on doors, no accusations of men being torn from their families under cover of darkness.

The long days of waiting and impotent frustration were over, the

October breezes sweeping away the last torpor of an indolent spring
and summer.

17

From Attorney General Akerman came a note of triumph and sadness.

> Nov. 18 [187]1
> Genl Alfred H Terry
> Louisville, Ky

My dear sir,

I stayed at Yorkville over two weeks. I doubt whether from
the beginning of the world until now, a community, nominally
civilized, has been so fully under the domination of systematic
and organized depravity. If the people of the North really
understood it, there would be an outbreak of indignation
unparalleled since April 1861. To those, however, who have not
been there, or are in a similar state of society, the truth is
incredible; but if half of it comes forth, and is credited, the
country will sustain all that has been done, and will insist that
Congress shall furnish, and that the Executive shall apply,
remedies still more energetic.

All that you said to me about Major Merrill, I found to be
true. He is just the man for the work—resolute, collected, bold
and prudent, with a good legal head, very discriminating between
truth and falsehood; very indignant at wrong, and yet master of
his indignation; the safer, because incredulous at the outset, and,
therefore, disposed to scrutinize remarks the more keenly. He has
performed a difficult service with admirable success.

Though rejoiced at the suppression of KuKluxery, even in
one neighborhood, I feel greatly saddened by the business. It
has revealed a perversion of moral sentiment among the

Southern whites which bodes ill to that part of the country for this generation. Without a thorough moral renovation, society there for many years will be—I can hardly bring myself to say savage, but certainly very far from Christian.

Very truly yours

Amos T. Akerman

The jailhouse in Yorkville was bursting at the seams.

Major Merrill ran a tight ship, though, under trying circumstances. An infantryman, rifle in hand, stood sentry at each of the grated double doors that guarded the entrances on the second and third floors. There was not enough room for the prisoners' bedding on the floors of all the cells, so some slept in the corridors. The Eighteenth Infantry's medical officer inspected conditions daily, determined that no disease would break out despite the close conditions, and none did. The prisoners were allowed outside two to three hours a day for exercise in a nearby field, guarded by more infantrymen and three cavalrymen on their horses. From ten to twelve each morning visitors were permitted. Rows of saddle horses and teams stood hitched to fences along the roadside as their friends crowded in. Most of the prisoners acted cheerful and confident; some grumbled that their cotton and corn would go to waste and ruin; one who had already confessed he had helped murder a Negro spent hours crying and moaning, "I shall be hung! I shall be hung!"

The locals called confessing "puking," and men who confessed "pukers." Pretty soon everyone was puking. Merrill hired a stenographer and could barely keep up. Hundreds of men who hadn't been arrested came to the camp to turn themselves in; all Merrill could do was take their confessions and send them home on their own parole, holding only those who confessed to the most heinous crimes. Then he didn't even have time to take the confessions of the men who voluntarily surrendered, so busy was he taking the testimony of the men already arrested. His stenographer worked every day, early afternoon to midnight, then went back to the hotel and got up to do it again the next day. Sometimes the stenographer's wife transcribed his notes back at the hotel while he was at the major's headquarters taking down more.

Five hundred York County men turned themselves in; a hundred or two hundred fled, including fifty whose arrests had been ordered, and most of them were the ringleaders. A half dozen men who agreed to testify in court insisted to Merrill he damn well better arrest them, too, and make a good show of it so it would look like they'd had no choice when they appeared in court and told what they knew. Merrill obliged. But the few top men in the jail still weren't talking.

One raw November night, already more than halfway to midnight, an orderly entered the major's office bearing a slip of paper. The major, his stenographer would later recall, read it with barely concealed excitement. "Bring him here at once!"

"At last," Merrill said when the aide had left, "one of the big ones wants to puke." The stenographer had never seen Merrill so excited. The major paced the floor nervously.

Fifteen minutes later the man was brought in. Merrill opened the door himself, saying nothing, waiting for the man to begin.

"Major," he said, "my little boy is sick; he is dying; my wife sent me word; I want to see him; may I go home on parole? I give you my honor to come back."

Merrill was speechless for a moment. "How old is your boy?"

"Fo'teen."

"How ill is he?"

"My wife don't think he'll live to mo'n'n."

"How far is it?"

"Fo'teen miles."

"How will you get there?"

"Afoot."

"When will you return?"

"Day after tomorrow sundown."

Merrill paused again, looking the man hard in the eye. The stenographer felt he could almost see the contending thoughts going through Merrill's mind: the need to make a split-second judgment on nothing more than a look or a tone of voice, the price he would pay if he were wrong, the inhumanity of turning down the request if it were the honest truth and the man as good as his word.

"You may go."

The man was off in an instant in the cold November rain.

Late in the afternoon, on toward sunset the second day following, the major abruptly interrupted his work and invited the stenographer to take a walk through the camp with him. He fussed with odds and ends of the tents they entered, kept glancing to the west.

Then he startled his companion with an exclamation. "There he comes! I knew he would!" The prisoner walked toward them down the main street of town, and when he reached them said, "Major, my little boy is still living but the doctor says he will die before morning. I want to go back." Again the man pledged his honor to return, sundown the next day, and again permission was granted. The next day Merrill casually inquired of his orderly late in the day whether the prisoner had come back; yes, he had returned at four o'clock, after burying his boy.

On the last day of November the *Yorkville Enquirer* reprinted an appeal that was making the rounds across the state.

[CIRCULAR.]

Eminent counsel from the North have been employed to defend the men prosecuted under the Ku Klux act of Congress. This has been undertaken in order that ample justice may be done, and to the end that the constitutional questions involved may be considered. This is deemed a public duty. In order to carry out this purpose, it is necessary to raise the sum of $15,000. Your county has been assessed $2,000, which you will please raise and transmit to Columbia to the committee in charge.

WADE HAMPTON

M. C. BUTLER

The prisoners were transferred to Columbia for trial in the United States court. Merrill went a few days later to deal with matters, which dragged on to weeks. He telegraphed his adjutant to send three bottles each of his wine and whiskey.

In Columbia, the prisoners were out-and-out heroes. The ladies of the city called regularly with sparkling conversation and supplies of provisions donated by the merchants of the city; the reverend doctors and students of the theological seminary came with words of solace; General John Smith Preston, famous orator, famous fire-eating secessionist, brother-in-law of Confederate cavalry hero Wade Hampton, came with a five-gallon keg of beer and stirring oratory: "Well, gentlemen, we are all in jail in South Carolina; the only difference is, you are under shelter, and those of us who are on the outside have to dodge the storm as best we can."

The eminent counsel retained by the white citizens' subscription, two former attorneys general of the United States no less, spent two weeks arguing the finer points of constitutional law, heaping derision on the very notion that the powers of Congress to enforce the Fourteenth and Fifteenth amendments could extend to the acts of individual citizens; assault and murder were state crimes, not the business of the federal government. They disputed the rules of the federal courts for challenging jurors; they raised highly technical questions about the law of conspiracy; they insisted that even if the law making it a federal crime to engage in conspiracy with the aim of hindering a citizen from exercising his right to vote were valid, the alleged offenses had not taken place on election day, and thus the charges in this particular case were not valid.

Finally the first witness was called. A cavalry officer was sworn; he described going to a house on Major Merrill's orders in October and there searching a locked desk drawer and securing a copy of the Ku Klux constitution and bylaws. The constitution was read into evidence. It swore the members to secrecy on penalty of death; swore them to oppose the "radical party"; swore them to fight for the constitution "as bequeathed to us in its purity by our forefathers."

Colored witnesses told of being whipped and threatened for having voted the Republican ticket; "damn you, we'll make a democrat of you tonight," his assailants told one man as they beat him. A colored woman described her rape by the Ku Klux in such graphic terms that the court reporter noted that it was "of too obscene a nature to permit of publication."

The Democratic newspapers remarked the next day that it was inconceivable that such "gentlemen of wealth and refinement" would have found any attractions in such a "filthy-looking fright of a negress."

Most of the defendants pleaded guilty; most of the leaders had already got away. In passing sentence on the parade of prisoners who lined up to plead guilty, Judge Hugh Lennox Bond was indignant but his options were limited. "Some of your comrades recite the circumstances of a brutal, unprovoked murder done by themselves, with as little apparent abhorrence as they would relate the incidents of a picnic, and you yourselves speak of the number of blows with a hickory, which you inflicted at midnight upon the lacerated, bleeding back of a defenseless woman, without so much as a blush or a sigh of regret," said the judge, and then passed sentences of fines of a hundred dollars or less for most and prison sentences of a few months for a few, in the United States Penitentiary in Albany, New York.

One of the few Ku Klux leaders on trial was Dr. Edward T. Avery, of Rock Hill, at the eastern end of York County.

As Avery's attorney began presenting his closing arguments, the district attorney interrupted.

MR. CORBIN. If your honors please, I don't notice the defendant in court. I have just asked the counsel where the defendant was, and the reply I received was—that was for me to find out.

MR. MCMASTER. I repeat it now.

THE COURT. Do you know where your client is, Mr. McMaster?

MR. MCMASTER. I beg the court will excuse me from answering that question.

THE COURT. Had you any knowledge from your client that he was going away?

MR. MCMASTER. I hope the court will excuse me from answering.

THE COURT. The clerk will lay a rule on Mr. McMaster to answer the question, or show cause why he should not be thrown over the bar.

As a matter of fact, Dr. Avery was on his way to Canada, leaving three thousand dollars in bail behind him.

As the proceedings wound on in Columbia, there were rumors of political wheels turning in Washington. Amos Akerman's fellow cabinet members were getting tired of his twice-weekly accounts of atrocities from the South, impatient to wrap the business up and move on; they were muttering that he was getting to be a bore on the subject; he had Ku Klux "on the brain." The army commanders were antsy to get the cavalry back to its business of fighting the Indians out West, to get out of the degrading business of acting like so many police constables down South. The United States courts couldn't possibly handle the hundreds of pending cases anyway, not with one judge riding the circuit and funds so short that the district attorney couldn't even hire a stenographer with any regularity.

In the second week of the new year of 1872 Merrill received a letter from Akerman acknowledging he had been forced out as attorney general, and at least hinting why. "I thank you for your kind remarks in reference to my resignation. Perhaps I should violate confidence, and possibly should make mistakes, if I were made to state what I suppose to be the causes of the state of things which made that step proper on my part. My successor is an able and experienced man, and in administering the office will be free from some of the hostilities that have obstructed me. I shall always remember with pleasure my visit to Yorkville and the companionship of yourself, your family and your mess. And it is comforting to believe that I have borne some part in the exposure and destruction of that terrible conspiracy. Hoping that the turns of life may bring us together again, and with very best respects to Mrs. Merrill, I am, Yours very truly, Amos T. Akerman."

A few weeks later Company C of the Eighteenth Infantry was ordered to leave Yorkville, the first of a series of departures that would continue steadily over the coming year.

In July of 1872, Merrill woke one morning with his left side and tongue paralyzed. Those symptoms wore off, but for the rest of the year the thirty-seven-year-old officer was constantly plagued by sleepless nights, constipated bowels, loss of memory, blinding headaches, dimness of vision.

Discipline of the troops encamped at Yorkville deteriorated further. "I have no doubt, from various sources of information, and from careful observation, that desertions are encouraged and facilitated by Ku-Klux and their sympathizers," Merrill reported in September. "There is every moral conviction that no effort has been spared by these persons to breed dissatisfaction among the men." The men who deserted were virtually impossible to catch, owing to the ease with which they could get away and the refusal of the local population to offer any help or information to aid in their recapture.

The South Carolina newspapers were now calling him "Dog Merrill."

Now wild rumors were constantly being spread about town, readily believed: Merrill would be removed from his command owing to disapproval of his conduct; the Supreme Court had overthrown the Enforcement Acts; and so on and on. "The readiness with which they were credited, and the congratulatory comments of the hearers, not unfrequently coupled with threats of what would now happen to the negroes and to such white men as had been witnesses, go to show how deep-seated are the causes from which all this lawlessness has sprung," Merrill reported.

In his report of January of this year, the major noted, he had expressed the hope that it would not be long before the military could be withdrawn completely, once the better men of the community began to exert their influence in the wake of the suppression of the Ku Klux. "I regret to say now that events since then do not justify that opinion, and that I am forced now to think it was premature. Public sentiment does not condemn law-breaking, or demand its punishment, except in cases where negroes are the law-breakers, or in gross cases of whites against whites. In the courts the sacredness of the obligation of an oath is disregarded, to an extent and by individuals of a social grade that would be incredible elsewhere; it is done, however, with impunity. Public sentiment excuses and palliates it when done in the defense of the Ku-Klux. As matters now stand, the only protection which citizens can look to with any assurance is the General Government; the only laws justly enforced are those of the United States; and even this would avail but little if it were not for the moral effect of the presence of United States troops, and the feeling among the people that violation of United States law will be promptly and fully investigated, and the perpetrators brought to justice."

With failing hopes, the cavalryman appealed directly to the new attorney general. George H. Williams, former senator from Oregon, was not quite the worthy successor Amos Akerman had described. Williams's chief interest in his new position seemed to be the opportunities it presented for personal gain; the talk of Washington was how Mrs. Williams was riding about in the finest carriage in town, finer even than the president's. It would soon come out that it had been paid for with department funds, as had a good share of the Williamses' lavish living expenses.

Merrill had heard reports that clemency was now being actively considered for the convicted men in prison in Albany; it was another attempt by Washington to get the matter wrapped up and over with and things back to normal. Merrill wrote Williams: "I beg to invite the attention of the Department to the facts that there are in this county alone some *five* or *six hundred* members of the Ku Klux who are of varying minor grades of guilt who are quietly at home, on their personal recognizance, untried, and in whose cases it is to the least degree improbable that any further action will ever be taken. Most of those men have been personally engaged in outrages. In only a small percentage of the cases are they of a degree of guilt which elsewhere would not be brought to condign punishment."

In selecting the original cases for trial only murders and the worst outrages were chosen to begin with, Merrill continued, which meant that a degree of clemency had already been shown far in excess of what any reasonable men would expect in any other place. Hundreds of witnesses would find their lives at risk were the guilty now set free.

Within just the previous two days a white man, a prominent witness, had his throat cut ear to ear and now lay between life and death. The victim of one of the most notorious of the early Ku Klux murders in York County, a worthy and industrious colored man, had left a widow with a large family. They had been in comfortable circumstances through the man's industry and thrift, but now she was driven from her home and was "ekeing out a miserable existence on the charity of the United States, being kept from starving only by the small quantities of bread and meat which by order of the War Department I am allowed to issue to her."

Merrill was all in favor of mercy to the convicted prisoners, as soon as it could be shown there would be no renewal of their crimes; but justice demanded that he remind the department of their victims, too. And then there was the fact that the overwhelming majority of whites here would "attribute clemency to the Ku Klux to a desire for their favor, or construe it into a confession that wrong had been done them."

"Nothing but the deepest conviction, slowly reached" lies behind these conclusions, the cavalryman wrote. "The very worst of these men if released tomorrow would be received here by most of the whites not as criminals to whom a great government had magnanimously granted pardon, but as heroes whose sufferings had been martyrdom for the rights of the South."

In spring of 1873 the pardons began. The attorney general ordered that all remaining cases be suspended and that no new indictments be brought, except in "flagrant cases of murder."

In March of 1873 the men of Company K of the Seventh Cavalry boarded the tiny train of the Kings Mountain Rail Road at the tiny depot in Yorkville and began the ten-mile-an-hour rickety first leg of their journey back West to the plains, to fight the Indians. In July the hundreds of men who had fled the state to escape prosecution were granted clemency to return to their homes.

Lewis Merrill was detailed to report to the Department of Justice for special duty for a few more months, then granted a year's sick leave to recuperate from "general prostration of the nervous system incident to protracted and severe mental labor in the discharge of his duties."

When he returned to duty in 1874, he was out in Dakota for just a couple of months before an urgent summons brought him back to the South again. This time it was to Louisiana, where a real war had broken out.

IV

"PLAIN HONEST CONVICTIONS OF A SOLDIER"

18

Before he started scribbling off letters to the newspapers, James Longstreet had a reputation as secure as any Confederate war hero's.

Right after the war Andrew Johnson had pointed to Longstreet as one of three Southerners who had caused "too much trouble" ever to be pardoned. (Robert E. Lee and Jefferson Davis were the other two.) Longstreet was Lee's senior corps commander and his stalwart companion in battle. Lee always pitched his tent near Longstreet's and enjoyed his good humor and sociable instincts; Longstreet gave advice, and Lee listened, even if he often didn't take it. Lee called him his "old war horse."

He was a messy bear of a man, six foot two with unkempt beard and hair and a big chest, and he was technically an Edgefield man, born there in South Carolina though reared in Augusta and backwoods Alabama. He could ride better than anyone who better looked the part of the model Southern cavalier. He was the best fence jumper in the whole Confederate army. When he was accidentally shot through the neck by his own men while aligning the troops for an attack in heavy underbrush and spent weeks convalescing, Lee sent him a fine horse from Virginia. Longstreet named his son Robert Lee Longstreet.

Longstreet learned the hard way what most of his fellow commanders, North and South, never did, that by standing on the defensive an outnumbered force could let its attacker bash himself to pieces first, and then could chew the pieces into mincemeat with a well-timed counterattack. At the Second Battle of Manassas, Longstreet three times urged Lee to hold off the kind of blundering frontal attack over unknown ground with flanks exposed that had brought so many to grief; three times Lee remarkably agreed, and three times subsequent reconnaissance proved Longstreet right. The next day the Union army attacked Stonewall Jackson's troops in the center of the Confederate lines, and Longstreet, on the right, immediately wheeled his artillery

and enfiladed the attackers; then without even waiting for Lee's orders
sent his entire right wing wheeling into the Union flanks, too, thirty
thousand men turned and got moving in under half an hour, and the
defeated bluecoats staggered back to Washington much as they had
the last time they clashed on that same battleground.

In 1863 at Gettysburg, Longstreet again proposed turning the
Union left with a flanking maneuver. This time Lee didn't listen. The
Confederate commander had appeared nervous and irritable that day.
Longstreet had surveyed the Union position, securely ensconced on the
high ground of Cemetery Ridge, and wanted to move east and south
across the Union army's lines of communication, find a solid defensive
position of his own between the Union troops and Washington, and
wait for the Yankees to do the attacking. Lee said no; the men would
see that as a demoralizing retreat. "The enemy is there, and I am going
to attack him there," he said, pointing to the hill.

"If he is there, it will be because he is anxious that we should attack him," countered Longstreet, "a good reason, in my judgment, for
not doing so."

Lee again said no; they would attack the next day. Longstreet was
up long after midnight, preparing his two divisions to be ready for
action the next morning, stole a couple of hours' sleep, and was up at
three in the morning that second day of July.

At dawn Lee sent out a reconnaissance party from his staff to sur-
vey the ground, discover the Union positions, and find a suitable line
of attack. Lee's chief of artillery, an odd man named William Nelson
Pendleton, an Episcopal priest supremely unqualified for the military
post he held, an "old granny" and a figurehead, as his fellow officers
called him, joined the reconnaissance and sent Longstreet and Lee a
note reporting his findings.

At eleven o'clock that morning Lee gave Longstreet his orders to
move into position to attack the left end of the Union line. Lee's guide
first led them on the wrong road, in full sight of a Union signal post
atop Little Round Top, an isolated tall hill at the south end of the
ridge. They had to countermarch and then back again on a more shel-
tered path. At about four o'clock they were in place, and Longstreet
gave the order to attack. At once both his division commanders sent

urgent messages asking that the attack be realigned: the Union troops had shifted their position and were occupying the ground right in front of them; instead of hitting the Union line on its exposed left flank up on the ridge they would be heading right smack head on into troops in the wheat field and peach orchard in front of them. But Longstreet had already been twice rebuffed by Lee and ordered the attack to go ahead at once. Lee then also personally rejected a further appeal the two division commanders made directly to him.

Still, it almost succeeded; only bitter, desperate fighting on and around Little Round Top by the men of Adelbert Ames's old regiment stemmed the tide. The Twentieth Maine, no longer the ragtag insubordinate farmers they once were, had at the last minute gone at the double to reinforce the signal post on the exposed hill and keep the rebels from seizing the spot, from where they could have enfiladed the whole Union line up Cemetery Ridge had they gained it. After the battle the men sent their tattered battle flag to General Ames, their old commander, the man they had once wanted to shoot themselves.

The next day Lee ordered Longstreet to send one of his three divisions, Pickett's, charging right across three quarters of a mile of open ground and take the center of the Union ridge. Longstreet again spoke up. Such an attack was impossible, he told Lee. "The fifteen thousand men who could make successful assault over that field have never been arrayed for battle," he told Lee. He had spent the night scouting the situation and believed the flanking move was still possible. Lee impatiently shot it down.

Longstreet returned to his officers, said, "It is all wrong, but he will have it," and did the best he could to do the impossible. He massed a hundred and fifty guns and opened up the heaviest artillery barrage of the whole war to try to clear the way for the men who would soon follow. He kept a calm exterior, but when the final moment came he could not speak. Pickett said, "General, shall I advance?" and Longstreet only nodded, and in half an hour two-thirds of the men were lost, just mowed down like wheat before scythes by the Union guns above. Longstreet took the disaster with iron self-control, and told himself he would take the blame on himself and spare Lee, but in his official report he still noted that the order for

attack "would have been revoked had I felt that I had that privilege."
He later admitted that that day at Gettysburg "was one of the saddest
of my life." The two generals remained friends but Pickett never for-
gave Lee. The romantic haze of Southern chivalry that soon envel-
oped Pickett's hopeless charge left Pickett unmoved. "That old man
had my division massacred," he said.

One day in the week before the surrender at Appomattox, Pendleton
had approached Longstreet and confided that a group of officers had
met the night before and had decided to advise Lee to surrender; knowing Longstreet's special friendship with the general, would he deliver
the message? Longstreet replied that the Articles of War prescribed the
death penalty for counseling surrender, adding, "If General Lee doesn't
know when to surrender until I tell him, he will never know."

The first historians of the conflict were unanimous in their praise
of the man known as Lee's "most trusted lieutenant." Lieutenant
General Longstreet had been faithful, diligent, obstinate, and brilliant, far and away Lee's ablest corps commander. Lee told one historian that he considered Longstreet's generalship to be the best in the
world, literally second to none. The historians agreed, too, that Lee
had blundered badly when he twice ignored Longstreet's wiser counsel at Gettysburg.

After the war Longstreet thought he'd head out to Texas but
stopped in New Orleans and liked it there well enough to stay for a
while. He became a cotton factor and the president of an insurance
company and got involved in the financing of railroads and was soon
making fifteen thousand dollars a year from his investments.

In the spring of 1867 the editor of the *New Orleans Times* invited
eighteen prominent ex-Confederate leaders living in the city to con-
tribute their views on the recent Reconstruction acts of Congress.
Longstreet replied at once, writing not one but two letters.

He began by saying he was speaking with the "plain honest convictions of a soldier." He said that, as he saw it, the South had fought,
and fought well, but had lost; they were a conquered people. It was
accordingly their duty to accept the terms of the victor. Even if they
were in a position to resist, it would be wrong to do so. He himself
had lost his rights of citizenship under the Reconstruction acts, as

someone who had sworn an oath of allegiance to the Union and then engaged in rebellion, but that was one of the "hazards of revolution, and I have no better cause of complaint than those who have lost their slaves." To claim now that Southerners need not concede anything to the victor was tantamount to claiming they hadn't known what they were fighting for in the first place.

He hoped he might be forgiven the "bluntness of a soldier" to remind his fellow Southerners what *had* been decided at Appomattox. "The surrender of the Confederate armies in 1865," he wrote, "involved: 1. The surrender of the *claim* to the right of secession. 2. The surrender of the former political relations of the negro. 3. *The surrender of the Southern Confederacy.* These issues expired upon the fields last occupied by the Confederate armies. There they should have been buried. The soldier prefers to have the sod that receives him when he falls cover his remains. The political questions of the war should have been buried upon the fields that marked their end."

One of the gravest errors, Longstreet went on, was the opinion that "we cannot do wrong, and that Northerners cannot do right." There were good and bad in both sections. But one must now bend to the other. The war had decided which.

Finally, there was a practical side to the question. The quickest way, for that matter really the only way, for the South to reassume its political part in the nation was to obey the law of Congress, however distasteful that might be. The Reconstruction acts provided a clear process for ending military supervision and restoring civilian rule.

In June he wrote again to the *New Orleans Times*. He had first shown this letter to his uncle, a well-known judge, lawyer, newspaper editor and publisher, humor writer, Methodist minister, and college president. "It will ruin you, son, if you publish it," he told his nephew.

Longstreet's letter began by acknowledging that it was quite true, as had lately been rumored, that he had now gone well beyond his previous statement and was actively endorsing the Republican party. He asserted that his only object in doing so was out of a desire to relieve his late confederates-in-arms from the "unnatural condition" they had been placed in by the progress of revolutionary forces beyond their control. He would not presume to meddle with politics were it a time of "ease and comfort." But "these are unusual times, and call for practical advice."

It was a simple matter, he went on. In the current state of disorder one side or the other must make concessions. "The war was made upon Republican issues, and it seems to me fair and just that the settlement should be made accordingly." People resort to war, the "blunt soldier" explained, when all other options have been tried and exhausted. Before the war the principles that divided the parties were debated by the greatest statesmen of the country. Compromises were attempted and failed. Finally, resort was made to the sword. "The highest of human laws is the law that is established by appeal to arms. The sword has decided in favor of the North, and what they claimed as principles cease to be principles, and are become law. The views that we hold cease to be principles because they are opposed to law. It is therefore our duty to abandon ideas that are obsolete and conform to the requirements of law."

The first response to Longstreet's new letter was harsh and predictable. The second response was harsh and awful, but for now only hinted at by the editorial which appeared the next day in one of Louisiana's white establishment newspapers. Under the headline "A Soldier's Blunder," the editorial expressed regret "that a brilliant reputation in war should have been put to such peril by political utterances so feeble."

Longstreet's business dried up and social acquaintances began shunning him and his family on the streets. Across the South editorials denounced his embrace of the Republican party as "illogical," "puerile," and "muddled." His old friend and comrade, the Confederate general D. H. Hill, wrote in his magazine *Land We Love* that he hoped Longstreet's endorsement of Republican principles was meant as some kind of a joke. If not, then either his "theology or his loyalty is at fault."

Longstreet wrote to his old confederate-in-arms Robert E. Lee asking for a public word of support. "It is evident to my mind that our side or the other must make concessions or our political status will never be established. Either those who have conquered or those who have been conquered must make concessions or we shall ere long be on the same road that Mexico has pursued for the last twenty-five years.

"I fancy that few of our brave men that have fallen in the late struggle would have risked their lives if they had supposed that the war was to settle nothing. And yet, if the claims of both sides are good nothing has been settled.

"As I have said you can relieve the distress of the people at once if you can bring yourself to endorse my views. I know that you will not unless your heart approves. I pray you therefore apply yourself to the subject, with the earnestness that the times demand of us all, and if it be possible let us lift up the country from this despondency. If you can come to approve my views, please write me or publish a letter to that effect. It will be better to publish a few lines, for I expect to go to Mexico next week and shall not be back under fifty or sixty days."

Lee replied five months later that he "avoided all discussion of political questions."

In 1869 Grant, the newly elected Republican president, appointed Longstreet to the post of surveyor of the port of New Orleans, a plum federal patronage job that paid six thousand dollars a year. The following year he accepted an appointment as adjutant general of Louisiana's state militia, under the Reconstruction government.

The attacks on Longstreet so far had been limited to his postwar politics; his reputation as Lee's able lieutenant and comrade remained untouched. But when Lee died in 1870 the gloves really came off.

The Reverend Pendleton, Lee's former artillery chief, declared himself the keeper of Lee's "sacred memory." He toured the South seeking donations to erect a statue and mausoleum on the campus of Washington College in Lexington, Virginia, where Lee had become president after the war. He recited over and over a eulogy of the Virginia general who became more saintlike with every telling.

The reverend would begin with a recitation of familiar wrongs. The Northern states had committed a crime against the Constitution—by comparison to which secession "sinks into utter insignificance"—when they refused to enforce the fugitive slave law. The abolitionists had incited national bloodshed with their "fanatical fury." Masquerading as morality, an appeal to "higher law," in truth all of that "slavery agitation" was nothing but "criminal disingenuousness." It was mere pretext for "political plans" to overthrow the Constitution's safeguards, "substituting the rule of mere numbers," "supplanting reason and right by brute force."

Yet the saddest certainty was that the end of such evils had not even yet been approached; "the cruel vengeance which seeks to reverse divine ordinances and make the inferior African our equals and rulers" can but bring to mind the chaos of morals and opinion that marked the fall of the Roman Empire.

Pendleton then went on to extol Lee's virtues as a Christian, a gentleman, and a military man.

In 1873, on the occasion of the third celebration of Lee's birthday since his death, Pendleton revised his speech. It was now an unvarnished attack on General Longstreet. The mistakes at Gettysburg were all Longstreet's, not Lee's. If Longstreet had not deliberately disobeyed the orders Pendleton had heard with his own ears Lee give him—to attack *at dawn* on July 2—victory would have been certain. "The delay thus occasioned was, it can scarce be questioned, the loss to us of that battle," the reverend declared, "and with it the cause of constitutional government. There can hardly be a reasonable doubt that, had the attack been made in the early morning of that day as intended, General Meade and his force would with comparative ease have been swept away. Then gladly had been accepted our equitable terms of peace."

Lee was blameless; his vision and courage were true. Longstreet was not merely painfully slow to move; he had committed "culpable disobedience" and "treachery."

Simply, he was the man who lost the Confederacy. That Lee had taken the blame on his own shoulders for the debacle at Gettysburg only showed how perfect a Christian he was.

It was as complete a fabrication as ever crossed the lips of a man of the cloth. Pendleton's claim that he had heard Lee order Longstreet to attack at dawn of July 2 was flatly contradicted by what Pendleton himself had written in the reconnaissance report he had sent Lee and Longstreet that same morning.

Longstreet now wrote Pendleton asking him to produce one scrap of evidence to support his claims, or to give the names of the unnamed officers who, Pendleton had alleged in his speech, had witnessed Lee's "mental anguish" when the attack failed to materialize at sunrise on the second.

Pendleton replied, refusing to offer any facts, merely suggesting sarcastically that Longstreet must be happy that the South had lost the war, given his well-known political views.

Longstreet replied, "School-boys may be misled by you, but even with them I fancy that only the most credulous may be temporarily misled. The impertinent tone and language of your letter are in keeping with your disposition to propagate falsehoods."

Pretty soon the entire South believed the falsehoods, for the entire arsenal of the defenders of Lee's sacred memory was trained on Longstreet too. Scarcely a Confederate veterans' reunion, a Lee memorial service, or an issue of the *Southern Historical Society Papers* failed to include an attack on him. Longstreet had always been slow, they now said. He had been slow at Gettysburg; he had also been slow at Second Manassas, leaving Jackson to do all the hard work, then trying to steal the credit at the end.

Finally, they even robbed him of his friendship with Lee.

In the version Pendleton and other Southern generals were soon retailing, Jackson, not Longstreet, had been Lee's great friend and confidant and most trusted lieutenant. (Jackson, like Lee, was now safely dead and couldn't say otherwise.) Lee had only pitched his tent next to Longstreet, the keepers of Lee's sacred memory now explained, to keep an eye on him, because he was always so slow to get moving. "Lee was never really beaten. Lee could not be beaten," they said. But like any mortal—like even Jesus Christ himself—he could be betrayed.

Longstreet was not just a scalawag; he had now become Judas.

19

On a late summer day in 1874, General Longstreet rode his horse down Chartres Street through the silent French Quarter, south to the United States Custom House on Canal Street, and could see the barricades in the streets beyond. Every wall he passed was plastered with the placards that had suddenly sprung up across the city the day before.

> CITIZENS OF NEW ORLEANS: FOR NEARLY TWO YEARS YOU
> HAVE BEEN THE SILENT BUT INDIGNANT SUFFERERS OF OUT-
> RAGE AFTER OUTRAGE HEAPED UPON YOU BY AN USURPING
> GOVERNMENT. MONDAY THE 14TH OF SEPTEMBER CLOSE
> YOUR PLACES OF BUSINESS WITHOUT A SINGLE EXCEPTION,
> AND, AT 11 O'CLOCK, A.M., ASSEMBLE AT THE CLAY STATUE
> IN CANAL STREET.

Even the curbs at every street crossing were covered with long strips of paper, pasted there where everyone would see them as they walked about town on their business, repeating the time and place of the meeting.

Five thousand citizens had responded to the call that morning in New Orleans; doctors, bankers, lawyers, journeymen, clerks, and laborers, all gathering there at the foot of the statue of Henry Clay, the same spot made famous in city legend thirteen years before, when a prominent local physician had rallied the citizens of New Orleans to enlist in the Confederate army, leading them in a singing of the *Marseillaise*.

It was now about a quarter to four o'clock. As he advanced with five hundred white and colored troops of the Metropolitan Brigade past shuttered shops, bringing a Gatling gun, two twelve-pound brass cannons, and four smaller artillery pieces with him, General Longstreet, the man Robert E. Lee had called the world's greatest general, was violating one of his oldest principles of battle. He was taking the offensive against a superior force.

It had been his plan all along to stay at the State House, the palatial old St. Louis Hotel that had been taken over by the state government in June as its new capitol building. He had 475 colored troops of the regular state militia in the State House itself, armed with rifles; he had parked his artillery in Jackson Square nearby; in Pirate's Alley off the square thirty cavalry horses stood in a row tied to the St. Louis Cathedral fence; in the Cabildo, the old Spanish capitol that anchored the near corner of the square next to the cathedral, the Metropolitans crowded into the Third Precinct Police Station rooms on the ground floor and the Supreme Court rooms on the top. The surrounding streets were closed off. It was a solid defensible position. He would wait for the trouble to come to him, as was his wont.

The trouble in the city had been brewing for days, and Longstreet was well informed about what was afoot. When the Metropolitans were mustered into militia service they brought their thirty detectives with them, and some of them had infiltrated the White Leagues when the clubs began forming that summer, and they knew that the leagues were expecting a large shipment of illegal guns on the steamer *Mississippi*, which had just arrived that Saturday night and would begin to be unloaded that Monday. Worried about the loss of prestige they would suffer if the state authorities intercepted those arms, the White League leaders had then decided to precipitate a crisis and go for broke. The pretext would be a mass meeting called to deplore the violation of their "right to bear arms"; and in a sense the White Leaguers did want to test the waters to see if they could get a crowd whipped up enough to support desperate action. But in truth their plans had already been well laid. Longstreet was fully expecting an armed attack on the State House. His plan accordingly was to stay there, on the defensive with nearly a thousand men, and wait for them to come.

The mass meeting had broken up around noon with cries from the crowd, five thousand strong, for the "immediate abdication" of the state's Republican governor, William P. Kellogg. A delegation of five was chosen, and they set off in carriages for the State House.

At one o'clock the milling men broke into deafening cheers as the carriages returned. The delegation read out the governor's reply. He could not possibly receive a message from an armed assemblage in defiance of law. "Hang Kellogg!" the crowd shouted. "We'll fight!" "Call out the troops!"

A speaker exhorted the crowd to go home at once, get their arms, and be back by two-thirty. From his headquarters two blocks away the last Democratic candidate for lieutenant governor, the loser in the election two years earlier, issued a proclamation calling on Louisianians between the ages of eighteen and forty-five to assemble under arms "for the purpose of driving the usurpers from power"; then issued General Orders No. 1 from "Headqr's. Executive Department of La.," naming ex-Confederate colonel Frederick N. Ogden as the "Provisional General of the Louisiana State Militia."

All of this was so much show, since people around town had seen armed men who looked like they meant business gathering since early morning, first by twos and threes, then dozens, then hundreds. They took up posts at every street corner, and built barricades along the key thoroughfares.

At around two o'clock a detachment of the White Leaguers marched over to city hall and demanded the immediate surrender of the building from the mayor; they then marched in and cut the fire alarm and police telegraph wires. The governor then told his militia commander that it was time to take action and to wait no more. So Longstreet had reluctantly ordered the change in plan from defense to offense.

Now as Longstreet's men approached Canal Street they drove back the pickets that had been posted there and halted in front of the Custom House. Canal ran roughly east–west; so did Poydras Street, a few blocks farther to the south, and that was where the White League barricades had been set up. The barricades, the people in the city amused themselves by saying, were done after the "Parisian fashion." At Poydras and Camp a fortification of old lumber, barrels filled with earth, and dry-goods boxes had been thrown up. A block west, at the corner of Poydras and St. Charles, the men had run a streetcar off its tracks and used that to block the intersection, pulling up the pavement to make a ditch in front. Mattresses, wagons, iron plates prized out of the streets, piled five or six feet high, filled other intersections along Poydras.

Behind the barricades stood hundreds of armed men. Running the whole length down to the levee, eight blocks to the east, Poydras Street was a line of battle. Despite their civilian garb—suits, bowler hats—the armed men were disposed in a manner that, as any trained military eye could see at a glance, spoke of experience and discipline.

Longstreet did not have to look hard to see the trap, either; the one he had spent four hard years of fighting scrupulously avoiding. If he were to attack at the barricades he would be attacking at the center of the enemy line, leaving his left flank exposed to an enveloping movement and allowing the White Leaguers to roll him up with an open line of advance to the State House behind him.

Longstreet's men were still facing south, toward the line of barricades, their guns positioned to hurl enfilading fire down the cross streets. One of his horsemen was shot in the leg. Everything then started happening very quickly. The White Leaguers began moving double-time down Poydras Street toward the levee, toward Longstreet's left. Longstreet wheeled his line left and sent his troops down Canal Street to parallel them and not be outflanked.

A few minutes later he personally appeared at the head of Canal Street to inspect the position the men had taken up. It was all wrong. He told the head of the Metropolitans, General Badger, to get his position right down on the levee and close the flank. But it was already too late, and the shooting began.

From their dangerously exposed spot at the head of Canal Street, the Metropolitans opened up with their Gatling gun and twelve-pounders, firing south toward the White Leaguers at the head of Poydras Steet. A rain of bullets came back. From behind cotton bales and piles of freight, from behind a slow-moving freight train they sent creeping along the tracks by the levee, from windows of nearby buildings, the White Leaguers fired on Badger's gunners, and several dropped dead in an instant. Badger leapt down from his horse to help serve the guns.

Letting out a rebel yell, two companies of White Leaguers charged the guns down the open levee.

Longstreet heard the old Confederate battle cry and turned pale. Badger fell with four bullets in him, a broken arm, and a shattered leg that would shortly have to be amputated.

The Metropolitans ran. One of the White League captains later said that it was only with the greatest difficulty that he had restrained his men from firing particularly at General Longstreet.

Longstreet tried to rally his troops in front of the Custom House, but a company of white Metropolitans went over to the enemy and the sniping from the buildings continued and some of the colored troops took refuge in the Custom House and the rest retreated all the way back to Jackson Square. It was all over in less than fifteen minutes. Thirty-one men lay dead on the streets and close to a hundred were wounded. Most of the dead were White Leaguers, most of the wounded Metropolitans. Longstreet, hit by a spent bullet and slightly injured, galloped his horse back to Jackson Square and took personal command of the artillery he had left there covering the approaches to the State House.

"General" Ogden had his horse shot out from under him on Tchoupitoulas Street, and knocked his head on the pavement, but was all right.

During the night Longstreet inspected the ammunition on hand. There was enough to resist a single assault, no more. The small contingent of United States troops at the Custom House had stayed out of the fight and were still staying out; they would not, or maybe really could not, supply any ammunition to the state troops. The state didn't have any. The next morning Longstreet surrendered the State House, and went home.

The respectable white citizens of New Orleans and the Democratic newspapers of the city greeted the Fourteenth of September like any other military victory they had cheered during four years of fighting the Yankees. The Democratic lieutenant governor, now installed in the State House, issued General Orders No. 2. He congratulated "the troops in the field" and briefly reported what was known of the losses sustained by "our enemies."

At noon on Tuesday the White League companies staged a victory parade, after ceremoniously escorting the arms shipment from the *Mississippi* to the center of town. The location where the martyrs had fallen was solemnly noted. The newspapers were filled with reports from the company commanders describing in conventional military terms the role each had played, courteously praising the ladies who had been conspicuous in coming to their aid with food and refreshments, wrangling over any failures to distribute proper credit for the victory achieved:

[THE NEW ORLEANS BULLETIN]

Editor New Orleans Bulletin:

In your account of the charge made of the metropolitan artillery by the citizen soldiery, at the foot of Canal street, on the evening of the 14th, which appeared in your Sunday's edition, you unintentionally overlook the fact that among those who were conspicuous for their heroism and courage on that day, and the first to reach the deserted guns of the flying metropolitans were the gallant members of Capt. John Glynn's company.

The other companies (including my own) who were present and participated in the capture were those of Capts. Pleasant and Lord, who have received merited eulogies from press and public.

Feeling assured, Mr. Editor, as an old fellow-soldier, you will award to the brave boys of Capt. Glynn's company their just measure of praise,

I remain, very truly yours,

W. T. Vaudry

Capt. Com'g Co. A, C.C.W.L.

(C.C.W.L. stood for "Crescent City White League.")

Longstreet took to bed with a severe illness, and remained there for most of six months.

On Wednesday the sixteenth of September a train pulled into the New Orleans depot at 10:00 P.M., a man majestically stepped forth from one of the cars, a brass band struck up, and huzzahs echoed down the platform. He was the Democratic candidate for governor who had lost the last election, one John McEnery; he had laid low in Vicksburg to stay out of trouble if the business went awry; now he returned to take possession of the office by virtue of the military victory just won.

From the other end of the car stepped a man a newspaper reporter on the scene described as "a quiet elderly gentleman." He was the commanding general of the Department of the Gulf of the United States Army, William H. Emory.

The next day the two men met formally. The general read a proclamation from the president. It ordered the persons who had combined together with force of arms to overthrow the state government of Louisiana to disperse. McEnery said he was familiar with the document. The general said he was under instructions in no circumstances to recognize him as the legal governor of the state. McEnery denied there had been an "insurrection" and protested this act of military interference in state affairs, but said he had no desire to resist the armed force of the United States, and would order his "state troops" home and turn over the State House—but only to the army; he insisted on putting on a show of bowing to overwhelming external force, not conceding to his political rival.

Once again the United States Army was called upon to stage a "military pantomime." A company marched down Canal Street, fifes and drums marking their cadence, turned north into the French Quarter, formed into files in front of the State House; a general officer brilliantly uniformed stepped forth to formally demand McEnery's surrender. The now unseated governor stepped forward to read his reply, voice breaking with emotion, before withdrawing amid a crowd of weeping supporters and leaving the general to take possession of the governor's chair.

By the end of September, Emory had eight hundred troops of infantry and artillery in New Orleans. Along the waterfront and steaming on the waters of the Mississippi nearby were seven ships of the United States Navy, mounting a total of fifty-one guns. The army quickly turned the State House back to Governor Kellogg. In the city, at least, peace reigned.

But Kellogg was in fact governor of little more than New Orleans. General Emory reported: "Nearly every parish in the State, following the example of New Orleans, is more or less in a state of insurrection. Red River Parishes west of Alexandria are in such a condition that I do not think order can be maintained without the use of Cavalry."

In a few days six companies of the Seventh Cavalry were once again on their way east from Dakota. Major Lewis Merrill was ordered to head to Shreveport, five hundred miles up the Mississippi and Red rivers from New Orleans, and take command of the cavalry and other troops in the northern part of the state. His new command was designated the District of the Upper Red River.

20

Cuttings from the Louisiana press from the election of 1874.

[THE SHREVEPORT TIMES]

There has been some red-handed work done in this parish that was necessary, but it evidently has been done by cool, determined, and just men, who knew just how far to go, and we doubt not if the same kind of work is necessary it will be done.

We say again that we *fully, cordially, approve* what the white men of Grant Rapides did at Colfax; the white man who does not is a creature so base that he shames the worst class of his species. We say, again, we are going to carry the elections in this State next fall.

———•———

[THE FRANKLIN ENTERPRISE]

We ask for no assistance; we protest against any intervention. We own this soil of Louisiana, by virtue of our endeavor, as a heritage from our ancestors, and it is ours, and ours alone. Science, literature, history, art, civilization, and law belong alone to us, and not to the negroes. They have no record but barbarism and idolatry, nothing since the war but that of error, incapacity, beastliness, voudouism, and crime. Their right to vote is but the result of the war, their exercise of it a monstrous imposition, and a vindictive punishment upon us for that ill-advised rebellion.

Therefore we are banding together in a White League army, drawn up only on the defensive, exasperated by continual wrong, it is true, but acting under Christian and high-principled leaders, and determined to defeat these negroes in their infamous design of depriving us of all we hold sacred and precious on the soil of our nativity or adoption, or perish in the attempt.

Come what may, upon the radical party must rest the whole responsibility of this *conflict,* and as sure as there is a just God in heaven, their unnatural, cold-blooded and revengeful measures of reconstruction in Louisiana *will meet with a terrible retribution.*

[THE NATCHITOCHES VINDICATOR]

The white people intend to carry the State election this fall; this *intention is deliberate and unalterable.*

[THE ALEXANDRIA DEMOCRAT]

The people have determined that the Kellogg government has to be gotten rid of, and they will *not scruple about the means,* as they have done in the past.

[THE SHREVEPORT TIMES]

We know the results of the election in every parish; the returning-board cannot change the count of a single precinct without perpetrating fraud and violating the constitution and the most sacred rights of the people. Therefore we should simply give the members of the board to distinctly understand that unless they return the elections as they were returned at the polls, they and those they seek to "count in" will pay the forfeit with their lives.

We have no appeals to make to our fellow-citizens of New Orleans. We know that the men of the 14th of September will do their whole duty as freemen and Louisianians zealous of their liberties. But throughout the country parishes there should be concert of action, and that action should be prompt and emphatic. In every parish where the officers elected by the people may be counted out by the returning board, the people should use hemp, or fall on the defeated candidates counted in. To localize the proposition: If Geo. L. Smith is counted in over W. M. Levy, or if Twitchell is counted in over Elam, let Smith and Twitchell be killed; if Johnson and Tyler in De Soto are counted in over Scales and Schuler, as the New Orleans Republican thinks, or if Keeting, Levisce, and Johnson, in Caddo, are counted in over Vaughan, Horan, and Land, then let Johnson, Tyler, Keeting, Levisce, and Johnson be killed; and so let every officer from Congressman down to constable in every district and parish of the State be served.

Human life may be precious, but the lives of all these carpet-baggers and radical politicians in Louisiana are valueless compared with the worth of a single principle of justice and liberty.

[THE SHREVEPORT TIMES]

If a single hostile gun is fired between the whites and blacks in this and surrounding parishes, *every carpet-bagger and scallawag that can be caught, will, in twelve hours therefrom, be dangling from a limb.* We do not say this in a spirit of braggadocio; we say it in the interests of peace, and we know what we are talking about.

21

There was a weary sense of familiarity in the dispatches Major Merrill filed from his new post in Louisiana; three years on and four states over, the same lies, the same brutal calculus.

[TELEGRAM]

DATED Headquarters Department of the Gulf
New Orleans, La., Ten, 27, 1874 (Received 12:58 p.m.)
TO Adjutant-General United States Army, Washington, D.C.:
The following, received last night, is the dispatch that I refer to
in my cipher of this date.
W. H. Emory
Col. and Bvt. Maj. Gen. Commanding

TO Assistant Adjutant-General
Headquarters Department of Gulf, New Orleans:
Telegram received. If what I have already seen is a fair sample
of discussion and comment, can only say that it is based on
falsehood. I expect abuse, as a matter of course. The facts are
that only five arrests have been made; that no more than these
were even contemplated; that neither myself nor any other officer
or soldier was present at either the arrests or hearing. Whatever
mischief is done elsewhere, is not by the facts, but by the
falsehood of the White League leaders in regard to it. No civil
authority or machinery of any kind, local, State, or national, has
for a long time existed here, and the community was fast
drifting into a state where any uncontrolled lunatic could set a
match to the mine. My action was taken to set civil functions
going and restore respect for civil law, to remind community that

this was not a state of war. My name was appended to affidavit, because any one else who signed it would have been killed, and not to constitute myself prosecutor, which I have not done. This is a difficult position, and not of my own seeking; if my ability to conduct this command is doubted, I would be only too glad to be relieved of a great responsibility which I did not seek, but shall not shirk.

Lewis Merrill,

Major Seventh Cavalry, Commanding District.

———•———

Headquarter District of Upper Red River

October 27, 1874

Sir: I have the honor now to add as follows. The previous report was made so hurriedly that in reading it over I find that it fails to convey fully an idea of the situation here.

Upon my arrival here I found that the whole community was on the verge of anarchy. The Kellogg representatives of the civil authority were violently ousted from their offices at the same time that the State government was overthrown in New Orleans. The legal mayor of the town had practically abdicated, and his duties were being discharged by another man. The local police had been disbanded, and its place supplied by a volunteer force, consisting of white citizens, many of whom are no doubt good men, but all are partisans of the so-called white man's party, and a very large proportion are more or less violent members and supporters of the White League. No civil process of any kind emanating from State authority can be issued or enforced for want of the legal officer to issue it.

The peace and good order of this whole section are at the mercy of any one who can get followers enough to begin a riot. Bad as such a state of things would be in any quiet and orderly community, it has the great aggravation here that the majority of the white people are wild with passion, and under the control of a few reckless leaders who, at best, are mere crazy revolutionists, and who have fully determined that they will bring on a conflict if possible, openly saying that such a course will compel the National Government to intervene and destroy the present State government, and set up a military government in its place. This purpose is hardly veiled and is not infrequently an open boast.

As may be easily imagined, no negro or white man of opposing politics outside of the town, where they were at the mercy of the White League, dared say that his soul was his own; in the town, where they kept their courage alive by contact with each other, they made several attempts to hold meetings, in each instance being stampeded and broken up by a few men instigated by these leaders. In one instance a large number of those engaged in a political meeting were stampeded into a disorderly flight from the court-house by one of the White League leaders jumping up in the midst of a speech and denouncing the speaker as a liar, at the same time drawing a pistol. Such was their terror and apprehension of violence that they fled because they expected the next act would be a pistol-shot.

I found, as before repeated, that such an absolute reign of terror existed that no man dared take the initiative, and I do not doubt that the fear of death as the consequence to any individual who made the affidavit was well founded. Such is the universal statement of men of all shades of political thinking, and even now it is well understood that numerous threats of assassination have been made against myself, and I am constantly cautioned by men who deprecate violence that I must be prudent. The most abusive stories were set afloat, such as that the whole town was to be arrested and confined in a stockade which Captain Parker was then building; that it was especially designed to arrest certain women, and probably send them to New Orleans in irons; and hundreds of other rumors, each as incredible as the last, readily taken up and given currency.

In any event I feel I can safely say that, even should a riot occur here, I can in great measure prevent it from running into a general massacre of the negroes.

I am, very respectfully, your obedient servant,

Lewis Merrill

Major, Seventh Cavalry, Commanding District.

In the middle of November, Company G of the Seventh Cavalry rode into Shreveport. They had been gone a month, on Merrill's orders, accompanying the deputy United States marshal as a posse comitatus to serve arrest warrants in Coushatta and Natchitoches.

Captain McIntosh told Merrill what they found. In Coushatta they had ridden out to the site where six white Republicans had been murdered back in late August. The dead men had been buried where they had been killed, three each in two graves about two miles apart. All were officeholders or Republican party leaders in Coushatta; they had been arrested by an armed force of fifty local white men, who had seized control of the town claiming they were preventing a "negro insurrection." They were held in a store overnight, then told they would be released and escorted to safety in Shreveport, sixty miles away, if they agreed to resign their offices. About thirty miles from town the party was suddenly "ambushed" by another gang of white men, who shot three of the prisoners dead on the spot, and pursued the others and killed them after a short chase.

McIntosh located the grave sites. They had been undisturbed since August. A letter to one of the murdered men from his wife lay on the ground. McIntosh's men dug up the bodies. They had been stripped of their valuables. One had been so perforated with bullets that it was only with the greatest care that the body could be moved without falling to pieces. Another had had his private parts shot off. "This," McIntosh said, "may account for what Mrs. Dewees stated to Deputy Marshal Stockton, October 18, namely, that she is virtually a prisoner in her own house, at Mansfield; that she was not permitted to see the corpse of her husband, or visit his grave, and that being warned not to attempt it on pain of death, she had been unable to do either."

In Natchitoches, the editor of the *Natchitoches Vindicator* newspaper had thrown a chaw of tobacco in the deputy marshal's face when he was arrested on a warrant, and made loud threats about what he would do to the captain.

Major Merrill was now in command of five companies of infantry and three companies of cavalry and but found he was bound to his desk in Shreveport by one crisis after another. The five men who had been arrested on his affidavit were charged with violating the Enforcement Acts; all had signed a public proclamation declaring they would discharge any man who worked for them who voted the Republican ticket, and that was a plain violation of federal law, and all Merrill had done was to attest in an affidavit to the fact that he had seen the proclamation; but he spent weeks explaining his action to his higher-ups because of all the howls the white press put up about it.

The *Shreveport Times* accused the major of persecuting honest citizens and "bedraggling his uniform in the filth of partisan politics."

The *New Orleans Bulletin* called him a "political bummer with shoulder straps."

He spent another two weeks untangling a legal mess one of his lieutenants had gotten into, running up a huge telegraph bill trying to sort things out from a hundred miles way as it became clearer and clearer the whole thing was a political setup of the shrewdest and most malicious kind.

What had happened was that Lieutenant Hodgson of the Seventh Cavalry had set off with Deputy United States Marshal Seelye and fourteen troopers to serve several arrest warrants for violations of the Enforcement Acts. The first town they rode into, they had three men to arrest, including the town's mayor. An angry crowd gathered around and threatened to come after the troops and free the men by force. At the second town, Vienna, they made a fourth arrest, and headed back for Monroe, Louisiana. A mile out of town Seelye told Hodgson he'd better cut the telegraph wire to keep the White Leaguers from getting word of where they were. Hodgson, fearing his men were in imminent danger, did it.

A few days later, in Monroe, a posse appeared in town. There were several hundred armed men, most on horseback. They claimed they had an arrest warrant for Hodgson and Seelye, for contempt of court for failure to comply with a local judge's habeas corpus writ ordering their prisoners brought before him. It was all news to Hodges and Seelye, but they had little choice but to go with the men back to Vienna.

Merrill got a wire about it and immediately sent an order to the commander of the Third Infantry company in Monroe, one Captain Head, to send every available man to Vienna after them. "That you are further instructed, and will, at all hazards, protect the prisoners against any illegal violence; and this you are hereby instructed to do. A company of cavalry will report to you at Vienna at once."

That should have been clear enough, but to add to Merrill's woes the man was a fool, and a show-off, and in sympathy with the local whites. "Who accompanies Lieutenant Hodgson for protection?" the captain wired back. "Infantry in this afternoon from eighteen miles' march. Mules nearly dead, and cannot move infantry before Sunday, and then not more than six men, probably. I anticipate no danger."

Merrill shot back: "Go yourself at once with all the men you can take. If necessary, hire transportation for seven days' rations for your own command and five days' rations for thirty men from here."

Later that same night Merrill began sending frantic telegrams to Head, and to Hodgson in care of the jail in Vienna, and to everyone else he could think of, insisting that application be made at once to have the case transferred to the United States courts: "Employ competent legal advice. Refer attorney to Brightley's Digest of United States Laws, volume ii, page 112 and following—subject, 'Removal of cases from State courts,' especially sections six and nine."

Merrill wanted no display of military force, but he wanted no conciliation either; he wanted to assert the law and set a clear precedent to discourage the White Leaguers from getting up such tricks again. And the law was clear enough. Officials acting under the Enforcement Acts could not be arrested by state authorities. They had an absolute right to have habeas corpus cases transferred to federal jurisdiction.

Over the next two days Merrill sent telegram after telegram asking if a petition had been filed for transfer of the case. A lawyer from Monroe had been retained, but Merrill could get no satisfaction out of him.

Captain Head finally nonchalantly reported that the case had already been tried, and Judge Trimble had sentenced Hodgson to ten days' imprisonment and a hundred dollars fine. "No violence at all; prisoners treated kindly and courteously by everyone."

Merrill telegraphed to Head to bring the lawyer bodily to the telegraph office the next morning at nine o'clock and answer his telegraphed questions, viva voce, in person. The next morning Merrill stood in the telegraph office in Shreveport and the lawyer stood in the office in Vienna and they cabled back and forth, each dictating to and receiving their replies from the telegraph operators crouched over their keys and translating the clicks that came back.

Q. What is status of case this morning?

A. Hodgson charged with contempt of court for having refused to obey writ of habeas corpus; was tried yesterday; will file an application for rehearing, in the morning. Everything quiet here, perfectly, as much so as in Boston.

Q. Was not petition in case filed?

A. Confidently expect Trimble will remit penalty.

Q. Will you please read my question and answer it?

A. Nothing can be done today. Will telegraph you full particulars at 9 o'clock to-morrow morning.

Q. I want answer in regard to petition.

A. The judgment of the court, so far as the contempt is concerned, is final.

Q. Has the petition for transfer been filed?

A. As there is no other charge against Mr. Hodgson, there is nothing to transfer to the United States district court. The action tried yesterday is final.

Q. Will you follow such instructions as are given you in regard to the further conduct of this case?

A. Certainly, unless such instructions lead to a result prejudicial to the interest of my client.

Q. Without discussing your belief that present action is final, which is not the fact, make out and file, without any delay, the petition for transfer of case to the United States circuit court district of Louisiana. Take from the clerk of the court a certificate under seal, that the petition has been filed. Notify the judge in proper time that such petition is on file, and ask that he take such action as acts of Congress require. Do not fail to file petition without delay.

The next day, after a flurry of a dozen more telegrams, Merrill received a wire from the attorney stating that Judge Trimble had "reversed sentence and discharged Hodgson."

Merrill, exasperated, tried cabling Head again. "Without delay, give me a distinct and categorical answer to following: Was petition for transfer of Hodgson's case filed? If no, why not?"

Head replied that Hodgson had now been indicted by the grand jury on a new charge, of cutting the telegraph wire. The attorney sent his own wire, broadly hinting that Hodgson should beat it out of town, and singing Head's praises. "They give Hodgson till to-morrow morning to get out of the way. I advise nothing. Deem presence of Captain Head invaluable. He has formed and now controls public opinion. Retain him if compatible with the interests of the service."

Merrill, at wit's end, to Captain Head once more: "If it be possible to induce on your part, or Hodgson's, or his attorney's any obedience or attention whatever to instructions, do as follows: Request petition for transfer of case to United States circuit court to be filed as in former case directed to be done. The attorney you now have is evidently an obstinate ignoramus. If a better one can be found, employ him. Answer if you fully understand."

The matter was finally settled later that day with Hodgson's arrest by the military on charges of cutting the wire, to the prejudice of good order and military discipline. The attorney sent a final reply to Merrill's last communication. "Further communication with you on this subject is respectfully declined. Charges will be preferred against you for conduct unbecoming an officer and a gentleman. There is a wide difference between a gentleman and a blackguard; you furnish an illustration. I hold myself personally responsible for my words to you."

The military court quickly convicted Hodgson, and issued an unofficial reprimand as its punishment.

A subsequent investigation by Merrill found that the whole proceedings in Vienna had been engineered by a White League lawyer there, who had advised the judge on his tactics throughout.

He also discovered that the White Leaguers in Shreveport knew of every development in the case as soon as he did: again his wires were being read.

A colonel, Henry Morrow, was sent from New Orleans to write a report. Morrow talked to the white people and concluded that there was no need for more troops and said it was unfortunate that the army was stirring up such resentment by assisting in carrying out such unpopular arrests; he recommended it cease doing so. He talked to no colored people but vouchsafed that "the negro does not comprehend politics." He acknowledged that the situation in the Red River district was "bad." He concluded, "The present State government cannot maintain itself in power a single hour without the protection of Federal troops." People everywhere—white people everywhere, he meant—boasted to him that the government could be knocked down with a shove.

Merrill went down on the steamboat to New Orleans and testified before another congressional investigating committee. He told them that more than two hundred colored men had personally come to him and reported that they had been dismissed from their work or lands because they had voted the Republican ticket. Several delegations of colored men came to report many more such acts of retribution. He estimated that in just two of the parishes within his district, De Soto and Caddo, more than five hundred men had been so discharged and had little chance of reemployment.

He said he had received frequent threats on his own life, but thought that the White Leagues would not take so foolhardy a step as to assassinate a federal officer, given the consequences that would surely follow. Not that they would disapprobate the act "so far as the private citizen, Lewis Merrill, is concerned."

Q. Suppose you were to resign your commission and take off your uniform and go back to live there?

A. I should want to borrow a Gatling gun, at least.

V

"VOTE THE NEGRO DOWN OR KNOCK HIM DOWN"

22

Adelbert Ames bought a house in Natchez as he said he would, and came down to tend his constituency as a United States senator. One day in 1872 he journeyed across the Mississippi River to observe an election campaign in Louisiana. He came away disgusted with the low dealing he had seen. He wrote to Blanche, "It causes two different and conflicting emotions to rise up within me—the one, to abandon a life of politics where such things alone find place, and another, to buckle on my armor anew that I may the better fight the battle of the poor and oppressed colored man, who is regarded by the old slave holder only as an inferior, and not fit for the duties of citizenship."

They were often separated, and he wrote her almost daily, and she replied the same, their usual long, loving letters. "Do you know, my Love, that I begin to suspect that were you my wife during the war, my love for you should have caused me to have made but a sorry soldier," he once wrote from Mississippi. He always asked solicitously after their "beautiful children"; he assured her his health was good, that he was staying away from the parts of the state where the yellow fever and "the black vomit" had broken out. She replied full of little accounts of the babies' doings and asking occasional sharp and discerning questions about the political situation. She teased him, "Perhaps by this time you think more of votes than caresses—if so, I will not trouble you with them." They were both full of anxiety if a few days passed without a word from the other. He agonized over being away from his growing children.

But he was learning to speak to a crowd, coming to like it even and getting a little vain about it, too. He told Blanche he was no hand at the stories and jokes that colored audiences seemed to want from a political speaker. But pretty soon he found that he could hold an audience anyway. "Facts I have," he said. He boasted that he had spoken for an hour, two hours, three hours without difficulty; he could turn out a well-wrought phrase without stumbling; he even learned to stir up a crowd by asking "Is not that so?" at the right moment and getting them to stamp and applaud in answer. He enjoyed the infectious enthusiasm of the colored audiences. "Youse de man!" they'd shout. They'd come up afterward and tell him that the way he went after the Democrats, they must have "thought the day of judgment had come."

One time a prominent white Democrat had stood up and walked out in the middle of his speech, and the crowd had shouted to Ames, "Hit 'em again!"

He proudly sent Blanche a clipping from a Democratic newspaper commenting on his newfound powers as a speaker; the ultimate compliment, coming as it did from his vouchsafed political enemies. "Gen. Ames has been misrepresented by the Press; he is anything but 'addlepated' or foolish. His speech was extremely deliberate, his enunciation remarkably clear and distinct, his grammatical construction faultless, his manner calm and dispassionate, his rhetoric chaste, his sarcasm abundant, polished and cutting; there was no sign of haste or confusion, every sentence had the complete finish, the correctness and polish of an epigram. We have heard no republican speaker who has so favorably impressed us as a *speaker*."

Blanche worried about the fevers and the climate but she came in the spring of 1873 to Natchez for a few months with their second baby, a girl. On the boat a woman admired the baby and asked to hold it and said, "What a fine child! Whose is it?" and then when she was told the woman had exclaimed, "Oh, take it, take it,—It is a Yankee baby, take it," and bribed her six grandchildren who were traveling with her to sing "The Bonnie Blue Flag." Blanche, by now more amused than offended, wrote her mother that the same thing was constantly happening in Natchez. "Everyone asks on the street, 'Oh, whose sweet baby is that?' When they learn it is Gen'l Ames' the noses fly up and they start back as from an adder."

By himself again in Mississippi that summer, Senator Ames read *Nicholas Nickleby* by Charles Dickens and *Roughing It* by Mark Twain and played billiards and smoked a cigar for the first time since his marriage and threw the larger half of it in the fireplace unsmoked and decided he would run for governor in the fall. Blanche worried about some of the political company he was forced to keep as he stumped across the state, but he assured her that he was already so accepted as a leader in his political circle that rather than being dragged down by the bad habits of his fellow politicos, they were deferential to his better ones, even to the point of avoiding profanity, knowing his dislike of it, and apologizing to him personally if they let a stray oath slip.

He had another two years yet to serve in the Senate. But his political blood was up now, and he saw a chance to vindicate himself, and solidify his political position, and probably guarantee his election to the Senate for another term down the road. The other senator from Mississippi, James L. Alcorn, led a rival faction of fair-weather Republicans, Republicans in name only; he was an old Whig planter and was sounding less like a Republican every day. He had opposed the Ku Klux bill, had denied the reports of outrages and murders coming from the state, had put in a part of a term as governor and dismissed nearly all of the appointments Ames had made as provisional governor and installed hundreds of Democrats in their place, and hardly a colored man among them. He had grandly suggested that if there were any Negroes fleeing persecution elsewhere in the state, they could come to his county, Coahoma, where he would extend them his personal protection. He had stood on the Senate floor and denounced Ames as "a sort of brevet brigadier Senator" who had "the senatorial toga flung upon his shoulders before he had taken off his soldier's coat."

With the overwhelming support of the colored delegates, Ames beat out Alcorn's man for the Republican nomination for governor 187 to 40; then Alcorn announced he was going to run against Ames himself, as an "Independent Republican."

Ames wrote to Blanche, "He can do no harm. We prefer he should run. It is the easiest way for us to get rid of him. He will make a great noise, but it will be the last of him."

Ames canvassed the state nonstop, counting the days till November that would bring both the election and the first frosts, and with them the days of healthy weather that would bring a reunion with his wife and children. He had seen his boy but a single week since the spring. "This is not living," he wrote to his wife. "When you run for Governor you will understand how the minutes and hours slip by, and nothing is done but talk," he told her another time.

On the Mississippi River steamboat *Belle Lee* heading down from Greensville to Vicksburg on a cold late October day with a north wind chopping the river he wrote her, his pen shaking to the vibrations of the paddlewheel slapping the water. "My pleasantest hours are those in which I think and dream of you and our babies. I suspect I am much out of place as the leader of a great party in a state, for my whole heart and life is not in the work, but rather with those I love, so far away. The smile of my wife, or the laugh of my boy has much more that is gratifying in it to me than the loud applause of the audience to which I make my political harangues.

"I am in my stateroom with my overcoat on and am glad to know that the cold wind which makes it necessary comes from the north where my Love is, and that she too feels its piercing shafts—for the cold means November, and November means the end of our separation. Is this strange love talk? But then love talks unlike anything else, being full of strange freaks and fancies."

On election day he finished with a speech in the morning in the southwest corner of the state, then rode forty miles, ten and a half hours, through mud and rain in an open buggy with one very large horse, one pony, a "reluctant driver," an umbrella, and a piece of oilcloth wrapped around his knees to try to keep him dry, to get home to Natchez. They crossed a dangerously swollen bayou with the horse and the rear wheels of the buggy touching the stream bottom and the pony and the front wheels floating.

He waited in Natchez for the returns to come in. On the fourth day he cabled Blanche, "My majority about thirty thousand, legislature about forty republican majority. Shall leave for Northfield in a day or two. A. Ames." His little boy slipped and bumped his head at his grandfather's house in Lowell, and old Benjamin Butler consoled the lad saying, "Never mind, my boy, your Father is Governor of Mississippi."

23

Albert T. Morgan ran nothing like so energetic a campaign that fall of 1873. In Yazoo City he was under a doctor's care, consuming quantities of quinine and confined to bed. His term in the state senate was up and he was running for sheriff, because he frankly needed the money. It was a lucrative office; the sheriff was by law also the county tax collector, and the position was legitimately worth five to ten thousand a year in fees.

In addition to serving in the senate, Morgan had been president of the board of supervisors of Yazoo County; that job paid a pittance, ninety dollars a year, but it had given him a chance to prove himself by deeds to his constituency. He had put in place a total reform of the county's finances and services. When Morgan's board came in they found the county was broke and ten thousand dollars in debt; that debt consisted mostly of county warrants that were trading on the open market at forty-five cents to the dollar. The scanty records showed that the planters who used to run the county had used up most of the old school fund making fifty thousand dollars' worth of unsecured "loans" to themselves. His old landlady and nemesis Mrs. White held one of the largest outstanding notes. No effort had ever been made to collect either interest or principal. Some of the individual "loans" were as much as six thousand dollars. The Whites had also received a generous allowance from the county poor fund, on the grounds that they were providing support for old and indigent ex-slaves on their plantation. The tax rate was one and a half percent on property, but when Morgan began going through the records he found that the lands of the large planters were assessed at a pittance. Tokeba, which Morgan had paid seven dollars an acre a year to rent, was assessed for tax purposes for as little as a dollar an acre as its outright value.

The county had not a single public school building; the courthouse had been burned during the war and court was now being held in a

room over a storehouse; the jail was a rickety brick structure surrounded by a rotting, tumbling-down board fence and with but a single
usable cell; roads and bridges had been left unrepaired for years.

Morgan's board raised the land assessments, still to nowhere near
their true value, but at least so that an acre that rented for ten dollars a
year was assessed for at least that much; they raised the tax rate to two
and a half percent; they built sixty schools and a fine new Beaux Arts
courthouse in the center of Yazoo City, stuccoed brick with a Greek
pediment over the entrance and an octagonal cupola housing the new
town clock and a bell; they repaired the jail and the washed-out
bridges and roads; and they paid down the debt.

Though he made but one speech, and though he spent less than a
hundred dollars for his campaign from start to last, and that just for
traveling to attend the primaries in each precinct, and though he made
it a point of honor that he never spent a dollar for whiskey, cigars,
liquor, and other such customary and expected treats to the voters,
Morgan was elected sheriff of Yazoo County by a vote of 2,365 to 431.

Morgan's predecessor as sheriff was a man named Hilliard. Morgan had helped him get the job. Now he refused to vacate his office.

The laws of the state required the sheriff to post a huge bond for
performance of his duties, $105,000. If he failed at any time to main-
tain a valid bond in the full amount, the court could remove him from
office. Only the largest landowners could normally provide that kind
of security—which meant the sheriff usually found himself firmly
under their thumbs. Now Morgan found all of the wealthiest men of
Yazoo County arrayed against him. "Not more than a handful of land
owners may defeat the will of two thousand out of three thousand
voters, and, when they combine, as they have here, secure entire control of the offices," Morgan wrote his friend General Ames, enclosing
a plea for help in raising the bond.

But finally Morgan found enough smaller property owners willing
to pledge his surety, and the county board certified his election, and it
brushed aside an absurd and legalistic challenge from Hilliard claiming that he should be allowed to keep his position (though he was not
contesting the vote). Hilliard was ordered to vacate his office in the
courthouse forthwith.

When Hilliard left that night he set three men to guard the rooms for him. That night he also sent a man to Morgan, and told him he would give him five thousand dollars if he let him stay in the job another month—until he had collected the year's taxes and pocketed the fees.

Morgan sent the man packing, and the more he thought about it the hotter he got. He tossed and turned all night, unable to sleep as his indignation ate at him. His wife saw that he was fretful and couldn't understand it; he tried to spare her the details. He later reproved himself for not treating her as the true wife she was, worthy of his full confidence. His youngest child, the four-month-old baby, was crying and colicky. Finally at dawn, after a sleepless night, he arose and headed for the courthouse. When he walked into the sheriff's office he found that the guard had dwindled to one, Hilliard's nephew, who was sweeping the floor.

Morgan told him politely that he had come to take possession of his office; he had been elected, given bond, taken the oath; the office books and papers were now his and he had come to claim them. The man offered no resistance. He asked if he could go behind the desk to get his things. Morgan said no, but he would see that they were sent to him. After the man left Morgan opened the desk drawer and found the man's pistol.

Soon several of Morgan's deputies and friends arrived. An hour and a half later Morgan looked out the window to see Hilliard leading a crowd of thirty men walking quickly toward the building. Morgan rushed out and tried to halt the crowd on the street, warning them to keep the peace. They ignored his hail and strode past him, then went on at a run to the courthouse steps. As Morgan reached the base of the steps he heard a crash of shattering wood and the echoing boom of gunshots from within. He bounded up the steps and a bullet sang past him. In front of the sheriff's office down the hall the door had been smashed down, and his deputy inside was trying to fight off the attackers, who were shooting into the office. Hilliard and some of his men turned toward him. The firing continued. From the courthouse entrance Morgan fired two or three shots in return, driving the crowd from the hall. Hilliard fell to the floor.

One of Morgan's deputies was severely wounded. Morgan sent for a doctor. Within minutes a messenger from the mayor arrived saying that several men had sworn out a complaint against him, for the murder of Hilliard.

Things got stranger in a hurry. Morgan's lawyers, all prominent members of the white establishment, urgently advised him to seek a hearing on his charges first, before any of Hilliard's men could be arrested and brought to trial. They assured him that he would not actually be confined in jail. So Morgan filed a writ of habeas corpus, and the judge, a chancellor of equity, immediately ordered him to jail. The chancellor then came to visit Morgan in his cell and explained that while he did not believe he would be convicted by any court in the world on the charge of murder, he was denying him bail for his own safety.

The chancellor then promptly found that the coroner, who by statute acted in place of the sheriff, had insufficient bonds to assume that office; and there miraculously appeared before him at the same instant a man put forward by the local white Democrats, complete with adequate bonds already prepared, and the chancellor appointed him sheriff. The local newspaper fanned the story that Morgan had shot Hilliard point-blank in the head as Hilliard was trying to flee.

From his jail cell Morgan wrote his friend Adelbert Ames a letter outlining the facts. "My colored friends are true as steel. They watch the street corners & by ways, and even watch the jail to prevent assassination or any sort of violence to my person.

"It is damp and cold in my cell and I find great difficulty in writing," he concluded.

Two days later he wrote again. "I have no doubt it is the purpose of those controlling to keep me here until an election can be had for Sheriff—I cannot, do not dare to write you all the particulars, here. I fully believe my life is in great danger by violence."

The chancellor himself became worried enough that he ordered Morgan transferred to the jail in Jackson. The first attempt to move him was met by a large armed mob, under the command of the temporary sheriff. Morgan was finally smuggled out at night under a heavier guard and spirited aboard a steamer on the Yazoo River.

Morgan tried appealing to the state Supreme Court, but there was no written record of the habeas corpus proceedings, or even of the chancellor's decision.

Finally the legislature passed a special bill transferring the sheriff's office in Yazoo County to Morgan's deputies while he remained in jail; it passed another bill allowing for a second habeas corpus hearing in cases where the loss or destruction of the hearing records made an appeal impossible. The chancellor who had first heard Morgan's case, who had a temporary appointment anyway that had never been confirmed, was dismissed, and Ames named an eminent professor of law from the university at Oxford, Mississippi, in his stead. The new chancellor wrote a lengthy opinion that carefully sifted all of the testimony and ruled that even on the prosecution's evidence there could be no possible conviction on a charge greater than manslaughter, and ordered Morgan released on five thousand dollars bail. Two grand juries investigated and brought no indictment.

Morgan returned to Yazoo City and reclaimed his office.

24

The Ameses moved into the governor's mansion at almost exactly the same time Albert T. Morgan moved into the Jackson jail.

Ames's attempt to take possession of the house was an uncannily familiar business: again the occupant would not leave. The previous governor was now contending that the election should never have been held at all; instead of November 1873 it should not have taken place until November 1874. He was challenging it in court. Meanwhile, he wasn't budging.

For nearly two weeks Ames, with his wife and their two small children—Butler was now two and a half, Edith, nine months—stayed uncomfortably at the hotel by the depot. The noise of the trains passing through the night woke the children, and the children woke the parents, and no one was getting much sleep. Finally the state Supreme Court ruled that the election was valid, Ames was sworn in, and that same day, late in the afternoon in a heavy rain, the family moved into the mansion.

It was grand but shabby, "a great barn of a house," Blanche wrote her mother, occupying a whole block of the downtown, nicely shaded by trees, with a columned portico in front and lots of dilapidated furnishings within. The rooms were twenty-five feet on a side, had thirteen-foot ceilings; the faded upholstery and curtains and worn carpets gave it the air of a slightly disheveled hotel. The entrance hall was elaborately plastered and gilded, the stairs painted faux green marble, the genuine white marble of the mantelpieces so begrimed with soot that no one would have guessed what they were made of. Three convicts were sent from the state penitentiary to do the heavy cleaning and put the house in order, watched over by a guard with a huge pistol stuck in his waist. Some women from the penitentiary were to come the next week and wash the lace curtains.

The cook was a trouble. Blanche had her hands full trying to teach her that "lard is not the staff of life," and not to shout "Oh! gal Oh! gal" to get her attention: "You are to say Madame when you want anything of me." They got a cow to supply milk for the children, and cream for their coffee and tea.

Blanche wrote her mother, "The great question which disturbs the residents here is 'Shall we call on Mrs. Ames?' Quite a number have called, and the rest will probably follow." The ladies came, all "lynx-eyed," rigid politeness on both sides. "But one is constantly on guard," said Blanche.

Blanche's mother, the wife of a politician longer than she, offered advice. "Yours is a difficult part. Never forget to adorn yourself. That you are not apt to forget. Keep back any spirit of retort, which you have a spice of, and your beauty, gentle manners, and good breeding will prove an efficient aid to Gen. Ames. He is on the topmost wave of political triumph. You both have ability enough to keep there, if some ugly accident does not intervene."

On another occasion she added, "If you always remember that you are the observed of all observers, and are careful to neglect or offend none, you cannot go wrong. But this, to be sure, is greater than the labour of Hercules.—But you are bonny, and can do it."

The ladies called but society remained frosty, and by the time they had been there two months Blanche had not ventured beyond the gates of the mansion more than half a dozen times, all of those to return calls. They contented themselves with small entertainments for the fellow "carpet-baggers," as Blanche cheerily described them, teas, suppers, regular croquet parties on the lawn of the governor's mansion.

The governor's inaugural message was received with cautious praise by the Democratic papers. The new governor called for rigid economy and strict accountability of government funds, and followed up with a long list of suggested reductions in the cost of government. He proposed compulsory schooling, a minimum of three months a year for all children between the ages of five and fifteen, to fight illiteracy; the encouragement of manufacturing; the ownership of the soil by the man who tills it, to avert thereby the evils of a permanent class of "peasantry or tenantry," as found in "monarchial counties." He sternly disapproved of a scheme afoot to invest $320,000 in federal land grant funds, intended to support a state university, in a "paper railroad," the Vicksburg and Nashville.

Ames said in his message that it was true that the colored people were uneducated and poor. "But this is their misfortune rather than their fault, and a spirit of fairness would so treat it." He deprecated all talk of a racial line in politics. If the colored people are Republicans today it is because of "the firmly rooted conviction that it is necessary to be so to avert impending destruction. They have always acted on the defensive." But they ask for nothing but their rights. "Believing that their safety depended on their ballots, they have never attempted to secure an advantage over their opponents by fraud or violence at the polls. They have never forgotten, in securing their own rights, to guard with jealous care the rights of others. There is no just cause for asserting that their action tends to a war of races."

"There should be no cause for division, much less for war, if the same freedom of thought and action claimed by the one race for itself be accorded to the other."

At the end of the legislative session in April the Ameses steeled themselves for the one large, formal reception that custom demanded, inviting all of the state officers and legislators, "without ladies." The custom, Blanche found, was to put a notice in the newspaper, serve nothing but confectioner's cake and cheap champagne—"nigger champagne" was apparently the usual local term for it—and deal with a "great deal of rowdyism and drunkenness" that always followed. "Gen'l. Ames is quite determined to make a change," Blanche wrote her mother, and she worked for weeks organizing something more fitting: thirty-six chickens with an equal weight of celery, made into salad with a dressing she made from six dozen eggs, oil, vinegar, mustard, and a little cayenne pepper; twenty-four pounds of lobster made into salad, with lettuce; six large roast turkeys; four hams; ten large frosted cakes; and twenty-seven loaves of bread, "nicely sliced and buttered." There were sardines and olives; four dishes of strawberries; two and a half gallons of ice cream; ten pounds of mocha coffee brewed in a large urn; and a centerpiece Blanche created herself with three huge bunches of bananas, three hundred bananas in all, and stacks of oranges, and flowers. The next morning the yard was littered with banana skins and orange peels. Cigars were offered after supper. "Some *gentlemen* took three and four." It was a success.

The spring of 1874 brought heavy rains that sent the Mississippi over its banks, inundating farm fields and leaving thousands without food or a roof to sleep under. A. T. Morgan telegraphed from Yazoo City: "What about rations cant we get any sent by river from Vburg immediately action is very essential." Reports of families living on nothing but parched corn came to the governor's office. From Washington came a telegram reporting that Senator Alcorn was blocking the relief bill for the state. "Senate Committee reported sixty thousand for Mississippi. Alcorn made an onslaught upon it + as a result of the discussion the bill has been recommitted. Telegraph immediately somewhat in detail the facts of the conditions of the sufferers it is represented that the suffering is exaggerated." The aid arrived and the governor telegraphed Morgan. "Shipped 10,000 rations 7500 pounds of pork 10000 pounds hard bread 1500 pounds beans."

The summer of 1874 brought a drought; a stream of ants that reached the sugar bowl on the table in the governor's mansion, somehow getting across the jars of water that the legs of the table had been placed in to thwart them; a pistol in the mail, sent by Blanche from Cape Ann, Massachusetts, where she and the children had again repaired for the hot months; and harbingers of unease. "I do not imagine it will be of any use," Ames wrote back to her when his pistol came. "However I will carry it as of old." She wrote, "I cannot say that the house in Jackson seemed exactly like home to me, Del, yet I was happy there and the thought of going back is not unpleasant. We shall have another quiet winter together and the life there is such as to render us very dependent upon each other."

Blanche, pregnant again, lay awake at night, and sent her husband a letter asking that he send her his personal note for five thousand dollars. This was the interest earned so far on the money her father had given her when they married, and she wanted to be sure it was secured for their children if she should die in childbirth; this way it would not be tangled up with his debts or money troubles, if he ever had them. He did as she wished, and she sent her gratitude and apology. "Your letter enclosing note came this morning. Do not think me morbid or unhappy, Love, because I made such a request of you. No doubt all women, without really fearing death, think of the possibility at such times and govern themselves accordingly. Perhaps it is something of the same feeling you may have had going into battle. Full of hope, yet counting the chances."

She went on. "Tomorrow Butler, as you remind me in your letter, will be three years. I cannot realize it. Four happy years I have been married. Each succeeding one more full of love and content than the last. I have to thank you, Del, for all your gentleness and loving kindness to me during these four years, which has made them the happiest of my life. You have humored my whims, been forbearing with my faults, and seemed so content with your wife, that you have left me nothing to wish for. I have, and do appreciate this, Dearie, and my only desire is that you should feel the same. If you do not, tell me wherein I can add to your content, and I am sure I shall not fail you."

One lady in Ames's regular five o'clock croquet party stopped coming, because of a rumor spread about town that she had "played croquet in Vicksburg with negroes"; she would not call on the governor until "the story is shown to be false."

He read that his name was being mentioned as a possible vice presidential candidate. "If I know myself, I never possessed so little political ambition as today. Events are constantly transpiring which cause me to look with disgust on many things which I am forced of necessity to meet. My purpose is to give a good government, and let the future look to itself."

Two of his political comrades were staying with him in the mansion, and they "remorselessly drank all my whiskey and brandy, two bottles of the former excepted, and made way with my cigars!"

He shopped for a billiard table, but decided $350 was too much money, especially with the national economy in a "stagnation" and the principal and interest on his debts swelling "into frightful proportions."

Autumn brought a sweep for the Democrats in Congress, even General Butler thrown out by the voters of Massachusetts in the tide of dissatisfaction over the depression.

In November, Blanche and the children, including two-month-old Sarah, headed south once again. It was an oddly ill-fated journey. The horses pulling their cab in Boston slipped in a snowstorm and fell down. The boat to New York ran into a heavy headwind and choppy seas that made them all seasick and twelve hours late. They missed their train and lost their reservation, and when they left New York the next night the train got a broken wheel in Pittsburgh and they had to shift first to one car and then another. Ames came to meet them in Louisville, where they had to change stations, and accompanied them back to Jackson, where they arrived twenty hours late. He had telegraphed ahead for the carriage and a baggage truck to be waiting for them, but when they pulled in at five in the morning no one was there. And so they trudged home along the deserted early morning November streets of a Southern city, babies, bundles, and all.

In December word came from Vicksburg that 500 armed white men had surrounded the courthouse and run the Negro sheriff out of town under threat of death, and installed a white Democrat in his place. When the sheriff returned with a posse of 125 poorly armed colored men to reclaim his office, the white mayor of Vicksburg had declared "martial law," appointed an ex-Confederate colonel to direct military operations, and seized the sheriff. The posse agreed to return home after a parley. While they were talking a body of armed white men on horseback flanked them. The colored men had gone half a mile when the men on horseback opened fire. The posse tried to return fire but had only pistols and shotguns, and they were picked off by the whites at long range with Winchester rifles. The shooting around Vicksburg went on for some days. A hundred and sixty men from one of Louisiana's armed White Leagues came over to assist.

From A. T. Morgan came a bit of news that he had secretly picked up in Yazoo City: "If it can be done, an examination of the files in the Telegraph Office at Vicksburg will discover the fact that the mayor of the city of Vicksburg telegraphed the attorney for the Grangers here on the Wednesday or Thursday following the riot there—'Coons in the canebrakes, have taken a hundred scalps. We are masters of the situation. R OLeary Mayor of Vicksburg.' What would the world say of it if it could be known. Can't you get hold of it? I can not get away to come to Jackson now, so confide this to you through the mails—Do not let it be known except to the proper persons. M"

Another telegram became widely known:

Trinity Texas December 12 1874
To President Board of Supervisors
Do you want any men? Can raise good crowd within twenty
four hours to kill out your negroes.
J. G. Gates and A. H. Mason

Ames summoned an emergency session of the legislature to issue the necessary call to the United States government for protection against domestic violence as prescribed by the federal Constitution. The president issued the orders, and Mississippi waited for two more weeks. At last word came.

New Orleans La Jany 5 1875
To Gov Ames
I have tonight assumed control over the department of the Gulf
a company of troops will be sent to Vicksburg tomorrow.

P. H. Sheridan
Lieut Genl

The troubles abated, but the sick sweet taste of blood remained.

The summer of 1875 brought to the again lonely governor's house in Jackson the sound of a Scotch air sung to a neighbor's piano wafting through an open window, an occasional cart rattling by, hungry and numerous mosquitoes in the bedchambers, solitary evenings spent reading a history of England and *The Way We Live Now* by Anthony Trollope, little appetite for dinner, and a note from the White League of Claiborne County listing the Republican officeholders they intended to assassinate: "Our brothers in your section will look after you—Send out your negro troops & Gatlin Guns and we will wipe them from the face of the Earth which they disgrace—We have the best rifles and eager for an opportunity to use them. 'There is life in the old land yet.'"

Alone in the governor's house, Ames took to having a glass of beer with his dinner, which he disliked, but hoped it might put some weight back on him.

At the gate of the mansion he bought a pail of thick-skinned native grapes from a man for forty cents.

A fitful and uneasy wind stirred the dust in the streets.

25

Jackson Miss.
Sept. 2 '75

Dear Blanche:

This is a very hot day. The thermometer ranges well up towards 90° in my room. Walking up to the office and back suggests a moderately heated furnace. As I have so little to do now-a-days I do not go office-wards till about midday. At half past two I aim to be at the restaurant.

The only business just now is to listen to reports of outrages by the Democracy. Today a telegram came that a Republican meeting in Yazoo City where Col. Morgan was speaking was attacked and one or two Negroes killed, and quite a number wounded. Of arming and intimidation by these white liners reports come from all sides. They will do anything to carry the state. So far has this intimidation gone that I cannot organize a single company of Militia. In fact, months ago when I was laboring to do so, leading Republicans came to me and besought me not to. Today everybody is against it, and I can get no one to take a commission. The old rebel armies are too much for our party, and the colored men dare not organize even though they know their liberty is at stake. You see how unsatisfactory my position is.

Love, kisses and caresses for the babies and yourself from
Adelbert

Jackson Miss.
Sept. 3 '75

Dear Blanche:

I had a call from a lady this morning before daylight. Col. Morgan was addressing a "club" of Republicans in Yazoo City, a few evenings since, when some white liners interrupted, broke up the meeting and killed two men. Col. M. escaped. Immediately the city was filled with armed men. Companies were marching to and fro and pickets and sentinels established as in active warfare. The only way our friends there could communicate with us was to send a lady, a sister-in-law of Col M., his brother's wife, to us. She came in on the night train and at once came here to the Mansion with Mr. Cardoza, and related the facts. The Democracy are organized into military companies and have assumed control—taken military possession of the county. I shall issue a proclamation ordering them to disperse and retire to their homes. Of course I can do nothing by physical force, but my proclamation will, I hope, pave the way for national interference. The canvass here is waxing warm, and I shall have to remain constantly to my post.

I send you, Sweetheart, love in abundance.

<u>Adelbert</u>

Jackson Miss.
Sept. 5 '75

Dear Blanche:

I had finished my letter to you yesterday and was looking for George to mail it when Capt. Fisher came to me out of breath and out of heart to tell me of a riot which had just taken place at Clinton (a village ten miles west of here) and from which he had just escaped, with his wife. He was speaking when the riot began. It was a premeditated riot on the part of the Democracy which resulted in the death of some four white men and about the same number of Negroes and quite a large number of Negroes wounded. There were present at a Republican barbecue about fifteen hundred colored people, men, women and children. Seeking the opportunity white men, fully prepared, fired into the crowd. Two women were reported killed, also two children. As the firing continued, the women ran away with the men in many instances, leaving their children on the ground. Today there are some forty carriages, wagons and carts which were abandoned by the colored people in their flight. Last night, this morning and today squads of white men are scouring the country killing Negroes. Three were killed at Clinton this morning—one of whom was an old man, nearly one hundred years old—defenseless and helpless. Yesterday the Negroes, though unarmed and unprepared, fought bravely and killed four of the ring-leaders, but had to flee before the muskets which were at once brought onto the field of battle. This is but in keeping with the programme of the Democracy at this time. They know we have a majority of some thirty thousand and to overcome it they are resorting to intimidation and murder. It is cold-blooded murder on the part of the "white liners"—but there are other cases exactly like this in other parts of the state. You ask what are we to do. That is a question I find difficult to answer. I told you a day or two ago that the whole party has been opposed to organizing a militia and furthermore I have been unable to find anyone who was willing to take militia appointments.

The Mansion has been crowded all day long with Republican friends and Negroes from the field of battle. I have run off to the northwest chamber for my daily chat with you, leaving a crowd in the other rooms. There has also been a crowd at the front gate all day long. The town is full of Negroes from the country who come to escape harm.

I anticipate no further trouble here at this time. The "white liners" have gained their point—they have, by killing and wounding, so intimidated the poor Negroes that they can in all human probability prevail over them at the election. I shall at once try to get troops from the general government. Of course it will be a difficult thing to do.

I send a world of love,

Adelbert

[Copy Telegram, sent Sept. 7, 1875]
To His Excellency,

U. S. Grant, President

Washington, D.C.

Sir:

Domestic violence, in its most aggravated form, exists in certain parts of this State. On the evening of the 1st of September unauthorized and illegal armed bands overthrew the civil authorities of Yazoo County, took forcible possession of the county, from which the Sheriff, the peace officer of the county, was compelled to flee for safety, and is still a refugee. The Sheriff of this county (Hinds) reports that since the 4th instant, he has been unable, after every effort, to maintain the

peace and protect life. He reports various murders by
unauthorized armed bodies, who are scouring the country.
Warren county is also reported as being in a state of terrorism
from the demonstrations of still other unauthorized armed bodies.
A feeling of insecurity pervades in other counties than those
named. After careful examination of all reports I find myself
compelled to appeal to the general government for the means
of giving that protection to which every American citizen is
entitled. A necessity of immediate action cannot be overstated.
Adelbert Ames

                                Yazoo City Miss Sept 9 1875
Your Excellency,
Eight days have now passed since the assault of the "White
League" on our club and their occupation & possession of the
town and seizure of authority. I have caused letters to be written
to you, telegrams sent to you, and, by every means in my power,
sought to reach you that we might get help from some quarter. I
have been unable to get further word from you or from Jackson
than was brought by my brother's wife on her return.
Can nothing be done? I am in great danger of losing my life.
Not only that, all the leading republicans, who have not run
away, in danger. They are all secreted like myself, not with me,
however. I get word from them occasionally. The town is so
strongly guarded by pickets, police, & men, women, & children
from every door-step, porch, & window, besides armed men
who patrol the streets at night, that none can get away if they
would. The league here have adopted a new policy, which is to
kill the leaders and spare the colored people, unless they "rise."
A certain element here headed by Dixon, H.M., and men like
him who have been and are still doing all they can to drive,
provoke the colored people to show fight. They seem anxious to
"distinguish" themselves. The larger, and so far the stronger,
class are doing all they can to prevent this, but all seem to dread
the Dixon men. At the same time Dixon is the lion of the hour.
Lawyers and others tell him he has won a victory he deserves

great credit for. Halder openly boasts on the street that he
killed Dick Mitchell. He took his pistol. The colored people—I
have been speaking only of whites—in the country are very much
excited. They have acted discretely so far. They have no arms,
save occasionly a shot-gun, and cannot get ammunition even for
these. I have done all in my power to prevent them coming to
town. I could not do much in my position, of course. They have
exhibited no bad blood so far as I have been able to learn. The
patrolls have been to the country and warned some of the
country leaders to leave. During the first few days the town was
filled with all sorts of rumors of the "niggers rising." I am
satisfied they are mainly hatched by the Dixon men. Every time
any such story was started the citizens would be called together
and patroles set out to warn or drive them off. These means
seem to be used to "rouse" the "indignant" whites to action as
whiskey is given to soldiers just before a battle, or approval and
acquiescence in the conduct of the leaguers in killing republican
leaders and driving off others. Last night they were called
together—the white citizens again. Within twenty yards of my
hiding place, on either side, were stationed two pickets. Men
were passing & repassing all night. I heard one man say to
another as they passed by, "if they catch him they will hang him."
I can see & hear a great deal that goes on. Much comes to me by
messengers which is exaggerated. I am giving you what I see &
hear, and the messages I get after sifting & comparing them. I do
not feel like running away from here, even if I could. I might get
shot in the back, or more roughly handled, even, than that.

My friend, I fought four years; was wounded several times;
suffered in hospitals, and as a prisoner; was in twenty-seven
different engagements to free the slave and save our glorious
Union—to save such a country as this! I have some love left for
my country, but what is country without it protects its
defenders? I have had a letter from my wife. She takes it bravely,
but her condition is such I fear the consequences. I know how
you are situated. I do not blame you. I would not give you more
pain than you already feel at your inability to help; but can't you

get an officer to come here? Is there no protection for me? Can't
an officer of the camp there be sent here? I don't want troops if
Ohio is to be lost by it; I prefer to die first. Indeed, I am ready to
die, if it is necessary, and good result from it; but to be butchered
here by this mob after all I have done is too cruel.

Respectfully yours &c.

A.T. Morgan

Jackson, Miss.

Dear Blanche:

Today I issued a proclamation commanding the illegal
military companies to disband: and I also telegraphed the
President to make an inquiry before formally making a
requisition for troops.

You may read to your Father such portions of my letters as
touch on the political situation. Tell him that in '60 and '61 there
were not such unity and such preparation against the government
of the U.S. as now exist against the colored men and the
government their votes have established. Gibbs and Raymond
report that Gen. Augur is ready to act but that he requires
authority from the President. He holds, as I have told you our
party generally does, that the organizing of the militia of colored
men precipitates a war of races and one to be felt over the entire
South. He says thousands in Louisiana are ready to come here to
fight the Negro. As it is, the power of the U.S. alone can give the
security our citizens are entitled to. If it is not given, then no effort
will be made by the Republicans to carry the election.

I send you love.

Adelbert

Bay View on Cape Ann

Dear Del:

I shall write you only a short letter, just to remind you that
there is someone here for you to love. . . .

Love. Kisses and caresses

Blanche

26

Cuttings from the Mississippi press from the election of 1875.

[THE JACKSON CLARION]

"Now, therefore, I, A.A., do hereby command all persons belonging to such organizations to disband." Ha! ha!! ha!!! "Command," "Disband." That's good.

[THE YAZOO CITY HERALD]

What impudence. Our dapper little Governor Ames comes to the front with a proclamation ordering the disbandment of all the military companies now organized in the State. If he had brains enough to know his right hand from his left, he ought to know that no more attention will be paid to his proclamation than the moon is popularly supposed to pay to the baying of a sheep-killing dog.

[THE JACKSON CLARION]

Ames is organizing a war of races with all its attendant horrors, in our otherwise peaceful state. The time has arrived when the companies that have been organized for protective and defensive purposes should come to the front. There are three of them in the city of Jackson. There are others in Hinds—let still others be formed all over the state as speedily as possible, and armed and equipped with the best means that can be extemporized for the occasion. We hope to see a large and imposing display of these defensive organizations as soon as practicable. Let every citizen hold himself in readiness to join one or other of these companies for the emergency that the bold, reckless, and desperate adventurer, who is in the executive office, seems determined to force upon us.

———◆———

[THE JACKSON CLARION]

Appeal after appeal has been made in vain to the colored people. No more appeals will be made to them.

———◆———

[THE COLUMBUS INDEX]

Below we give a list of the presidents of the negro clubs in this county. In the coming election these must be *marked men*. We request every beat committee to save this list for future reference.

———◆———

[THE WESTVILLE NEWS]

VOTE THE NEGRO DOWN OR KNOCK HIM DOWN.—We have tried policy long enough. We must organize on the color-line, disregarding minor considerations. The white man's party is the only salvation for the State. Show the negro his place and make him keep it. If we cannot vote him down, we can knock him down, and the result will be the same. Either the white man or the negro will rule this country; they cannot both do it, and it is for the white men to say who the ruler shall be. Let us have a white man's party to rule a white man's country, and to do it like white men.

———◆———

[THE VICKSBURG HERALD]

Much as we deplore bloodshed, and much as we lament violence, we believe that every riot will carry a plain lesson to the intelligent electors of Mississippi. To put down this riotous, revengeful feeling, we have just got to put down the Ames ring.

Just so long as the Ames power rules Mississippi, just so long will white men be compelled to sleep with guns handy to reach.

———•———

[THE VICKSBURG MONITOR]

The same tactics that saved Vicksburg will surely save the State, and no other will.

———•———

[THE YAZOO DEMOCRAT]

CARRY THE ELECTION, PEACEABLY IF WE CAN, FORCIBLY IF WE MUST.

———•———

[THE YAZOO DEMOCRAT]

Try the rope.

27

After two weeks in hiding Albert Morgan slipped out of his place of concealment in his brother's house one night disguised in old clothes, and made his way cautiously to the stable where his hostler had left his sorrel mare saddled and ready, and rode out of town. Nine miles out of Yazoo City some colored people at a prayer meeting at a Negro church warned him of a white company occupying the town ahead, and lent him a guide to lead him a circuitous route to Jackson.

He got there the next morning, alive and with more details of what had happened at the meeting in Yazoo City two weeks earlier.

He had begun to speak when the man his brother had nicknamed the Human Hornet, one Henry M. Dixon, had come in. Dixon was a small, wiry, nervous man with light hair, thin lips, and a girlish face who had harried Morgan and his brother for years. He also had the nickname "the rope-bearer"—for the part he had played in some lynchings. He commanded a group of men who went about in military style wearing ribbons that said "Dixon's Scouts" on them.

Dixon and several other white Democrats in the hall started heckling and interrupting Morgan. Morgan made a reference to the board of supervisors. A Democrat in the audience shouted out, "There ain't one of them fit to be there."

"What do you say of Mr. Rowe, born here and raised here, a man of property and means here, and a good citizen?" Morgan retorted. "What have you to say of Captain Bedwell?"

Dixon leapt to his feet and began shouting, "He's a thief! He's a thief!"

A colored man answered, "No! No! That is all you know about it!" And Dixon pulled out his pistol and shot him.

Morgan, up on the stage, commanded the peace; then they started shooting at him. The lights over the hall where Dixon and his men were went out but the lights on the stage shone brightly. The end of the table where Morgan was standing took three slugs; the wall behind him was tattooed with bullet holes; somehow they all missed him. He scrambled out a window and fell fifteen feet to the bricks below. The alarm bell at the market house was ringing, and white men with rifles were running toward there.

A few days later Dixon and his Scouts went out and hanged the colored Republican leaders in every supervisor's district in the county.

After they hanged one man they went into town, brought back a magistrate, reassembled on the spot as a coroner's jury, and declared that the deceased had met his death by hanging at the hands of persons unknown.

They killed Morgan's deputy, a white Republican.

The next seven weeks to the election passed in a nightmarish succession of images limned in terror and lies.

The Democratic state chairman telegraphed Washington, "Peace prevails" throughout the state.

Ames pleaded for federal troops. The United States attorney general, a conservative former Democrat, replied. He had just heard from the president, he informed Ames; the president had told him, "The whole public are tired out with these annual autumnal outbreaks in the South."

Ames pleaded for troops again. "Let the odium, in all its magnitude, descend upon me; I cannot escape the conscientious discharge of my duty towards a class of American citizens, whose only crime consists in their color, I am powerless to protect," Ames wrote; again to no avail.

From all over the state messages poured into the governor's office: sheriffs in nine counties run out of their offices or unable to keep the peace; Republican candidates told to take their names out of the running or be killed; Republican ballot tickets intercepted in the mail and destroyed.

Fifty men, armed with needle guns and sixteen-shooter Winchesters, had fired from the windows of the Vicksburg mail train on Negro men and women working in the fields.

Shots were fired into the governor's mansion.

Senator Alcorn personally showed up with a double-barreled shotgun and a gang of armed men at a political meeting for the colored Republican sheriff in his home county, and left six colored men dead.

"Profound peace and good order prevails," the Democratic committee wired Washington.

Too late, much too late, a company of state militia, colored men under arms and under the command of State senator Charles Caldwell, was formed, and Caldwell declared himself ready and willing to march to Yazoo City and restore Morgan to his office; but Morgan called off the expedition when he learned that Dixon had nine hundred men mounted and armed, waiting to head them off and boasting of leaving the ground soaked in blood; when he learned that the one white state militia company that was to accompany them was planning to fire a few blank cartridges and then go over to the other side and help hang Morgan and slaughter all of the colored soldiers, to a man.

Caldwell's militiamen, under the governor's orders, marched yet, marched thirty miles west from Jackson to deliver a hundred rifles to a newly formed company that lacked arms, boldly defying the threats of the white liners, returning triumphant and unharmed—only to be disbanded three days later when Ames accepted a "peace treaty" with the Democrats, negotiated by an emissary from Washington, under which both sides agreed to abandon all further resort to arms.

Still the killing went on.

From Yazoo City, two weeks later, came another desperate letter to the governor: "I beg you most fully to send the United soldiers here they have hung six men since the killing of Mr. Fawn. They won't let the Republicans have know ticket they will not permit any at all. Now they are going to have war here—send help—they told Mr. Richman if he went to the telegraph office tomorrow they would hang him—help—help—help—help."

From Noxubee County: "The democrats was in Macon town in high rage, raring around and shooting of their cannons all up and down the street, and shooting all their pistols also, Richard Gray shot down walking on the pavements, shot by the democrats, and he was shot five times, four times after he fell, because he was nominated for treasurer."

From De Soto County: "We as republicans of state of Mississippi do ask you to tell us whether we are to be murdered by the whites of the state or not—with out any protection at all Dear Sir did not the 14th Article and first section of the constitution of the United States say that no person shall be deprived of life nor property without due process of law it said all persons shall have equal protection of the law but I say we colored men don't get it at all."

The peace treaty became a farce even to the credulous man from Washington who had negotiated it. With every new report of a killing or outrage the governor went wearily to the man from Washington, who would take the report to the head of the Democratic committee, who would the next day produce a half dozen or a dozen telegrams or a dozen affidavits from the locality in question, all swearing to a state of perfect calm, or solemnly asserting that the Negroes who had been killed or outraged were the aggressors.

Even the credulous man from Washington finally acknowledged that the Democrats had never had the slightest intention of abiding by their agreement. A few days before the election he reported to the attorney general, "It is impossible to have a fair election on Nov 2nd without the aid of U.S. troops."

Ames told him there was no point now.

"No matter if they are going to carry the state," Ames told him, "let them carry it, and let us be at peace and have no more killing."

At the last minute the 215 United States troops stationed at Jackson, Vicksburg, and Holly Springs—all there were in the whole godforsaken state of Mississippi, a third of them sent there just to get away from the yellow fever in New Orleans—received orders that they could "prevent bloodshed in case of disorders." They could not, however, act to prevent disorders from breaking out, much less be employed to prevent intimidation at the polls, or beforehand.

Ames had written Blanche: "Through the terror caused by murders and threats, the colored people are thoroughly intimidated. They cannot be rallied unless we have U.S. troops and it is now too late for that.

"Yes, a <u>revolution</u> has taken place—by force of arms—and a race are disfranchised—they are to be returned to a condition of serfdom— an era of second slavery. Now it is too late. The nation should have acted but <u>it</u> was '<u>tired</u> of the annual autumnal outbreaks in the South.' The political death of the Negro will forever release the nation from the weariness from such 'political outbreaks.' You may think I exaggerate. Time will show how accurate my statements are.

"Last night I made up my mind to resign after the election when this revolution shall have been completed. Why should I fight on a hopeless battle for two years more, when no possible good to the Negro or anybody else would result? Why?"

A few days before the election he wrote, "Dear Blanche: This morning I received the babies' photographs. Butler's and Edith's are excellent. This has to be a short letter, as I have been prevented writing you till this late hour. I will add this only—politically we are beaten—and that through violence, murder and intimidation."

Violence, murder, and intimidation delivered a clean sweep.

The Democrats took a thirty thousand vote majority. In Yazoo County, where A. T. Morgan had been elected two years earlier with a two thousand vote majority, the Democratic ticket won. The vote was 4,044 to 7. The seven Republican votes were cast by the Democrats, it was said, in a spirit of "bravado," lest their victory appear too lopsided.

The Democratic citizens of Yazoo County took up a subscription and purchased a silver bowl for Captain Dixon. It was inscribed To THE BRAVEST OF THE BRAVE. The inscription went on to explain that it was given "in appreciation of his brilliant services in the redemption of the county from radical rule in 1875."

In the Mississippi House the Democrats gained a majority of ninety-five to twenty and in the Senate twenty-six to ten. They hadn't expected to get the Senate, but they wasted no time exploiting that windfall. They impeached the lieutenant governor, so that the state need not suffer the humiliation of a Negro governor when they got rid of Ames, and then they impeached Ames. The charges were so absurd as to make the farce transparent, but they didn't care; they had the votes.

One count accused the governor of violating the constitution by removing the unelected sheriff the whites of Vicksburg had installed at rifle point. Another accused Ames of filling two companies of militia with "men of the African race" and appointing Charles Caldwell, "a notoriously dangerous and turbulent and obnoxious man of that race," as their captain, in order to "provoke peaceful and law-abiding citizens to wrath and violence." Another accused him of firing two judges "for partisan purposes." Blanche proposed that he offer to resign if the legislature dropped the charges.

The Faustian bargain was easily struck. Adelbert Ames left the state the next day, never to set foot on its red blood-drenched soil again.

28

Albert T. Morgan got himself and his family out of Mississippi in January and never went back either. In Washington, D.C., he eked out a living for a while with a meager legal practice, representing a Yazoo County lady who had a claim against the government for some horses and mules and cotton taken by Union troops during the war.

Another United States senatorial committee convened to record the words of the victims after it was too late to help them. The Democrats now held the House; the mood of the country was now more one of fatigue with the travails of the South than anything like the righteous indignation of times past. The lingering Republican majority in the Senate had an air of resigned impotence, of going through forms with no expectation of results.

So on a July morning in the year of 1876, exactly one week after the nation had celebrated its hundredth year of independence, Albert T. Morgan came. Across the unfinished grounds of the Capitol where workmen were digging and hauling trees for Frederick Law Olmsted's grand new plan of walkways and plantings, through the throngs of sightseers, past the bronze doors of the Senate wing surmounted by the sculpture depicting Justice and History, along the buff and blue–tiled corridors brilliantly illuminated with frescoes symbolizing the people's business at each of the committee rooms he passed, the Roman goddess of war Bellona, the red-robed figure of Authority consulting the written law, he entered the closed doors of one of the plainer hearing rooms and sat down to tell his piece of the story of the Mississippi elections of 1875.

He had the tone of a man speaking for history, knowing there was nothing left to save but his own reputation. He spent a long day at the witness table, telling the whole story of his life in Mississippi, from the time of his arrival. He told of his treatment by Colonel and Mrs. White at Tokeba; how he lost everything when the sheriff seized his sawmill; how he had made his entrance into politics; the shooting of Hilliard and the legal ordeal that followed; and finally the tale of Dixon's armed men seizing Yazoo City and his escape, and the decision not to march the militia back.

He brought the documents that proved his account of the Hilliard affair; the certification from the county board that he had been duly elected and sworn in as sheriff; the ruling of the chancellor that carefully sifted all of the witnesses' testimony and freed him. He spent a good while going over the finances of Yazoo County he had been responsible for, how he had seen to building schools and a new courthouse, and had faithfully accounted for the money and left things better than he had found them.

He patiently and respectfully submitted to the cross-examination by Mr. Bayard, Democrat of Delaware, who among other things wanted to know if it wasn't true that black men could live and thrive in the low and fertile regions of Mississippi such as were found to the west of Yazoo City, whereas white men could not; Morgan explained that no, that was not the case, and indeed the colored people dreaded the swamp because of the malarial diseases there.

And when the senators were done, though he had been in the witness chair for hours, Morgan said: "I would like to make a statement, if there is no objection, in regard to myself."

"You can do so."

"I have been in public affairs in Mississippi since the organization of the party in that State, and I want to make this statement in defense of the colored people and in my own defense," Morgan began. "I have never been deceived or betrayed by them; they have been my friends, my warm friends and supporters; so also a large number of white people of Yazoo County.

"I want to say in addition, that with all my experience there, I have never in my life expended a dollar to buy or influence the support of the colored man in my behalf. Nor do I recollect ever having resorted to any means used by demagogues in politics to secure their favor. I reluctantly accepted office and was never beaten. I believe they gave me their support because, from the outset, I exhibited a sincere desire to see them educated and made good citizens; and I believe they appreciated that desire.

"Nor do I believe that colored men are cowardly. They are unused to guerilla warfare. I know they are not cowards. They are cautious and too intelligent to be drawn into a conflict in which they must necessarily be the only sufferers. I have seen them tried. They will fight for their rights and liberties if they have anything to fight with.

"I willingly assume the responsibility for the utter overthrow of government in Yazoo County last fall. It is not to be charged to the ignorance or cowardice of the colored people there. Like the colored people, I was unused to guerilla warfare. When the general arming of the whites became first known to me, I communicated the fact to the governor. Colored men in the county, many of them, consulted with me as to what Republicans ought to do. In every instance I counseled them against irregular arming, advising all to rely upon the law and its officers. I hoped by steadfastly pursuing this course, by offering no pretext for violence, we might pass the ordeal I saw approaching. As sheriff of the county, I knew it would be utterly futile to attempt to suppress violence, such violence as was exhibited, with a posse of colored men unarmed. I knew that I could not rely on the white Democratic citizens to aid me in the discharge of my duty under the law in such an event. The only safety, the only way to preserve the peace, seemed to lie in the course I suggested. Then, too, as an officer of the law, I was sworn to pursue this course."

When the Senate published the hearings later that year, the Democrats included a lengthy minority report of their own, in which, among other things, they dismissed Morgan as a man of "evil repute." They said, "He omitted to inform the committee that he had married a colored woman."

They heard from a colored man named W. H. Bell, another refugee now living in Washington, also trying to make a living in the law. He had graduated from the university in Pennsylvania, had gone down to Mississippi to teach school, was admitted to the bar, was appointed an election registrar. He was saved from being killed by the white companies that had gone around massacring colored men after the Clinton affray by the professor of the female college there, who hid his family and helped him get away through the swamps, to Jackson. After the election Bell was threatened constantly and his wife said they ought to get out of there. They boarded the train to Washington one night and a group of white men started acting in a way that made Bell uneasy, and then sure enough one pulled his pistol out and started saying something about him being at Clinton and what he was going to do to him. He tried to duck out of the train at a little stop called Michigan City and the men had followed him, so he got back on and managed a quiet word with the sleeping-car porter.

"There is some men in that car there that seem to be wanting to make an attack on me, and I want to get off within two miles of the next station."

Said he, "When the whistle blows that is your time to get off."

So Bell whispered to his wife to go on to Louisville and wait for him there with a colored friend of his, a member of the Louisville bar, and he asked the porter to look out for his wife and family and see that they got into a carriage when they got into Louisville and were taken to Mr. Harper's house, and then the whistle blew and he jumped off the back of the train at full speed, and walked until he found some colored people's house and stayed the night there and then walked the rest of the way to the next station and laid low till three the next morning and caught the night train for Louisville.

The committee traveled to Jackson, where they heard from others. They heard from Sheriff Lee of Monroe County, a white man, an Alabama native, a captain in the Third Texas Regiment in the Confederate army, one of a number of white Republicans in the county. He told how he went to the courthouse on the morning of the election, and shortly after that there arrived a cavalry company of sixty to a hundred men, and an infantry company of some sixty men armed with needle guns and revolvers, and about fifty men formed as an artillery company armed with huge brand-new army-style pistols and a twenty-four-pound cannon in tow, which they set up. And then the captain of this group addressed the colored men waiting to vote, some three hundred, and told them that if they didn't leave in three minutes they were going to fire the cannon and shoot down every one of them. "Not one of you shall cast your vote here today," he told them, and they didn't.

The sheriff told how a few days before the election a prominent Democrat came to him with a proposition that if he withdrew from the race his Democratic opponent would make him his first deputy and let him run the office and collect the perquisites and pay of the sheriff, and they would also give him two thousand dollars right there on the spot, and he had declined.

He told how the cavalry company had blocked the fords of several rivers to keep the Negroes from reaching the polls, and the captain of the armed men testified too and freely acknowledged that they had done that but only to keep the colored men from "massing and taking possession of the polls," not to intimidate them or prevent them from voting.

Out of fourteen hundred Republican voters in that precinct a grand total of ninety cast their ballots.

A prominent Monroe County Democrat, a lawyer, a member of Congress before the war, an ex-major general of Mississippi troops in the Confederate army testified before the committee. He explained that the whites had acquired the cannon "just for rejoicing," though he allowed that it had been "brought up to the polls." He offered his views on a good many points. "The negro is by nature dishonest, by nature destitute of all ideas of virtue," he told them; he opined that no "gentleman" could associate himself politically with the Negroes. "I don't think a gentleman would sleep, eat, and scent niggers after they had been working all day."

They heard from George K. Chase, the credulous man sent from Washington who negotiated the peace treaty, and he kept saying "the niggers" in his answers when the chairman asked him something about the Negroes.

Q. The Negroes would see them?

A. Yes, sir; the niggers.

And they heard from Adelbert Ames, who was on his way to Northfield to work in the family mill business and see if he could make it a going concern, and who wrote Blanche a little later from there, "Of course I shall give importance to my business whatever it may be by and by, for I must have <u>money</u> - <u>money</u>—this word I have to repeat constantly to myself."

His testimony like all the rest was given in secret and would only later be published, but he gave an interview to a newspaperman while he was in Washington and spoke with a bitterness that emerged not as hot rage but cold steel.

He contemptuously dismissed the excuse that the white Southerners had opposed the Republican governments in the South on the grounds of high taxation and fiscal extravagance. He had facts and figures at his fingertips. The debt of Mississippi was but half a million dollars, and that was entirely for improvements to public buildings and the construction of a new normal school and a colored college. The tax burden of the state as he left it was one dollar per capita a year, including interest on the debt. In New York state it was sixteen dollars; in New York City thirty-six dollars. "So much for relative indebtedness." And no one, not even his bitterest enemies, had accused him of dishonesty or misappropriation of public funds, because they could not.

What was the sentiment of the ruling element of the whites? asked the newsman.

"In one phrase—hostility to the Negro as a citizen. The South cares for no other question. Everything gives way to it. They support or oppose men, advocate or denounce policies, flatter or murder, just as such action will help them as far as possible to recover their old power over the Negro. Everything that stands in the line of their march to this end is overthrown. Any man who stands by the constitutional amendments—it makes no difference whether he is a Northern man or a Southerner—they are bound to get rid of, in order that the Negro may be compelled to do their bidding in politics. They care nothing for human life. The lowest estimate made by the most moderate Republicans of murders committed to carry the last election has been put at three hundred."

How did he account for such an overwhelming majority of Negro Republicans?

"The Negroes cannot forget that they were once the slaves of these Democratic politicians, who sold their wives and children away from them with as little regard for their rights or feelings as if they had been horses or sheep; that every dollar of the produce of their labor in those times was taken from them. They dare not trust them where their political rights are concerned. More than that, they have seen every effort of the North to enfranchise and protect them fought step by step, sometimes in sullenness, sometimes with bloodshed but always resisted to the uttermost. They remember that just as soon as Andrew Johnson gave these men a chance they enacted a black code, which would have kept them in a state of servitude worse than that of slavery. They heard them declare in defense of those infamous laws that the Negroes would not work unless under the lash. They have seen them oppose every effort to have them made voters, jurors, office-holders, or to have their children educated. They have known their teachers to be whipped and killed, and their churches and school-houses burned. They remember the Kuklux, who whipped, drove out, and killed thousands. They remember that the laws for the punishment of these outrages were met with persistent and obstinate opposition at every stage. They know that the same is true of the Enforcement act, of the Civil Rights bill, and of all other measures, state and national, that had for their object the security and maintenance of their civil and political rights. They would have joyfully extended their confidence, I believe, to the native Southerners if they could have trusted them. But, as the history of Mississippi and other Southern states has shown, they would have been guilty of great folly if they had done so."

The reporter wanted to know about the outbreaks of violence in Mississippi; had the Negroes ever begun a riot themselves?

"On the contrary," replied Ames. "I have never heard of a single case in which the Negroes were the beginners of any disturbance in the state. You must have noticed that in the riots that the Negroes are charged with having instigated, it is always the Negroes who are killed. If they were permitted the free use of their franchise, which the Constitution confers on them, not a single disturbance would be heard of. It is invariably the case that the whites begin the assaults, kill some, disperse the others, and then charge that the 'Negroes have risen,' or were about to rise, in insurrection, for the purpose of exterminating the whites."

"Can you give me a brief narrative of the outrages in Mississippi?" asked the reporter.

"Yes; but it would require an hour or two."

"Excuse me, then. Only one question more: What remedy do you suggest for this state of things? How can the Negro be protected in his rights?"

"Only by the nation. The nation must protect this class of citizens in its rights at home just as it would protect the rights of any other class abroad. Unless this is done they will practically be defrauded of their citizenship and reduced to a state of servitude."

"Military interference?" asked the reporter.

"No—national protection. 'Military interference' is a crafty phrase, invented to make odious the first and chief duty of all Governments— the protection of the citizen. The military forces in Mississippi never interfered with any man's rights; they only prevented wrongs. If an American citizen cannot rightfully demand protection from his Government, what is the use of Government?"

And they heard, too, from the widow of Senator Caldwell, the colored man who on Governor Ames's orders had led his militia company on the march to deliver arms, who had been ready and willing to march to Yazoo City, even though it meant certain death, to confront the white army that had deposed Albert T. Morgan as sheriff and that was occupying the streets of Yazoo City like a Confederate cavalry brigade.

She told the senators how her husband had gone out on a fox hunt on Christmas day. He had come home in the evening and an acquaintance had insisted he come down to Chilton's cellar to take a drink for a Christmas treat, and had drawn him by the arm and he had reluctantly gone, and when they had clinked glasses that was the signal, and someone shot him through the window.

And then a friend, Preacher Nelson, had carried him up to the street because he said he didn't want to die in a cellar but in the open air, and when he got up there a whole crowd of white men were waiting, and they said "dead men tell no tales," and they pumped forty shots into his body. And before he died he said to the white men who had shot him, "Never say you killed a coward."

Preacher Nelson told her that a braver man had never died than Charley Caldwell.

VI

"THE PASSION-STIRRING EVENT AT HAMBURG"

29

In South Carolina there arrived a letter from Mississippi, full of useful advice.

Greenville Jany 7, 76

Dear T.

I cannot tell you exactly how they did in other parts of the State, but will give you a sketch of the modus in Washington County, where the odds were the most terrible and where success has been the most complete.

First, look at our geographical position and political situation, consider the odds against which we had to contend, and in contemplating the result of a determined effort, you will feel that it is entirely practicable to redeem So. Ca. if the people choose so to do. Our registered vote shows 6390 voters; of this number not over 1200 at the outside are white. The only town in the county Greenville with a population of 2000—the whites slightly outnumbering the blacks.

Still, we determined to carry the election at all hazard, and, in the event of any blood being shed in the campaign, to kill every white Radical in the county; we made no threats, but we let this be known as a fixed and settled thing; the white leaders knew that we meant it. So, instead of fomenting strife, they counseled peace. When they had a political meeting, and we could find it out in time, we sent speakers to meet them and denounce their rascality. They, afraid to provoke a contest, which, end as it might, would be the signal of instant death to them, replied to specific personal charges, only by vague generalities—and the moral effect on the negro was to our advantage; he saw his leaders cower and finally retire from the contest, and this prepared him to submit to what was to follow.

To such an extent was this intimidation, not of the negroes, but of the white aspirants for office, that, when the election day came, none of them even came to the poll to vote. All that is necessary is to obtain the result, no matter how, and Mister Nigger accepts it as satisfactory.

The success of our plan depended, at last, upon our being in condition to make a fight if necessary, and to impress on the leaders, the individual danger each of them ran if <u>any disturbance</u> took place. To accomplish this, a thorough organization and arming were essential. Winchester Rifles and Colt's peace-makers kept the peace. Money freely contributed, and freely used accomplished much, not by buying votes, but in carrying out well devised plans, such as sending competent speakers stumping the county, attending all the meetings called by the other side, and abusing the candidates to their faces when they put in an appearance. Then, the day of the election, the white men went to the polls when they were opened at eight o'clock, and <u>remained</u> <u>until they closed</u>.

Be assured that if you determine to strike one good honest earnest blow to free the State, I will be with you, and I think that thousands from all the Southern States will be ready and willing to quietly take their arms and come, if needed—to judge from the feelings and expressions I have heard in this section.

Let your motto be <u>Suavitur in modo</u>, <u>fortiter in re</u>. Never threaten a man individually; if he deserves to be threatened, the necessity of the times requires that he should die. A dead Radical is very harmless—A threatened Radical, or one driven off by threats from the scene of his operations, is often very troublesome, sometimes dangerous, always vindictive.

Pray write to me again, for I am most deeply interested in all you may do in the coming campaign.

Yrs &c.

S. W. Ferguson

Copies of the letter were soon widely circulated in the state. In a small notebook, Martin Witherspoon Gary, Edgefield planter, lawyer, and ex-Confederate general, wrote a précis of the salient points from the copy he received.

"Plan of Campaign," he wrote at the top, and followed that with a list of things to do. He wrote in pencil, impatiently, a hurried hand:

1st   Determine if necessary to kill every White Radical in this county—2 Every mulatto Radical leader

3rd   Every negro leader—make no individual threats but let this be known as a fixed settled thing —

4th   We must send speakers to all of their political meetings, who must denounce the rascality of these leaders face to face. The moral effects of this denunciation will be of great effect —

5th   Thorough military organization in order to intimidate the negro

6th   Every white man must be at the polls by five o clock in the morning of the day of election, and must go prepared to remain there until the votes are counted

7th   Make no threats — "Suave in modo fortite in re"

8th   There is no use in arguments for the negro

Martin Witherspoon Gary was impatient that spring. Two years before he had bought a fine plantation house just outside of Edgefield Court-House. Right where the road from town turned sharply the entrance to Oakley carried straight on, up a long drive that almost seemed like a continuation of the main road, ending in a circle at the house. A magnificently broad flight of steps led up to the porch that ran the full width of the front, its roof supported by elegantly fluted square columns that framed the wide front door with its glass fanlight above.

One of the things he had done that year was to call together 137 local planters for a "tax union meeting." Gary, the ex-Confederate general, sat in the chair. The men took out a notice in the *Edgefield Advertiser* announcing themselves "ready to strike for white supremacy," and declaring that they were drawing up lists of Negroes to whom land would no longer be rented.

Gary had always been an unruly man. At Appomattox he refused to surrender, and galloped off the field instead. "Volatile" was the word that friends and foes alike used to describe him. He had a head as bald as a billiard ball and a hard stare and a long beak of a nose. He was known as the "Bald Eagle."

Now again he was spoiling for action and impatient with those who would compromise or surrender.

He stormed over the refusal of the Democrats to endorse a "straight out" ticket of white conservatives in the upcoming vote; there was even talk of the Democrats pledging to support the Republican incumbent governor for reelection.

In the spring of 1876 he got together with some of the other leading men of Edgefield. There was Matthew C. Butler, another ex-Confederate general, also a lawyer, the Democratic candidate for lieutenant governor in 1870, one of the men who had sent out the notice informing each county what their expected contribution was to be for the fifteen-thousand-dollar fund being raised for the Ku Klux trial defendants. Butler had also led a thousand armed white men hunting down a local colored militia captain the year before, but he had got away from them.

And there were the Tillman brothers, Ben and George. Ben Tillman was a young man, not yet thirty; he was the last of eleven children and his father had died when he was two, but he was well on his way to becoming one of the largest landowners in the county between what he had inherited and what he had bought, some two thousand acres of land. George, the oldest, had killed a man he got into an argument with at a gambling table, playing faro one day before the war; after lying low in California, Mexico, and Nicaragua he had come back to face trial and was sentenced to two years in jail and a two-thousand-dollar fine, and he resumed his practice of law from his jail cell and was elected to the state senate while he was there, too. Ben had been old enough to fight the last year of the war, but before he could enlist was incapacitated by a tumor that an army surgeon then cut out from behind his left eye. He survived the ordeal but lost the eye.

Ben Tillman had recently joined the Sweetwater Sabre Club, forty-five young white men from Edgefield and Aiken counties who met at the Sweetwater Baptist Church. It was about eight miles north of the town of Hamburg. The men bought themselves uniforms and sabers and army pistols, and many had improved carbines and Winchester rifles, and a large majority had shotguns, and there was good agreement among the members of the Sweetwater Sabre Club that nothing was so useful as a shotgun to mow down a bunch of men at short range. They had a system of couriers who could spread the alarm and get everyone assembled anywhere in the area on two hours' notice.

One day during that spring of compromise that so incensed Martin Witherspoon Gary, the Bald Eagle had got these men together and told them that "one ounce of fear was worth a pound of persuasion." He told them, and they agreed, that they should "seize the first opportunity that the negroes might offer them to provoke a riot and teach the negroes a lesson." They agreed, as Ben Tillman later recalled, that "nothing but bloodshed and a good deal of it could answer the purpose of redeeming the state." The idea was to set about "terrorizing the negroes at the first opportunity," and "having the whites demonstrate their superiority by killing as many of them as was justifiable." The idea was to force the hand of the whites of South Carolina who were holding back.

Hamburg was the place for it if any place was. Nothing could be easier than to provoke trouble there, since young white rowdies were doing it all the time. Edgefield and Aiken men had to drive through Hamburg to cross the bridge to Augusta, and they were often causing trouble, razzing the colored town constable, galloping their horses down the sidewalks, sticking their faces right into the public town well to take a drink and ignoring the posted notice to dip water out only with a clean vessel, shooting off their guns and whooping and cursing the "radicals" outside the house of Samuel J. Lee, the colored man who was a county commissioner of Aiken, and who had been in the legislature and Speaker of the House for a while.

The colored town marshal, Jim Cook, would sometimes arrest the white rowdies and haul them in and fine them five dollars, which they resented. William Nelson, a colored man who was the constable who served Prince Rivers's magistrate court, and Samuel B. Spencer, who was a successful colored businessman and cotton buyer, got into some altercation with a particularly cocky local white youth, Thomas J. Butler, one time in 1874. Tommy Butler's daddy owned a plantation just a couple of miles out of town and Tommy went around talking about the main street through Hamburg as "my road" or "my father's street." There was some kind of trouble, and Tommy Butler's father went to Trial Justice Rivers and swore out a complaint alleging that "he has good reason to fear that William Nelson will do or cause to be done some bodily injury to his minor son Thos J Butler," and Rivers required Nelson and Spencer to put up a bond of two hundred dollars each for one year to keep the peace toward the said Thomas J. Butler.

In July of 1876 Tommy Butler was twenty-two. On the Fourth of July he and Henry Getzen, who was married to Tommy's sister, were in a buggy driving through Hamburg. They were coming from Augusta, and the way from Augusta was across the wooden bridge that Henry Shultz had built, then as soon as you got to the South Carolina side of the river you made a sharp turn left onto Market Street, which paralleled the river. You crossed the South Carolina Rail Road tracks just where you turned left, then a few hundred yards down Market Street you went under the trestle of the Charlotte, Columbia & Augusta Rail Road, which came cutting right through the town block on the right. And then you came to the corner of Market and Centre streets, where the two-story brick-front Sibley Building stood. The way to Edgefield Court-House was to take a right on Centre, and on up the steep bluff above. The way straight on Market led to a few dozen more houses and then on out of town to the Butler place and the fields.

There would later be some dispute about whether the two young white men had sat in their buggy on a street in Hamburg for half an hour watching things first and had then circled around the block, or whether they had come just that minute from Augusta as they headed down Market; and there was plenty of dispute about whether the men of Company A of the Eighteenth Regiment of the South Carolina National Guard who were parading to celebrate the Fourth were taking up the entire width of the 150-foot-wide street or just a third of it, and whether the two young white men in the buggy could have gone around if they so chose: but there is no dispute that they did not so choose; and instead came right down the middle of the road, and whipped their horse into a trot as they did so.

There were a few hundred townsfolk watching the parade; they had gathered at three o'clock to hear a reading of the Declaration of Independence, and then at four thirty the militia company had put on its show of marching and drill. The company was on Market Street a block or so past Centre; and the two young white men later seemed to acknowledge that perhaps there was room for them to get by, but that would have meant driving through the grass and weeds, and anyway it was their buggies and wagons that had made the ruts down the middle of the road going to and from the Butler place and that was where they wanted to drive, not on the side. The colored militiamen parading with rifles and bayonets shouldered and the two white men in the buggy came to a halt facing each other.

"Mr. Getzen, I do not know for what reason you treat me in this manner," said Dock Adams, the captain of the company, a resident of Hamburg, a boss carpenter by trade.

"What?" Getzen replied.

"Aiming to drive through my company."

"Well, this is the rut I always travel."

"That may be true, but if ever you had a company out here I should not have treated you in this kind of a manner. I would have gone around and shown some respect to you."

"Well, this is the rut I always travel, and I don't intend to get out of it for no damn niggers."

There was more cursing from Tommy Butler. He later solemnly averred he had been "very mild and peaceful" throughout the confrontation, to which a colored member of the militia company said when asked about that, "It is the first time that he ever was" if that was the case.

After several minutes Adams ordered his company to "open order" and let the white men in the buggy drive through. There was some grumbling from some of the men in the ranks who said they would rather stand there all day and all night than move aside like that, and more words were exchanged. Adams tried to silence them. The white men in the buggy reached for their pistols and threatened to shoot anyone who stuck a bayonet in their horse. It commenced to rain, and Adams was able to convince the company to head on back toward their drill room in the Sibley Building. The town marshal, Jim Cook, showed up and shouted after the white men in the buggy that he would arrest them if they ever came through town again, but they were several hundred yards down the road at that point and weren't about to stop or turn back.

The next morning Tommy Butler and Henry Getzen and Tommy Butler's father showed up at Prince Rivers's trial justice office on Market Street to swear out a complaint against Dock Adams for obstructing the road. Rivers sent Adams a summons and held a hearing. Since Adams didn't have a lawyer Rivers allowed him to cross-examine Getzen, but things got so heated that Rivers found Adams in contempt for the language he used and ordered the hearing postponed three days, to Saturday, the eighth of July, at four o'clock in the afternoon, to give everyone a chance to cool off.

30

At three o'clock in the hot sun of a very hot Saturday afternoon on the eighth day of July in 1876 in the town of Hamburg, South Carolina, a buggy pulled up to the door of Trial Justice Prince Rivers's office on Market Street. In it sat General Matthew C. Butler. He called to William Nelson, Rivers's constable, who was sitting at his desk inside the open door, his feet up on the door frame. Butler called from his buggy, without getting out.

"Where is Rivers?"

"Mr. Rivers is at his house, I reckon," replied the constable, "but he will be here directly."

In the street other buggies pulled up, and some men on horses, and there were Getzen and the Butlers and some other white men.

Some of them had pistols, and some of them had larger weapons. Tommy Butler had a shotgun, and Henry Getzen had a carbine.

"I have come here as counsel to these people," the general barked. "Go and tell him to come here to me."

Nelson kept his same attitude. He replied, "I am not Mr. Rivers's office boy; I am a constable, and I am here 'tending to my business. He told me that he would be here at four o'clock, and he won't come any quicker by my going after him."

"Do you know who you are talking to?"

"I am talking to General Butler, I believe."

"Well, God damn you, bring me some paper here."

Nelson motioned with his arm. "Here is the office, and there is the paper, and pen, and ink, sir, and there is the chairs for all the attorneys that wants to do business here to come in and sit down."

At that Butler jumped out of the buggy and came up to him. "God damn you, you take your feet off the side of the wall when you speak to me. Give me the chair you're sitting on."

Nelson hesitated a moment, then got up. "All right, if this chair suits you better than the other, take it."

"You God damned leather-headed son a of bitch, you, sitting down there fanning yourself, God damn you."

"I am fanning myself sitting in my own office and 'tending to my own business," said Nelson.

"You God damned son of a bitch, you want to have a hole put through you before you can move. God damn you sitting down there with your feet cocked up."

"Well, General, I am not dead, but if you are going to kill me, why just kill me, and that is all you can do."

At four o'clock Trial Justice Rivers came and called the court into session and sent Nelson to fetch Dock Adams and the other officers of the militia company who had been summoned to give their testimony. Pretty soon Nelson saw the street filling up with armed white men. There were about a hundred of them, on horseback, carrying pistols and sixteen-shooter rifles and shotguns. The road down into town from above was screened by the bluff, so there had not been much warning that they were coming.

Nelson went back to have a word with Rivers. He told him he thought there was going to be trouble. "I reckon not," Rivers replied, but Nelson said, "We better get away from this office." Meanwhile, Adams and the militia officers had sent word that they were not about to show up at Rivers's court under the circumstances because they were sure an ambush was being planned and they would be assassinated.

Ben Tillman later on never made any bones about what the Sweet-water Sabre Club understood their orders for the day to be. They were to attend the trial, and "see what would turn up." If the opportunity offered, they "were to provoke a row." If no opportunity offered, "we were to make one."

And so Tillman and his comrades were disappointed at first when word came that Adams and his men weren't coming to the trial. General Butler left the courtroom and found Samuel Spencer, the town's respectable colored cotton factor, and asked him to go to Adams and arrange a meeting and "settle the matter." Spencer found the men of the militia company in the drill room on the second floor of the Sibley Building. There were thirty-eight of them there, and the streets kept filling up with more white rifle club men, and the colored militiamen had barricaded the door, and now they certainly weren't about to go to any meeting with General Butler. But they sent word back through Spencer that they were willing to compromise to arrange things, and Butler sent word back, fine, what they had to do if they wanted a compromise was turn over their arms to him. He was not going to have Negroes drilling around like soldiers. They had no right to have arms when white men like himself could not have them. So they had to hand over their arms to him. And that was when the colored men knew they had a war on their hands.

Dock Adams sent another note back saying he couldn't possibly do what General Butler asked; the arms belonged to the state, and he was personally responsible for them, and he could not turn them over to a private citizen who had no right to demand them.

General Butler told Spencer there was no use "parleying any lon-ger": "Now, by God I want those guns and I'll be God damned if ain't going to have them."

He got in his buggy and rode over the bridge to Augusta, and

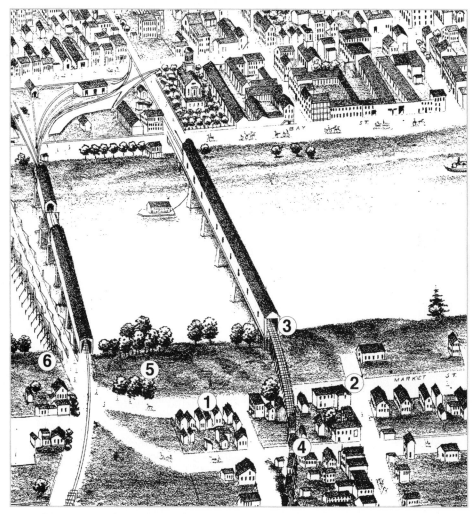

Hamburg, looking south across the river toward Augusta, Georgia. (1) Prince
Rivers's office on Market Street. (2) The Sibley Building at the corner of
Market and Centre streets, where the colored militia took refuge in their
second-floor drill room. (3) The abutment of the C. C. & A. Rail Road
bridge, where the white rifle clubs opened fire with guns and then a cannon.
(4) Where town marshal Jim Cook was shot dead trying to flee to safety.
(5) Where the militiamen were held prisoner in the "ring." (6) Where the
militiamen were executed, across the South Carolina Rail Road tracks near
the abutment of the wagon bridge.

came back half an hour later with two more companies of armed white men. Spencer and Rivers and some of the other leading colored men of Hamburg now came up as a committee to talk to him. Rivers was a major general of the state militia. He did not directly command the local militia company, but he proposed a solution. The men would turn their arms over to him; he would box them up and send them to the governor in Columbia.

"Damn the Governor," said Butler. "I am here as General Butler, not as the Governor of South Carolina."

Rivers asked Butler if he would guarantee the safety of the town if the arms were turned over. Butler replied that this would depend on how the men "behaved themselves" afterward.

John Gardner, the town's colored intendant, begged Butler to keep the peace and not fire on the militia, who were not injuring anyone. Innocent people would be murdered if that happened, he said.

Butler again answered that he would "have the arms of the damned militia whatever the consequences."

One of the white men pulled his pistol on Spencer, and Spencer was sure he was going to shoot him. Another struck one of their committee in the face with a switch and cut him. They got out of there.

From the top of the Sibley Building, Dock Adams and William Nelson could now see General Butler placing his men on the surrounding streets. Horsemen were positioned on the streets that ran to the north and east of the block that the building occupied. Ben Tillman and his fellow members of the Sweetwater Sabre Club paraded down Centre Street, turned left on the street that ran along the north side of the block, right on the next street that ran down to the river, and halted in Market Street by the C. C. & A. Rail Road trestle. They dismounted cavalry fashion, linked bridles, and seemed to be following the instructions of General Butler, who was pointing to the stone abutment of the railroad bridge along the river's edge, about seventy-five yards away. The men filed down and took up position behind it.

An order rang out, "All men having carbines or rifles step five paces to the front."

It was within half an hour of dark by now, and the first shot from down by the river flashed brightly against the black of the water behind. A bullet tore through the metal gutter on the roof right by Nelson's side.

For half an hour the firing continued. The men inside the building had only about three rounds apiece and waited to fire back, but when they did they fired one shot right into the head of McKie Meriwether, a twenty-five-year-old member of the Sweetwater Sabre Club who was down along the river bank firing up at the building with the others, and he pitched over dead.

A voice in the street below said, "Go to Augusta and get a keg of powder and we'll blow the damned building up." Another said, "Bring a cannon with you."

It was dark now and the full moon had not yet risen, and the colored militiamen began slipping out the back of the building to save themselves as they could. A half hour later the air was rent by the bass report of a cannon and the rippling rain of shrapnel against the brick face of the building and the cracking of splinters of the solid mahogany roof beams within. The cannon fired a couple of more times and then the rifle club men down by the river realized there was no return fire coming from the building any more.

Then came the sound of axes and hatchets at work throughout the block as the rifle club men started breaking down doors and smashing floorboards, searching for the hidden militiamen. Voices echoed around the square. "There is some damned nigger in this yard" . . . "There goes one of the God-damned sons of bitches!" . . . "There goes a god-damned nigger!" . . . "Stop, you damn son of a bitch" . . . "there's a nigger back there in that garden, go back there and get him" . . . "there is some God damn son of a bitch run in this hog pen, and he's not come out yet; get him out" . . . "come in here boys, there are seven more of the God damn sons of bitches in here" . . . "stop! stop!" . . . "you damned black son of a bitch, I'm going to kill you!" . . . "we've got the son of a bitch!"

William Nelson and Moses Parks had jumped over the fence into the next lot and were hiding in the shadows behind Davis Lepfeld's store on the northwest corner of the block and a voice shouted, "Who is there?" Parks made a run for it, tried to leap over the high fence on the north side of the block and there was a scramble of feet and shouting and then the Bam! Bam! and he dropped to the ground and a voice shouted "God damn him, I got him." Nelson crawled back on all fours into the yard of the house and came up against the brick privy and crouched there for a while. But the moon had come up and he heard a bunch of men nearby; he pulled a board up and crawled right into the sink of the privy itself.

From over by a peach tree near the railroad trestle another militiaman heard a second man a little later spring over the fence a little farther down the street and voices shouting at him to halt. And there were a lot of confused sounds of shouting and running footsteps on the street and the cracks of pistol shots and then the single boom of a shotgun. And then another man lay dead and the hiding militiaman recognized Tommy Butler's voice, and saw Butler looking down at the body and he was expressing great satisfaction that they had got Jim Cook, the town marshal, who was not a member of the militia company but must have known he was the most marked man in town and had holed up with the militiamen for protection and then tried to make a break for it. Butler then searched the dead man's pockets for the five dollars he had once been fined by the marshal, and not finding any money he lifted a nice-looking watch off the corpse and then the men cut out Cook's tongue and placed it in his hand and someone said, "Keep that till morning, and let them see what we have done."

"He'll chief no more in Hamburg," said another voice, "but in hell."

"By God, he is looking at the moon and don't wink his eyes."

By about eleven o'clock the rifle club men had rounded up twenty-seven of the colored militiamen and marched them a ways down Market Street just between the last house and the South Carolina Rail Road and surrounded them with a ring of men with guns, pistols, axes, hatchets, and grubbing hoes to keep them there. They were there for some time.

Ben Tillman and his squad had been in on the shooting of Cook on the street north of the Sibley Building, and two of McKie Meriwether's cousins were in his company, and they had come up and said it was a damned poor piece of work to have lost one of their best men and have only two dead Negroes to show for it. So they made their way up to the ring where the prisoners were being held. It was now two in the morning. Henry Getzen lived close enough to Hamburg to know some of the colored men, and he was accordingly given the task of designating the "meanest characters" among them.

Allan Attaway was a county commissioner of Aiken and a lieutenant of the militia, and when he saw Getzen approach the ring he called out to him. "Mr. Getzen, do what you can for me."

"God damn you, I will do what I can for you directly. I know you."

And a dozen or so of the rifle club men grabbed Attaway and marched him across the railroad tracks down into the field. "Turn around you yellow son of a bitch," a voice yelled, and then there was the sound of gunshots, and then the white men returned, without Attaway.

Then Getzen called out another man, David Phillips, and then Pompey Curry, and then Albert Myniart, and then Hampton Stephens, and each one was marched off across the railroad, and each time the sound of shooting came back across the night.

Pompey Curry managed to break away and run when his name was called and he was hit in the leg below the knee and fell to the ground and played dead and managed to crawl away and hide in the bushes when the men had gone back for their next prisoner. (When Curry survived to give a deposition against the white men, they were furious that they had been so careless.)

And then when they finished with the men Getzen had picked out, the rifle club men started arguing about what to do with the rest. One voice suggested they take them to the jail in Augusta and another said turn them loose and one of the Georgia men who had come over to help answered, "By God, if you do that you need never call in the assistance of Georgia any more." But one of the men who had led most of the executions, John Swearingen, Ben Tillman's brother-in-law, said they had lynched enough of them, and he said, "All you niggers hold up your right hands and swear you will never raise arms against the white men ever again and never give any evidence against them in court." And then he told them to go, and then the rifle club men fired some volleys after them when they were fifty yards down the road, inflicting a few parting injuries.

And then Ben Tillman and his fellows went up to the town spring and drank and washed, and John Swearingen yanked out the sign with the notice FIVE DOLLAR FINE FOR DIPPING ANY UNCLEAN VESSEL IN THIS SPRING and threw it into the middle of the road with a curse, saying Jim Cook would never fine another white man for that again.

It was past three in the morning, but from his house Samuel Spencer heard the sounds of doors being broken down throughout the town as the white men ransacked warehouses and homes. They destroyed Trial Justice Prince Rivers's papers, stole his clothes; elsewhere they took furniture and knickknacks and guns. They cut the ropes to wells and tore down fences.

Ben Tillman, for his part, pronounced himself "more than satisfied" with his "strenuous day's work," and when he and the boys reached Henry Getzen's place as the first streaks of red dawn were appearing in the sky, they stopped and ate some watermelons before continuing on their way home. Tillman would later allow that probably the killing of prisoners would not have happened but for the loss of "young Meriwether," but all was for the best as it turned out, since "the purpose of our visit to Hamburg was to strike terror, and the next morning when the negroes who had fled to the swamp returned to the town, the ghastly sight which met them of seven dead negroes lying stark and stiff certainly had its effect." They had been "offered up as a sacrifice," said Tillman, "to the fanatical teachings and fiendish hate of those who sought to substitute the rule of the African for that of the Caucasians of South Carolina."

What the colored people of Hamburg remembered most were the words they heard over and over from the white men as they shot and killed and cavorted through the night.

"By God, we've killed a sufficient number to prevent nigger rule any longer in Aiken County."

"We've put a quietus on nigger rule in Aiken County for all time to come."

"By God, we'll carry South Carolina; about the time we kill four or five hundred more, we will scare the rest."

"This is the beginning of the redemption of South Carolina."

31

For four days afterward they hunted Louis Schiller through the swamps. Schiller was a man they had especially wanted to get, almost as much as they wanted to get Dock Adams, who had slipped away somehow too. Tommy Butler's daddy had made his fortune before the war, everything he had, as a professional Negro hunter, and he still had his large pack of hounds and he brought them out and got on the trail.

Schiller, Ben Tillman said, was a "low Jew" who "had sold himself to the Negroes." He lived on Centre Street just next to the Sibley Building and had held some minor appointed offices like county auditor. He ran a printing business out of his home there, helped run a Republican newspaper, the *Augusta Times*. The plan was to hang him.

On the night of what they would always subsequently call the "stirring events" in Hamburg a squad of men came looking for Schiller at his house, and he had slipped up into his loft and then over onto the roof of the house next door, the one at the northwest corner of the block, which was where Davis Lepfeld lived and had his small store. From the roof he saw the gunfire coming from the river. Schiller had been through several battles—he had been a cavalry trooper in the Confederate army, the South Carolina Volunteers; he had ended up in a Richmond hospital with hemorrhoids and served out the rest of the war as a clerk, not a glorious career. But he did know war, and he said later he didn't think he ever heard the equal to the shooting that night. He passed the night on the roof, hearing his wife and children next door crying and screaming, hearing the men demanding to know where he was, beating the colored boy who worked for him to get him to tell, hearing the men breaking up everything in his house, his type cases being turned over, the furniture and doors being smashed to splinters with axes and the crockery hurled to the floor.

He hid out in Davis Lepfeld's house that night and the next morning he could see out the blinds that the rifle club men were still there patrolling the streets. His wife crept over and told him they had left some guards in the house to see if he came back. Lepfeld told him, "For God's sake, leave the house some way, because they are determined to come here and get you out."

On Sunday night he slipped out of the house and tried to make his way to a railroad station three miles up the road. Just out of town he came upon six armed white men standing in the road and he heard the click of their guns being cocked, and he stepped right off the road into the swamp. The water was low, which was both blessing and curse, for it made it easy for his trackers. He did manage once to take a pistol shot at them and lose them for a while. But he got turned around, and instead of getting to the road farther down he found when day came that he had made almost a full circle and come out near to where he had gone into the woods. The men again spotted him, and that was when Tommy Butler's father had gone home for his dogs.

From Monday morning to Wednesday morning he tried to escape them. He was barefoot by this point and his feet were swollen, and he had no hat or coat and he hadn't eaten since Sunday, and on Tuesday he got so desperate he made a break for it on the road, and they had spotted him and put the hounds on him, just like the old Negro hunters used to do, waiting patiently on the road for their chance. And he somehow managed to get into some bushes and get away from them, and somehow on Wednesday morning reached the town and found the intendant, John Gardner. On Wednesday night Gardner and some of the other leading men came and stayed with Schiller locked up in his house, and on Thursday he managed to get on the train to Columbia, having shaved off his moustache and hoping he wouldn't be recognized.

On the Sunday morning William Nelson had pushed aside the boards from the sink of the privy where he had been hiding and peered out cautiously. The body of Moses Parks lay about five feet from the gate of the yard.

Across the river in Augusta the ordinary stirrings of an untroubled city's Sunday morning were under way. At St. Paul's Episcopal church, just at the other end of the C. C. & A. bridge, the organ played; around the city the horse cars clanged on the streets; the morning newspapers arrived with advertisements offering to rent to picnic parties the park in Aiken on reasonable terms, and testimonials to Worcestershire sauce, and exhortations to have your signs painted at Miller's.

Nelson walked out of the block of his hiding place and saw Jim Cook's body a hundred yards down the street. He walked up to the ditch and washed himself as best he could and went home to put on some other clothes, and then came back to help carry the dead men lying at the head of the wagon bridge there in the field next to the South Carolina Rail Road into coffins.

Dock Adams made it from his hiding place in the woods to Aiken and slipped back to Hamburg to see his wife once or twice, but continued to lie out in the woods at night whenever he did so.

For weeks in the United States Senate the Hamburg massacre was discussed and debated, and the great newspapers of the nation carried the story on their front pages day after day.

The Democratic senator from Mississippi, sent by the newly redeemed Democratic legislature of that state, listened for several days to the debate, then rose to give his view of the matter. Of course such violence was terrible, he allowed. But, he hastened to add, "In those Southern States where disorders and violence occur there are governments of a peculiar character and type, invariably the governments of one character and type. They are governments which are called republican governments. And, sir, those State governments have invariably encouraged these disorders and these murders by their inefficiency, by their imbecility, by their cowardice, and by their connivance, for they have in every instance not only failed to punish these murders, not only failed to administer justice, not only failed to execute the laws, but they have used the occurrences to appeal to Congress and to the North for help in maintaining the power which they are so ruthlessly exercising."

THE HAMBURG RIOT, JULY, 1876

General Butler wrote indignant and scornful letters to the newspapers. A statement by the "so-called attorney general" of the state of South Carolina regarding the events at Hamburg, General Butler said, was based on nothing but "the *ex parte* statements of lying negroes." This man, elevated to his high office through the mere "accidents of war," said Butler, had produced a document "pregnant with partisanship and fragrant with the odor of radical falsehood."

The Hamburg events were nothing but an "unfortunate *émeute*," a "sort of spontaneous combustion," he explained. There was no political significance to it at all. He, General Butler, had been there in Hamburg that day solely in his capacity as a practitioner of his profession of the law. He had gone over to Augusta briefly on some other business, entirely unrelated to the Hamburg matter, while he was there. "Some parties unknown to me" brought the piece of artillery back from that city. He later left "the crowd arresting the negroes" and had gone home; as for how many were killed, or how they might have been killed, he had no personal knowledge whatsoever. The gentlemen from South Carolina who were present at Hamburg that day, however, were of "a class of people who do not commit outrages of that sort" as had allegedly taken place.

He, General Butler, had certainly not come to provoke a confrontation. But it was a fact that Rivers's constable, "a copper-colored negro," had sat in the trial justice's office "fanning himself very offensively." It was a fact that the town had "a negro intendant, negro alderman, negro marshals" and "this man Prince Rivers, wholly unfit for so important a station" as trial justice. It was a fact that the town had a colored militia company and that the placing of arms and ammunition in the hands of "these ignorant people" was "more than a crime"; it was "a cruel and inexcusable wrong, an unpardonable sin." The deaths that had occurred were accordingly solely the fault of the Negroes themselves. "This collision was the culmination of the system of insulting and outraging of white people which the negroes had adopted there. Many things were done on this terrible night which, of course, cannot be justified, but the negroes 'sowed the wind and reaped the whirlwind.'"

From his summer home in Newport, Rhode Island, Thomas Wentworth Higginson, Rivers's old colonel, wrote to the *New York Times.* "Allow me to call your attention to a remarkable circumstance in the recent Hamburg massacre, namely that after the captured militiamen had been shot down, the colored magistrate before whom the case had been brought was compelled to flee for his life, and his house was sacked. Yet all accounts agree in saying that his only share in the affair had consisted in an endeavor to keep the peace, he having gone so far as to advise the colored militiamen to give up their arms to him.

"Mr. Rivers, the magistrate in question, is well known to me, having been for more than three years the Color Sergeant of my regiment during the civil war. He is a man of uncommon mental and physical power, and a natural leader of his people. He could read and write even before the war, was thoroughly upright, courageous, and truthful; any statement of his was entitled to absolute confidence. He was not a man to hide himself or leave his home unprotected, except for all-sufficient reasons."

Louis Schiller and Dock Adams had been told that if they showed their faces in Hamburg again they would be killed, but Trial Justice Rivers did return, at least long enough to convene a coroner's court. He held an inquest over the dead men and took thousands of words of testimony and issued arrest warrants for eighty-seven men, including Matthew C. Butler and Benjamin Tillman. Seven of the men were charged with first-degree murder, the remainder as accessories before the fact.

The local newspapers played it for amusement value.

[THE AIKEN COURIER-JOURNAL]

The Hamburg "bloody-shirt," which the Probate Judge, Prince Rivers & Co. have been very busy in manufacturing for a Radical campaign banner to be used in the North, is completed at last. It is said that in rolling up the horrid undergarment to send to Washington the sight and stench so affected the Probate that he was taken with a cramp of colic spasm, and had to be transported to Aiken on an ambulance cart, where he now *lies* in a critical position. The bloody document when ready for mailing weighed exactly eight pounds.

The arrest warrants were turned over to the county sheriff, who, "like a wise and prudent man" (as Ben Tillman sarcastically put it) did not attempt to execute them.

But the sheriff did get in touch with the captain of the Sweetwater Sabre Club, and an agreement was struck whereby the men would turn themselves in at Aiken, and at the same time their attorney, none other than Martin Witherspoon Gary, would move for a habeas corpus hearing for the men to be bailed pending action by the grand jury.

This was also played for amusement value.

Ben Tillman went into Aiken and got the good ladies of the town to run up a set of homespun shirts for the men, and also bought some Venetian red and turpentine, and he brought them back and a high time was had manufacturing their very own "bloody shirts" that, the men said, *they* for once would wave at the *Yankees*. Some of the men insisted that pokeberries made a more vivid red than the oil colors, and used that instead. And when the day came they donned their red shirts and wore them outside their pants with their pistol belts buckled over them, and they loaded baggage wagons with provisions for horses and men and camping equipment, and mounted their horses and headed for Aiken. They camped for the night on a plantation two miles out of town, their host a sympathetic minister of the gospel.

The next day at four o'clock in the afternoon the surrendering prisoners mounted and formed into a column of twos and headed for Aiken in their homespun uniforms. At the head of the procession was another of Ben Tillman's creations, a huge standard he had ordered up specially for the occasion too. He had a carpenter make a huge flagstaff in the shape of a cross, and an extra-large-size shirt was stretched over the frame, and it was decorated with Venetian red, too, though in the form of bleeding bullet holes. At the top two large paper masks of a "grinning negro head" surmounted by a "kinky chignon" were tacked, facing each way. On one side of the standard was emblazoned in large black letters the words of Satan's appeal to the fallen angels: AWAKE, ARISE OR BE FOREVER FALLEN. On the other side it said NONE BUT THE GUILTY NEED FEAR. And when they reached Aiken they first paraded by the houses of all the nice ladies of the town who had run up their shirts for them, then they strung out in column of file a quarter-mile long and gave the order to gallop, and they tore full tilt through the streets of Aiken for half an hour, kicking up a great cloud of dust and receiving the cheers of the men, women, and children of the town, who waved handkerchiefs and shouted. The colored people of Aiken remained hidden indoors.

They repeated the performance the next morning, riding into town in a cavalcade of "well-conditioned, mettlesome steeds," as the local paper put it, accompanied by many carriages, buggies, and wagons filled with their supporters. In the courtroom General Gary and his fellow counsel spent the better part of the day entering into evidence 130 totally fraudulent affidavits that offered elaborate alibis for the accused, and that claimed to have discovered a plan by the dead militiamen "to kill out the whites." The court proceedings dragged on all day and into the evening, and the prisoners were constantly getting up and walking in and out of the room, and each time one of them retook his seat the sharp sound of a heavy pistol barrel slapping against the wooden benches would echo in the courtroom.

The attorney general of the state appeared in person and asked that bail be set at ten thousand dollars given the gravity of the charges; the judge decided a thousand dollars would be fair, but even this quickly became a farce, because the sheriff whispered to the clerk who was taking the bonds that he had better hurry things up "and let these men get out of town tonight else they may burn it and hang you before morning," and so the clerk let the men stand each others' bond, and one man who did not have ten dollars to his name signed twenty thousand dollars' worth of bonds, and this had been a source of great amusement to the prisoners. "In truth the whole performance was a laughable travesty on law," Ben Tillman said, "for if they had attempted to put us in jail I am sure few or none of us would have acquiesced; and we would have probably killed every obnoxious radical in the court room."

The white establishment *Charleston News and Courier* had started out deploring the murder of the Negro militiamen in cold blood after they had surrendered, and had argued that such goings-on could only harm the Democratic cause, but its editor found soon enough how out of step he was with forces on the march across the state. The first inkling came when readers and advertisers began a boycott of the paper. The next came when Matthew C. Butler appeared in person to deliver Martin Witherspoon Gary's challenge to the editor to a duel— for saying any such thing about the Hamburg incident.

Hamburg had fired up the straight-outers; they spoke of the "passion-stirring event at Hamburg;" there was going to be no turning back now. People had been talking about South Carolina adopting the "Mississippi Plan" for the elections, but now they were as likely to call it the "Edgefield Plan." Passionate appeals were made in the press for the white men of South Carolina "not to desert their old general, Butler, whether he had done right or wrong" at Hamburg. The *News and Courier* apologized in print for its past condemnations of the Hamburg murders.

A few days after the Hamburg rioters were bailed, Generals Gary and Butler showed up with six hundred armed men, pistols drawn, at a Republican political rally in Edgefield and demanded a "division of time" with the state's Republican governor, who was then forced to sit on the platform and listen to himself abused as a liar and a thief and the true instigator of the Hamburg massacre, which he had "got up" for political advantage. When he was at last permitted a half hour to speak at his own meeting his words were drowned out by rebel yells.

A few days after that the state's Democrats, who back in May had adjourned their nominating convention in a deadlock between straight-outers and compromisers, reconvened to nominate the Confederate cavalry hero Wade Hampton as their standard-bearer for governor.

THE RUBICON PASSED AT HAMBURG—THE STRAIGHT-OUT POL-ICY THE TRUE ONE declared the *Aiken Courier-Journal* in announcing these developments.

In the deaths and political marches of the two months that followed, Hamburg faded soon enough from view, then from remembrance. The state attorney general sized up the situation and decided no colored men would dare testify and no grand jury or judge would dare act, and ordered a continuation of the cases in Aiken, and so the grand jury was told not to proceed with any indictments for the September term of the Court of General Sessions.

Hundreds of colored men and women fled the town of Hamburg never to return. The intendant sent a plea to the governor that went unanswered. "Dear Sir, The recent occurrence at this place has had the effect of spreading gloom and distrust among the people. Yesterday a band of lawless men rode through the Town and bid defiance to the authorities. Though it might have been possible to have arrested, yet, I am satisfied that it would have precipitated another dreadful riot. Menace and threat seems to be the purpose of these disturbers of the public peace. I hope that you will have Deputy U.S. States marshal appointed for our Town immediately. John Gardner, Intendant."

Prince Rivers settled in Aiken, occasioning another sarcastic notice in the press.

[THE AIKEN COURIER-JOURNAL]

DISTINGUISHED ARRIVALS—Brigadier General Trial Justice Prince R. Rivers and family arrived in Aiken last week, and have taken a cottage for the season in lower Aiken.

General Butler wrote to the press again, protesting that he had been "grossly misrepresented" in a recent report on an "extemporaneous" speech he had given. What he had actually said was that he was "opposed to shooting down the poor ignorant negro masses." He had very carefully stated that in the event of a "collision" between the radicals and the Democrats, he, for one, would first shoot the governor, the United States senator, the Speaker of the House, and other carpetbag leaders; next the "miserable white scalawags"; and third the "black leaders." But he had said very clearly that he was "unwilling to hurt a hair upon the head of the negro masses." He added that he was not in the least concerned about the arrival of two companies of United States troops in his hometown of Edgefield Court-House: "We met them in time of war on the battle-field, and were not frightened by them."

The rifle club men certainly had little reason to be frightened now; there were a thousand federal troops in the state by the fall, but there were at least twenty thousand rifle club members, with at least ten thousand breech-loading rifles among them.

In October, the governor and the president of the United States each issued proclamations ordering the rifle clubs to disband. This provided further occasion for humor. A thousand uniformed and heavily armed men appeared at a Hampton rally a couple of weeks later with a banner bearing the legend THIS IS NOT A RIFLE CLUB. Other signs identified THE TILDEN MOUNTED BASE-BALL CLUB, THE MOTHER'S LITTLE HELPERS, THE FIRST BAPTIST CHURCH SEWING CIRCLE, THE CHAMBERLAIN BENEVOLENT ASSOCIATION (Chamberlain being the Republican governor).

The Democratic campaign that fall became indistinguishable from a series of military triumphs. Thousands of mounted men, armed with at least two pistols apiece, all wearing the now famous red shirts, some of them elaborately trimmed with blue or yellow, carrying torches, here and there a marshal with plumed hat and sword, led by a battery of artillery, all yelling the rebel yell, preceded Hampton's appearances across the state. In one town the torchlight procession numbered five thousand. The white ladies of South Carolina turned out with red ribbons in their hair and red sashes about their waists.

On streets where, eleven years before, the freedmen had paraded in humble celebration of freedom, Wade Hampton's men came now as conquerors.

32

Ben Tillman made sure to be on hand the day that fall when the Sweetwater Sabre Club got ahold of state senator Simon Coker, a colored man they did not much care for, and marched him out to a field and made him kneel and shot him dead, and then one of the boys had put his pistol right up to the dead man's head and shot once more, remarking as he did so that he remembered what a mistake they had made with Pompey Curry, and, "Captain, I did not want any more witnesses to come to life again."

And Ben Tillman was at his post bright and early on election day at a small poll in Edgefield County with his pistol, and when the vote was counted at the end of the day it was 211 to 2 for the Democrats, which was not very surprising, since he had not let any colored men vote. And General Gary had done much the same thing at Edgefield Court-House, where even the United States troops had not been able to do much more than clear a path about four feet wide to the ballot box between the armed white men; and when the vote was tallied for all of Edgefield County the Democrats had carried it by 5,500 to 3,000, which was impressive not only because it meant that the Democrats' vote had exceeded by 3,000 the total number of white voters in the county, but also because the total number of votes cast exceeded the number of voting-age men in the county by 2,000.

And when Hampton claimed a thousand-vote victory statewide the Republicans cried fraud, and a standoff ensued for months; and while the rest of the country forgot about the town of Hamburg, the Democrats of South Carolina did not, for one of the very first things Wade Hampton did to try to establish his legal claim to the office of governor of South Carolina was to fire Trial Justice Prince Rivers.

Rivers wrote to Governor Chamberlain asking what he should do.

Hamburg, S.C. Jan. 22d 1877

To His Excellency D. H. Chamberlain
Governor of South Carolina
Dear Sir,

You will find inclosed a true copy of a notice served on me by one Wade Hampton, that he has removed me from the office of Trial Justice, of Aiken County S.C.

Please let me know soon as possible whether I must submit to the notice or not, I am your obt Servt +c.

P. R. Rivers
T.J.A.C.
PS

Please gave me the date of my last appointment as Trial Justice of Aiken County by you.

[enclosure]
State of South Carolina
Executive Chambers
Columbia Jan 19th 1877
Mr Prince R Rivers,
Hamburg
Sir:

I am instructed by His Excellency the Governor, Wade Hampton, to inform you that he has removed you from the office of Trial Justice, for Aiken County.

You will, therefore, immediately upon the receipt of this letter, cease to exercise the functions of said office.

Very Respectfully,
Private Secretary

And in the harried governor's embattled office in the State House his secretary's pen scratched across paper as the governor dictated a hasty reply, and the wet ink was pressed into the onionskin paper of the letterbook, to preserve a copy for history.

January 30 [187]7
Prince R Rivers
Trial Justice, Aiken County
Sir,

I am directed by His Excellency the Governor to acknowledge
the receipt of yours of the 22nd inst and to say in reply thereto
that you are to pay no attention to communications such as the
copy enclosed by you to me, from Mr. Hampton or any of his
associates, but to continue to exercise the functions of your
office until notice from this office instructs you to cease.

Your last commission was dated Jan 18 1875

And in April, Rivers wrote once more, but he suspected by then
what the real answer was, regardless of what the governor's secretary
might be instructed to reply.

Hamburg, S.C.
His Excellency D. H. Chamberlain
Governor of South Carolina
Dear Sir,

I see that the President had ordered troops from the State
House. As that is true, do that compel you to give the State to
Hampton, or in other words what will be your situation in the
matter. Is there any hopes for the Republican Party of South
Carolina, or do you believe that the President will Sustain you
as Governor of South Carolina. Governor, I write to you for my
own confidential benefit. Governor I hope that you will answer
soon as possible, as I get no other papers but the Augusta, and
that I don't believe. Over-

I am your obedient Servant +c.
P. R. Rivers

This time he got a two-sentence reply, "As to the effect of withdrawing the troops you must wait and see. The Governor does not
know what may happen in the future."

And so the troops left, and Hampton came in, and the Democrats

in the legislature expelled two dozen Republicans to shore up their majority, and threw out the colored Republican attorney general, even though his election had never been in dispute, and seated Martin Witherspoon Gary as a state senator from Edgefield and elected Matthew C. Butler as South Carolina's new United States senator.

On June 1, Hampton dismissed Rivers as trial justice of Hamburg for good.

On the very last day of the special session of the legislature that Hampton had promptly called to repeal such radical legislation as state-supported college scholarships, the legislature revoked the town charter of Hamburg, and at two o'clock in the morning on June 9 sent the bill to Governor Hampton, who signed it, and that was the end of "Negro rule" in Hamburg.

The rest of the nation forgot about Hamburg, but the Democrats of South Carolina did not. In September of 1878, Prince Rivers and every once prominent colored political leader of Hamburg and Aiken County, along with the most prominent white Republicans who had stood with them, were indicted by the state for conspiracy to cheat and defraud, and for breach of trust with fraudulent intent.

The story, as the stalwart *Augusta Chronicle* told it, was that seven years earlier Prince R. Rivers ("Radical blackamoor"), John Wooley ("Radical scallawag"), ex-Speaker of the House Samuel J. Lee, and the others had all been in on a scheme to get a kickback on the purchase of the site for a new courthouse in Aiken County. The story was that they had agreed to buy the old Gregg Mansion, and would pay Gregg, the white man who owned it, an inflated price of fifteen thousand dollars, which was at least five thousand more than it was worth, and that Gregg would then slip three thousand of that back to them.

There were a few peculiar things about the story. The most peculiar was that Rivers and the others never saw the money. This was supposedly thanks to the "adroit and skillful maneuvering" of Gregg's agent, who swept the fifteen thousand into his own pocket with a look of serene innocence when the money was turned over, and thus "thwarted" the designs of the conspirators.

Another peculiar thing was that the attorney who appeared on behalf of Gregg at the trial was Martin Witherspoon Gary.

And then some other odd things started to happen. Rivers was convicted on the breach of trust with fraudulent intent count, with a recommendation of mercy to the court, and was allowed to post fifteen hundred dollars' bond pending appeal, whereupon the case was never heard of again. The conspiracy charge against Rivers and the other defendants then kept being continued from one term of the court to the next. Somehow it never came to trial. Then the case was moved from Aiken to the next county over, Orange County, and there it kept being continued too. And for year after year the case remained on the books but no trial was ever held, and then finally six long years later, in May of 1885, it was marked as "stricken off" the criminal docket with no further explanation.

There was an explanation, though it would have to wait a hundred years to see the light of day: Through the good offices of the editor of the *Charleston News and Courier,* and with the urging and enthusiastic support of United States senator Matthew C. Butler, the federal government in 1879 had agreed to drop the civil rights cases it had brought against the Hamburg murderers and Simon Coker's murderers and all the other white rifle club members who were never prosecuted by the state for the crimes committed in the bloody fall of 1876 that had brought them to office. The price the federal government asked in return was modest enough; namely, that the state of South Carolina would drop in return all the corruption cases it had brought in the meanwhile against former Republican officeholders of the state.

It was General Butler who personally suggested that "it would look very badly" to just have all the cases dropped at once, however; and he accordingly proposed that the cases ought to be continued for a while first. "I was very much in hopes that we should have had all the matters settled and peace and quiet restored all round," the general privately wrote the editor, "and whosoever takes the responsibility of preventing it will have much to answer for." He was sure that the United States district attorney would come around to his way of thinking, not keep holding out for dismissing the cases right away: "Read this to them. They ought not to ask for a <u>discontinuance</u> on our part, for it will be impracticable and unwise. A <u>continuance</u> of cases in state courts will amount practically to a nol. pros." Thus it was quietly arranged two days later.

The Democratic state attorney general was all for the plan, especially since, as his predecessor had written in a private note to Governor Hampton when the indictments of the Republicans were first broached, the corruption charges "would not stand test as legal evidence" anyway. But by publishing the indictments and then *not* bringing the cases to trial, they would achieve everything without even risking the backlash that an acquittal or hung jury would bring. "The press would revel in it, & we would politically guillotine every man of them."

And so Prince Rivers had been politically guillotined long before his case was finally dismissed in 1885.

And the years passed, and the state legislature got rid of the polling place at Hamburg and decided that the voters there could instead walk ten or so miles on election day if they wanted to vote, and they decided that all voters needed to reregister in May, which just happened to be planting season, and that local officials didn't have to tell anyone where they had to go to register, and if a voter did not reregister he would be struck off the voting rolls for life; and they decided that voters needed to place their ballots into eight separate boxes for different offices, and if they did not get it right their votes would be thrown out. So the political death of the Negro came to South Carolina as it had come to Mississippi, and Prince Rivers was no longer an object of interest to the newspapers as he had been in the days when he was the admired and reviled trial justice and mayor and political leader of Hamburg.

The local newspapers did have one final opportunity to revive the rich humor they used to enjoy so much in the days of Reconstruction. A dispute in the colored A.M.E. church in Aiken in 1885 resulted in charges being brought against Rivers for threatening the pastor and running him out of his pulpit. The *Aiken Journal and Review* printed a supposed interview with Rivers in Sambo dialect. Rivers then wrote the newspaper himself, a calm, articulate, wholly convincing, well-crafted, perfectly grammatical, and immaculately spelled statement of his side of the controversy. The *Augusta Chronicle* ran a short notice to the effect that the preacher, in the heat of the dispute, had accused Rivers of getting up the Hamburg riot and then siding with the Democrats. Anyone familiar with that "little unpleasantness," the paper noted, would know this could not have been true; because "it was generally believed that Rivers spent the night in the Savannah river to get away from those whom the preacher now says were his friends." At least some of the Democrats present that night, opined the editor, "who were anxious to see him on that eventful occasion, I am sure had no desire to congratulate him on his sudden conversion to Democracy."

Rivers died two years later in Aiken. He had spent his last few years there in the job that the editor of the *Edgefield Advertiser*, back in 1868, had suggested was his only "proper sphere."

He was working for a local hotel, driving a coach; sitting as erect as a statue, said the people who saw him. It was the same job he had performed in slavery.

VII

"GREED, THE FATHER OF SLAVES, WAS TOO MUCH FOR US"

33

The revenge went on.

Albert T. Morgan was given a job by the Republican administration in Washington as a second clerk in the pension office, and there he dutifully toiled until the Democrats gained possession of the White House in the person of Grover Cleveland. The new president appointed L. Q. C. Lamar, Democratic senator from Mississippi, as secretary of the interior, which oversaw the pension office, and Lamar fired him.

Morgan received a clipping from Yazoo City in the mail from one of his old enemies. The local paper reported that Morgan's old nemesis Henry Dixon, the Human Hornet, had had a falling out in a power struggle among the Democrats and tried to run an opposition ticket against the official slate, and suddenly the hero of '75 was a reviled man too. A resolution adopted by the local Democrats called Dixon "a murderer, a gambler, a bully, a thief, a man of violence, of blood, of lies, a man who will pack juries, a low, unprincipled demagogue in politics, and an infidel in religion." The local Democrats accused Dixon of having taken several thousand dollars off the body of Patterson, one of the colored men he had lynched when his rifle club had seized control of Yazoo County back in 1875. Dixon published a card defending himself, stating that it was well known that all of that money he had taken off the body of Patterson had gone for Democratic campaign expenses, in particular to serve "as a bribe to have the ballot-boxes stuffed, if necessary."

The next time Dixon appeared on the main street of Yazoo City a man with a double-barreled shotgun came up to him and blew him to kingdom come.

Morgan and his brother, back in '65, when they were looking for land and opportunity, had briefly visited Kansas, and Morgan recalled that now, and moved his wife and children there to Topeka and tried to practice law, and made a hash of it. His daughter later remembered him from those days as a "dreamer and an idealist," always defending the poor and helpless and neglecting to look after his own interests. In 1890 he went off to Denver to try to strike it rich mining silver, leaving his family behind, and he made a hash of that, too.

His four daughters grew into beautiful young women, and Carrie taught them to sing, and to support themselves they went on the road as a vocal quartet called "The Morgan Sisters" or "The Angela Sisters." Carrie traveled with them as their manager and "chaperone," a fiction intended to hide the truth about the girls' racial ancestry; they passed for white girls.

Albert Morgan never did come home after that. He moved into a cheap boardinghouse in Denver, and wrote idealistic and slightly cracked pamphlets about silver coinage, arguing that "money is not wealth," and his new conviction that "*no* man is fit to govern another," and once in a while he sent a letter to borrow money off his son, who had a steady job in Indianapolis as a railroad clerk. His son wondered after a while whether his parents ever really had been married, and wrote his father, who wrote back a slightly injured reply, "Bert, how can there be any doubt that your mother is my legal wife?" He told his son he could write to the county clerk in Jackson, Mississippi, and request a copy of their marriage license if he did not believe him.

He had never even thought of another woman, either. "On the contrary, where ever I have lived long enough to become acquainted with women, I have invariably announced that I have a wife and children living whom I love, and for whom I am making every sacrifice."

When he died all he had to leave his family was his soldier's pension, and even that raised some questions because the pension office could not believe the couple had not been divorced or legally separated, so long had they lived apart. "This is an unusual case," one official noted in the file. "It would look so," Bert replied, sending copies of letters to substantiate and explain the situation, "but my father never made a success and he became so disheartened that he was really too ashamed to come home."

The daughters in truth were ashamed, too; Nina changed her name to Angela and rewrote her past; she said she had been born in Washington, D.C., to parents named Alwyn and Carol Baldwin Morgan. She made a career for herself as a writer of feature articles for ladies' magazines and sentimentally spiritual poems for newspapers, and attracted some wealthy New York benefactors who were taken with her claims of being in touch with "cosmic forces" of the universe, of being able to feel showers of light radiating from the heavens through her hands and body. She gave dramatic readings and poetry recitals, as did her mother, who lived with her and became a Christian Science practitioner and "mental healer," and who moved with Angela from New York to Chicago to Boston to London as Angela constantly tried to escape from the financial straits she was always in.

Two of the other daughters wound up in a mental institution in Vermont.

Out in Denver, Albert Morgan had once written a friend a half-wise, half-mocking note about his own spiritual journey since the days of Mississippi; he said he was "the happiest man on the top o'Earth"; not excepting even J. Pierpont Morgan, John D. Rockefeller, King George, "or any son-of-gun for whom we fought, and bled an—lived to die for, all those blessed years."

He wrote William Lloyd Garrison II, the son of the great abolitionist leader, that the "immortal few" who dared to oppose slavery "left their work less than half done." He wrote as a man for whom practical politics had utterly failed and who now in his later years was seeking to salvage some meaning for all he had been through, and he grasped at the idea of spiritual revolution, for all mankind. He felt now that the evils he had fought in Mississippi had roots far deeper in the soul of man than the question of race alone; they came at heart from the greed that makes men exploit others for their own gain. "The negroes' color and physical peculiarities make it easier to defend encroachments upon his inherent right to life, liberty and the pursuit of happiness. In this fact we find the mirror of our own souls, and show the full measure of our own baseness when we put the blame on God. As I view it the race problem can be solved in no other way than by making common cause with all other races, and unite them in an effort to bring in a new desire; a desire for good for its own sake as preferable to evil however disguised."

He wrote a long, long memoir of his own trials in Mississippi, and published it himself at an expense he could not possibly afford, and on the last page his life and love became an allegory for the tragedy of the age. "Would you have me marry my daughter to a negro?" was the idiotic question he was always being challenged with, he wrote.

No! I would not have you do any such thing. But, since you have asked the question, I will venture to say that I would greatly prefer that you should marry your daughter to a negro than that you should consent that she be the mistress of one.

How dare I talk that way?

How dare *you* consent, as you have been doing for two centuries, that every woman of African blood shall not hope for a higher life? How dare you consent, as you have been doing for two centuries, that while your daughter may not marry a "nigger," nor yet be the mistress of one, your *son* may make my daughter his concubine, though he shall not marry her?

I have never denied nor been ashamed of the fact that my wife and my children have in their veins negro blood; "nigro taint" is the enemy's phrase. During all the dreary years that have passed since the enemy, by force and murder, took possession of my new field, stole our grand old flag from us, and occupied our temples, this woman and these children have been my refuge.

The world moves, though Yazoo may remain a dead sea. Have patience—wait.

Some day the telegraph, the telephone and the printing press will assemble the world in one congregation, and teachers will appear to instruct all in the language and justice of truth.

Lewis Merrill's enemies merely hounded him for the rest of his life. In the spring of 1876 Augustus Armes, the man Merrill had prosecuted for gross obscenity in the mess room, paid a call on Colonel Custer in Washington to dredge up the old business about the Lauffer case, and the two went over to the House Military Affairs Committee and tried to stir up some trouble about it once again. Merrill wrote a furious rejoinder to the *New York Times* and the *Army & Navy Journal* and testified himself before the committee, going over all the old ground about how Custer had first spread the story without informing him, how he had demanded an inquiry to clear his name, how Lauffer had backed down when challenged to produce his evidence. He also defended his acceptance of a twenty-thousand-dollar reward from the state of South Carolina for his arrests of the Ku Klux back in 1871; the state had announced a reward of two hundred dollars for each arrest and he had done it, and though it might have been unusual there was nothing improper, he insisted. Once again Custer backed down and claimed he never meant any harm.

Three months later, when Custer led 262 men of the Seventh Cavalry to their deaths at Little Big Horn, Merrill was on detached duty as military chief of staff for the Centennial Exhibition in Philadelphia, where his job was chiefly to ensure that proper protocol was followed in greeting foreign military visitors. Many of the men who had served with him fighting the Ku Klux in Yorkville and the White Leaguers in Red River died at Little Big Horn.

Merrill fought against the Nez Perces in Montana the next year, and then was stationed at various posts guarding construction parties of the Northern Pacific Rail Road as it pressed on westward. And finally in 1883 he came back east hoping to get surgical treatment for a tumor in his abdomen that had begun to form at the site of his old Civil War bullet wound. And when he was about to be retired for disability a few years later, Armes again started intriguing with the Democrats in the Congress to make trouble for him. Armes at one point got another of Merrill's old army enemies to write a letter purporting to support the story about his taking a bribe from Lauffer, and adding, "Maj Merrill was never a gentleman, and is a notorious <u>coward</u> + shirk." Armes kept up the attack with further letters, insisting "there is a little strategy being used somewhere to prevent Major Lewis Merrill from being retired before he is promoted to Lieut Col."

General Sheridan referred it all to Merrill for comment, who replied, "Deference to the authority which refers the letter is the only reason for giving any attention to the mouthings of this convicted blackguard and self convicted perjurer." Sheridan added his own endorsement to Armes's letter: "Armes is a chronic grumbler and I have very little confidence in any thing he says."

But the work had been done, and when, as the senior major in the army, Merrill was nominated for promotion to the single vacancy for lieutenant colonel that had opened up, the Democratic congressman from the Red River district of Louisiana raised a hue and cry and got the president to withdraw the nomination, against all precedent. The promotion went instead to the officer next in line, and Merrill was retired as a major. By a quirk of fate, the man who got the promotion was Henry Morrow, the officer who had come from New Orleans to inspect the situation in Merrill's district, and who had declared "the negro does not comprehend politics" and had urged that the army stop upsetting the white people of the state by protecting a government elected by Negroes. This was doubly a cause for cheer among the Louisiana Democrats.

Merrill sent a seventeen-page typewritten letter to the president of the United States closely arguing his "legal rights" to the lieutenant colonelcy, which did him no good at all. As his physical condition deteriorated he became more obstinate and cranky and also wrote some odd letters to get out of paying an overdue tailor's bill and the interest he had promised the widow of a fellow officer he had once borrowed five hundred dollars from. He had invested in real estate and some businesses and they had not done well. When a Republican again got into the White House, Merrill managed with great difficulty to have a bill passed raising his retired rank, and commensurate pension, to that of lieutenant colonel. Before he died he was breveted a brigadier general, "for gallant service" against the Nez Perces.

James Longstreet moved to Georgia and lost his hearing but kept his sense of humor even as he kept fighting his losing battle to vindicate his generalship at Gettysburg. He was not the clearest writer in the world and the more he tried to defend himself in print the more he attacked Lee, too, which infuriated his enemies all the more. They said he had revealed himself in these articles, and in his published memoirs, as a man consumed with jealousy of Lee; and even as the story of the dawn attack order was debunked over and over, the charge against Longstreet became rooted ever deeper in popular myth.

Longstreet became good friends with the Union general Daniel Sickles, who was something of a scapegoat for Gettysburg too, blamed in the North for failing to achieve a more decisive Union victory that day. The two attended reunions and celebrations together. Longstreet always enjoyed telling the story on himself of the time they were at a celebration of Grant's birthday in New York and Longstreet, almost stone deaf, couldn't a hear a word of what the speaker was saying but joined in the applause with everyone else, and at one point he noticed everyone very enthusiastically applauding and joined in with a particularly loud cheer himself, and kept going after everyone else had stopped, and then he had leaned over to ask Sickles what they were cheering for. And Sickles had shouted into his ear trumpet, "They were cheering you, General; the speaker had paid you a grand tribute."

And one time the two attended a Saint Patrick's Day celebration together in Atlanta, and both put away a quantity of Irish whiskey, and then the deaf Rebel and the one-legged Yankee took turns escorting one other to each other's hotel half the night, each insisting on doing the honor to the other.

But Jubal Early and some of the other Confederate leaders never let up; Jubal Early called Longstreet a "renegade" and a "viper"; and although Longstreet did go to a few United Confederate Veterans reunions, and though many of the common soldiers still loved him and were excited to shake hands with a link to the stirring days of their youth, he preferred going to the Northern reunions where he was welcomed as a soldier and nothing else. "Everywhere except in the South soldiers are accepted as comrades on equal terms without regard to their political affiliations. So I have come to regard it as a high compliment to be excluded from the U.C.V.," he wrote a friend.

He never mentioned the battle of September the fourteenth in New Orleans, and his Republican politics were thereafter pretty much limited to accepting sinecure appointments from Republicans in the White House; he was sent as minister to Turkey, was appointed

United States commissioner of railroads. The commissionership was at that point held by Wade Hampton, who tried to get the Senate to defeat Longstreet's confirmation, and when Hampton was finally forced to vacate the office he refused to speak to Longstreet or help in the transition.

In 1890 the aging soldier wrote a friend, "My arm is paralyzed; my voice that once could be heard all along the lines, is gone; I can scarcely speak above a whisper; my hearing is very much impaired, and sometimes I wish the end would come; but I have some misrepresentations of my battles that I wish to correct, so as to have my record correct before I die."

When he died fourteen years later the United Daughters of the Confederacy in nearby Savannah voted *not* to send flowers to the funeral, and 95 percent of the U.C.V. chapters across the South declined to pass the customary resolutions honoring the passing of one of their great generals.

34

Ben Tillman came to be known as "Pitchfork Ben" Tillman, and with his fierce one-eyed glower and plebian misshapen hats and profane speeches styled himself a populist. He said the Citadel in Charleston where the "aristocrats" sent their sons was nothing but a "military dude factory," that the South Carolina College where most of the rest went turned out "helpless" good-for-nothings, "too proud to beg, too honest to steal, too lazy to work." He cursed and ranted against the "Bourbons" and said he was for the little man.

He was elected governor and then United States senator, and for forty years he fought off attacks by the Bourbons and the real populists alike by reviving the horrors of "negro misrule" that he said the state had endured under Reconstruction. That was his ticket to power, and for forty years of political life he offered what he called "a solid front to all comers on the bond of white supremacy." He stood on the

"Pitchfork Ben" Tillman in his later years, as a U.S. senator.

floor of the United States Senate and jabbed his finger and said "we had to shoot negroes" and recounted again and again how the black man had "tasted blood," had been infected by unscrupulous Northern carpetbaggers with "the virus of equality" back in those dark days, and that the only way to make sure that it never happened again was for whites to remain united politically behind men like him who weren't afraid to tell the truth about how they had had to shoot niggers back then.

"The poor African became a fiend, a wild beast, seeking whom he may devour, filling our penitentiaries and our jails, lurking around to see if some helpless white woman can be murdered or brutalized," Pitchfork Ben said on the floor of the United States Senate, and he always reprinted his best such efforts in pamphlets that he sent to everyone. "We realize what it means to allow ever so little a trickle of race equality to break through the dam."

In 1895 South Carolina called a convention to rewrite the state constitution to disfranchise the last remaining colored voters who hadn't already been cheated or beaten out of their ballots, and Pitchfork Ben came and again retold the story of the "infamy" of those dark days, and how at any moment that sleeping viper might be "warmed into life again and sting us whenever some more white rascals, native or foreign, come here and mobilize the ignorant blacks."

The "hell hounds" who had masterminded it all the last time, he explained, had hated the South and were seeking revenge. They had concocted the most perfect scheme for "degrading us to the lowest level possible"—giving the ballot to our own ex-slaves. "The most fertile imagination, if it had been given a thousand years to concoct a scheme of revenge, could not have surpassed it."

And he continued: "How did we recover our liberty? By fraud and violence. We tried to overcome the thirty thousand majority by honest methods, which was a mathematical impossibility. After we had borne these indignities for eight years life became worthless under such conditions. Under the leadership and inspiration of Mart Gary—because he planned and brought about the Straight-out movement of '76— we won the fight. In 1878 we had to resort to more fraud and violence, and so again in 1880. Then the Registration Law and eight-box system was evolved from the superior intelligence of the white man to check and control this surging, muddy stream of ignorance.

"And this must be our justification, our vindication, and our excuse to the world that we are met in Convention openly, boldly, without any pretense of secrecy, to announce that it is our purpose, as far as we may, without coming into conflict with the United States Constitution, to put such safeguards around this ballot in future, to so restrict the suffrage and circumscribe it, that this infamy can never come about again."

As Pitchfork Ben told it the moral inversion was now complete. That decent men were forced to fraud and violence only showed to what extremes they had been pushed. The more brutally they treated their victims the more it proved that they had been the true victims themselves. The more the Northerners had stood up for the rights of the Negroes the more it showed how full of hate and hypocrisy they were. The more the federal government tried to interfere the more the nation and the Negro would suffer. Until the South was left alone by the federal government to handle the Negro as it saw fit, Tillman threatened, white Southerners would have "no conception of the word 'nation' except that it is connected with the word 'nigger.'"

Once again Mississippi had shown the way; the white men there had figured out how to take away the colored man's vote for good without directly violating the Fifteenth Amendment. Not that the colored vote amounted to anything by this point; the battle for political control was long won; the South, as Albion Tourgée had so acutely observed, had long since "reversed the judgment of Appomattox." But there was still the battle for memory and myth and appearances, and at Mississippi's 1890 constitutional convention one delegate had risen and addressed the 133 whites (130 Democrats, one Greenbacker, one "Conservative," and one "National Republican") and one Negro (Republican) in attendance:

> Sir, it is no secret that there has not been a full vote and a fair count in Mississippi since 1875, that we have been preserving the ascendancy to the white people by revolutionary methods. In other words we have been stuffing

ballot boxes, committing perjury, and here and there in
the state carrying the elections by fraud and violence. The
public conscience revolted, thoughtful men everywhere
foresaw that there was disaster somewhere along the line
of such a policy as certainly as there is a righteous judgment for nations as well as men. No man can be in favor of
perpetuating the election methods which have prevailed in
Mississippi since 1875 who is not a moral idiot.

"The old men of the present generation," wrote one reader of the
Jackson Clarion-Ledger, "can't afford to die and leave their children
with shot guns in their hands, a lie in their mouths and perjury on
their souls, in order to defeat the negroes. The constitution can be
made so this will not be necessary."

The solution, in Mississippi and later in South Carolina and a good
many other Southern states that followed her lead, was a section of the
constitution requiring voters to "understand and explain" a clause of
the state constitution to the satisfaction of a registrar, who would read
it aloud to them. A South Carolina delegate to his state's convention
said of the "understanding clause": "My 'understanding' is that this
will disfranchise every negro." (The problem with a simple literacy test
is that it would disfranchise a good many illiterate whites too.) The
convention also inserted into the state constitution a whole list of petty
crimes, conviction of which would lead to permanent disfranchisement; these included receiving stolen goods, bigamy, adultery, fornica-
tion, wife beating, arson, and larceny but excluded murder.

Albion Tourgée had seen the day coming when the whites of the
South would succeed in capturing the national memory along with
everything else.

Right after the war he had predicted that it was only a matter of
time before the romantic haze of the Southern cause would obscure
the jagged edges of the truth: "Within thirty years after the close of
the war of rebellion popular sympathy will be with those who up-
held the Confederate cause; our popular heroes will be Confederate
leaders; our fiction will be Southern in its prevailing types and dis-
tinctively Southern in its character," he had written. Tourgée be-

came a noted writer of fiction himself after the end of Reconstruction, and he wrote a novel called *A Fool's Errand* that was a fictionalized account of his own travails in the South battling the Ku Klux, but back when he made that prediction he was unknown as a writer and, as he later recalled, his assertion was regarded "as too absurd for refutation" at the time. In 1888 he could write that "there are yet seven years to elapse before the prescribed limit is reached, but the prediction is already almost literally fulfilled. Not only is the epoch of the war the favorite field of American fiction to-day, but the Confederate soldier is the popular hero. Our literature has become not only Southern in type, but distinctly Confederate in sympathy."

"The dashing Confederate cavalier," he sarcastically observed, had become such an inevitable figure of romance, that, "so far as our fiction is concerned, there does not appear to have been any Confederate infantry" at all.

And even histories, memoirs, and sketches had gone the same way, said Tourgée. There was a scarcely a word anymore about what the war had even been fought for. Books by the ton were being written about the war, but it was as if the generals and leaders of each side "were merely players in a great game of chess," as if "the question of loyalty to the Nation were a mere accident, for which the one class were entitled to no credit and the other deserving of no disparagement. This has gone so far that there was even a tendency to forget altogether the fact that a war could not be waged for the preservation of the Union unless some one was responsible for the attempt to destroy it."

If even the preservation of the Union was obscured in this haze of romance and armchair generaling then all the more was the colored man. The United Daughters of the Confederacy launched a campaign to ensure that the "slander" that the South had fought for slavery was expunged from schoolbooks, and orators at Confederate reunions hotly denounced such an infamous imputation. John Mosby, the partisan rebel cavalryman who had hanged Yankee soldiers from trees and terrorized the enemy's rear, wrote an old comrade that he was fed up with such "oratorical nonsense." He confessed, "I don't go to reunions because I can't stand the speaking." Mosby like Longstreet was one of those freaks of nature, a Southerner who thought it was the role of the defeated to accept defeat and move on; he supported Grant for president and became a diplomat in the American foreign service, and scarcely ever set foot in his native Virginia again. "Why not talk about witchcraft if slavery was not the cause of the war," he wrote his old friend. "I always understood that we went to war on account of the thing we quarreled with the North about. I never heard of any other cause of quarrel than slavery."

Mosby said, "I never apologized for anything I did during or since the war"; he said, "I committed treason and am proud of it"; he said, "I am not ashamed that my family were slaveholders, neither am I ashamed that my ancestors were pirates and cattle thieves."

But this was another voice in the wilderness, for the ladies of the U.D.C. and the rest of the South were shaping a memory in which the South had done no wrong; had fought not for slavery, but for great constitutional principle and "the most sacred rights of self-government"; had committed no treason, but had asserted its unshakable right within a "compact of sovereign States" to withdraw whenever it chose; had in the end submitted not to the greater right but merely to the greater force.

The story of Reconstruction was seamlessly sewn to the same fabric of romance the South had been weaving about herself forever, going back even before the war; the South as virtuous victim. The moral benignity and even superiority of slavery—the perfect harmony and kindest relations that existed between master and slave—the fanatical designs of the abolitionists, who cloaked base politics in hypocritical moral cant about slavery—the vengefulness of Northern radicals, who cloaked their hatred of the South in hypocritical moral cant about equal rights. So the U.D.C. ladies insisted that the schoolbooks also explain how the South had redeemed herself from the bayonet rule of Reconstruction, and how the Ku Klux had been formed for "self-protection against outrages committed by misguided negroes."

By the turn of the century this was what everyone knew. Dunbar Rowland, the state archivist of Mississippi and one of the most respected Southern historians of the day, gave a lecture in 1902 to the alumni association of the University of Mississippi that brought it all together. They met in Jackson, not far from the governor's house where Adelbert Ames had lived and lost the struggle.

"From early colonial times to 1860," the historian began, "the South was a garden for the cultivation of all that was grand in oratory, true in science, sublime and beautiful in poetry and sentiment, and enlightened and profound in law and statesmanship."

At the end of the war the South was in ruins, her "happy homes" laid desolate. Yet "there remained a strong and steadfast affection between the old slaves of the South and their former masters." Had that feeling of confidence been allowed to continue without the evil influence of the carpetbagger all would have been well, for "the Southern white man is the only man on earth who understands the negro character." The Northerner most definitely did not.

"The coming of the carpet bagger and the evil influence he gained over the negro" upset this harmonious condition. Negro suffrage, instituted by Northern radicals for nothing but "partisan political" aims, was the "crowning sorrow and humiliation of the South." It was cruel to condemn "a brave though fallen people to the suffering and humiliation which became their portion." Yet the "bitter humiliation of negro domination" was borne with fortitude and patience. The Negro was given "a fair trial" to prove himself "a worthy citizen."

Finally, when it became unbearable, the humiliation was overthrown, as was inevitable; for "the Anglo Saxon has never bowed his head to the yoke of an inferior race and he never will."

"No pen can adequately describe" what a bitter trial the South went through in those years, said the historian. But from her suffering we can at least learn for the future. The enfranchisement of the Negro is now recognized "by thoughtful students of events everywhere" for the "stupendous blunder" it was. "The greatest obstacle to the advancement of the negro" was not anything the white people of the South had done, explained the historian, but rather the black man's own "defective moral nature."

Yet, he concluded, "what an object lesson of love, and trust and faithfulness it would be if the beautiful relations existing now between the old slaves, who are rapidly passing away, and their former masters could be presented to every good man in the United States.

The old uncles and aunties of the South, as the old slaves are called, have never faltered in their devotion to their 'white folks' and thousands of them are cared for in their old age by their former owners."

Romance and official history and politics and popular memory fused into one, and voices like Albion Tourgée's expended their irony on deaf ears. But they tried now and then anyway.

Tourgée observed that in the novels of the South, the Negro was as reliable a stock character as the dashing cavalier; yet he "is only a shadow—an incident of another's life. As such he is invariably assigned one of two roles. In one he figures as the devoted slave who serves and sacrifices for his master and mistress, and is content to live or die, do good or evil, for those to whom he feels himself under infinite obligation for the privilege of living and serving. There were such miracles no doubt, but they were so rare as never to have lost their miraculous character.

"The other favorite aspect of the Negro character from the point of view of the Southern fictionist, is that of the poor 'nigger' to whom liberty has brought only misfortune, and who is relieved by the disinterested friendship of some white man whose property he once was. There are such cases, too, but they are not so numerous as to destroy the charm of novelty.

"About the Negro as a man, with hopes, fears, and aspirations like other men, our literature is very nearly silent."

So was the rest of the nation.

35

Adelbert Ames outlived them all, and his later life bore no tragedies. He made the "money money" he had told Blanche that he must have; he worked at the family mill business in Northfield, and worked in New York as a commission agent selling flour, and took a seat on the New York Produce Exchange. Blanche had inherited a fortune herself, two-thirds of a million dollars, much more than he ever made, and so they had houses on Cape Ann and in Florida and a villa on Lake Como. In his later years Ames became John D. Rockefeller's regular golfing companion in their winters in Florida. He lived to ninety-seven, taking his daily walks, looking like a military man to the very end, straight as a ramrod. The newspapers every once in a while would remember him, and a story would appear mentioning General Adelbert Ames as one of the oldest West Point graduates and one of the last fifteen, or ten, or eight living Civil War generals; and then he was the oldest West Point graduate and the last living Civil War general.

Their children all lived and grew into attractive and accomplished young men and women. The daughters went to Smith and Bryn Mawr and the sons to Harvard and West Point, and "little Blanche" became a highly regarded botanical illustrator and a prominent leader in Massachusetts in the campaigns for women's suffrage and the legalization of birth control. The younger son, Adelbert, Jr., became a lawyer, and then a painter, and then a pioneering expert in the theory of color vision and the physiology of the human eye. He so commanded this field that he created for himself that Dartmouth College appointed him a full professor with no duties but to pursue his research. He figured out the cause of a mysterious vision problem that produced debilitating headaches; he discovered it was the result of the two eyes perceiving the same object as different sizes, and he developed compensating lenses to correct the problem, and patients flocked to the Dartmouth Eye Institute for treatment.

Every once in a while a historian would write to Ames asking about the old days in Mississippi, and Ames would answer, never conceding an inch to the tides of latter-day sentiment. He had an exasperating exchange of letters in 1895 with one professor who had written in a magazine article that Ames, as governor, had run up the debt of Mississippi to twenty million dollars. "You have been extremely unfortunate in the selection of your authorities," Ames wrote him. "They have led you into making a $19,500,000.00 mistake in a $20,000,000.00 statement." The historian's "authority" had been the statements of Democrats during an 1890 congressional debate; the historian replied to Ames that perhaps differences in "bookkeeping methods" explained the discrepancy; in his forthcoming book he would "give the statement of each side and let each reader judge for himself."

Ames wrote back, and let him have it with both barrels. The historian was a Northern man who had fought in the Union army in the war, but he had bought the same line everyone else had. Ames told him it was preposterous to suggest that differences in bookkeeping could turn the actual debt of the state from the half million that he had left it into twenty million. Ames told him to go look at the official records instead of relying on the slanders of the "anti-Reconstructionists." And he went on to tell him a few more things; he compressed the whole tragedy of Reconstruction's overthrow into a few paragraphs that shook with a contained outrage unallayed by the passage of twenty years:

> The northern men in Mississippi as a class, were the brave youths who marched at your side for four years of bloody war. They were noble comrades, possessed of virtues equal to those of their associates; and were worthy sons of the fathers who founded this republic. They went to Mississippi under the same commendable impulses as had those who had populated this land from one ocean to another. They went to establish new homes. They took their whole capital and persuaded others to follow them.
>
> At first there was no political question. At first the enmity of a conquered people did not manifest itself. It was left for the union soldiers to practically solve the problem of reconstruction put upon them by a union Congress whose laws they had always obeyed and the wisdom of whose decisions it never occurred to them to doubt. Their only offense to the state of Miss. was an honest effort to obey the laws of the U.S. They incorporated into the organic laws of the State some of the best features found in the constitutions of northern states, to the great benefit of the state; they sought to build up, to rehabilitate especially as to the educational and eleemosynary institutions.

The offense of the union soldier was in reconstruction at all—in giving the negro the ballot. Political equality for the negro meant to the white, negro supremacy. Physical resistance resulted. The whole north conquered only after four years of fighting. The few union soldiers and their allies in Mississippi soon fell before the Mississippians and their reinforcements from Louisiana and Alabama.

"No negro domination"—"no force bill"—is the spirit of our modern Sermon on the Mount. The south is consistent.

The southern man has a motive in slandering the reconstructionists. He committed crime upon crime to prevent the political equality of the negro.

I hope you will find time at an early date to do an act of justice.

Another young historian, more diligent, wrote, obviously puzzled by the seeming contradiction between the accepted story line of plunder and misrule by the vandal horde of scheming carpetbaggers on the one hand, and the documentary facts of Ames's own personal rectitude on the other. But why had Ames made jurors of colored men as military governor? Why had he, a military man, taken political office? And what were in his view the merits of his administration in Mississippi?

Ames gave the young historian all his official papers to use and a few tart answers.

He had not made colored men jurors: the laws of the nation had.

As "incredible" as it might seem to the historian, as "ludicrous" as the explanation might seem now, he had taken political office because "it seemed to me I had a Mission with a large M." He had gained the confidence of the colored men by standing by them as military governor; "I was convinced that I could help to guide them successfully, keep men of doubtful integrity from control, and the more certainly accomplish what was every patriot's wish, the enfranchisement of the colored men and the pacification of the country."

As for the "merits" of his administration: "My dear Professor, when you appear before St. Peter at the gates of Heaven, what can you say in reply to his query as to the 'merits' of your earthly career? To say I acted conscientiously to the best of my ability does not seem to be sufficient."

The historian resolved his dilemma by vouching in his book for Ames's integrity as a man but concluding that he must have been led astray by "bad advisers" and by his "overconfidence in the mental and moral ability of the black race." The historian concluded that the responsibility for the violence committed by the whites of Mississippi must rest with the authors of Reconstruction in Congress and their "dangerous experiment" of giving the Negro the ballot.

Ames's fellow Reconstruction governors began to recant. Daniel H. Chamberlain wrote a long turn-of-the-century apologia for the *Atlantic Monthly,* explaining how naïve he had been as governor of South Carolina; he saw now that Reconstruction had been a "frightful experiment"; he saw now that it was "morally impossible" that a people of "force, pride, and intelligence" would abandon their "lifelong sentiments and prejudices"; the outcome had been as inevitable as the working out of a law of physics. He now saw that the Negro did not possess the "mental, moral, or physical capacity" to keep and maintain the precious right of self-government; it was folly to expect laws and constitutions to give the Negro what the Negro himself was incapable of holding on his own. The best hope for the future was to recognize the Negro's inherent limitations, "fixed not by us but by powers above us," not try to educate him with things like science and literature that for 999 out of 1,000 would be a "positive evil" for him to possess, but teach him handicrafts and manual skills.

Twenty years before these were the very views, almost to a word, that Chamberlain himself had derided as being "as illogical as they are immoral"; now the white South Carolinians were delighted that the former carpetbagger had come to see things so clearly, and warmly embraced the repentant sinner.

Ames never wavered, much less repented. He was never again

involved in politics after he left Mississippi and never published any defense of his actions, but to friends and enemies alike he stood by his record and the rightness of the cause he had fought for and lost. On the eve of the First World War, John R. Lynch, now a lawyer in Chicago, once the colored Speaker of the House of Mississippi and once a United States congressman in those days now so distant as to seem incredible, wrote to the old general, enclosing a copy of a book he had published; it was called *The Facts of Reconstruction.*

Another voice in the wilderness. Lynch went after the historical fabrications now universally embraced; he took bitter satisfaction in pointing out that while Governor Ames's administration had built schools, kept the debt low, and never been accused of peculation, the Democratic state treasurer who followed was discovered to have stolen $315,612.19 when he left office. The man had then gone silently to jail—the presumption being that the money had gone to pay for the arming and organizing of the white Democratic rifle clubs that had brought the party to power back in 1875.

Ames wrote Lynch back a warm and sad handwritten note of appreciation.

I have read with much interest "The Facts of Reconstruction."

In my time I have known many politicians and office holders state and national, but nowhere at no time have I met men more honest, more single minded or with higher ideals than those of the Republican party in Miss. in those days of which you write. We were all young, each and every one believed he was doing God's service and that the final result of his labors would be the elevation of an unhappy class of human beings. Unfortunately greed, the father of slaves, was too much for us. He who was a slave is now at best a serf. His road to life, liberty, and pursuit of happiness seems endless—thanks to the attitude of our Christian nation of this day and generation.

When the poor white of the south realizes that cheap serf labor degrades him then the first step towards the improvement of the condition of the colored man will be made.

But when will that time come—who can say? Perhaps you have a more speedy solution of the problem. May you make progress.

I enclose a check for (1.65×9=)$9.90 for six (6) copies of your book.

Yours truly,

A Ames

I am quite in accord with your estimate of the men you name in your book.

I thank you for your kind sentiments towards myself and the words by which they are expressed

In 1929, a few years before his death, Ames received an inquiry about his days as governor of Mississippi from Dunbar Rowland, the Mississippi archivist who had written of "the coming of the carpet bagger and the evil influence he gained over the negro." Ames was ninety-three; Rowland was sixty-four, born during the Civil War, a generation and a world apart.

Ames's answer came over a gulf as wide as the sea.

Dear Sir:

In reply to your courteous note of March 1st, I need only say that in those remote days it was the conviction in the National Congress that the protection of the negro was in the ballot.

I was a youth out of the U.S. Military Academy in 1861.

I forbade any legislation to put the state in debt. It was not done.

One's views of human affairs are modified by time.

The days are many before Christ's Sermon on the Mount will be our practical religion.

Mississippi like other states has a weary task before it.

And so the old general sailed, and golfed, and traveled, and passed his summers on Cape Ann where the family had built cabins for all the children to come and stay, and they came to visit bringing the eighteen grandchildren, and the old general attended a reunion of

Civil War veterans once a year, and rarely spoke to his family or acquaintances of the past except occasionally to tell of the time he had been caught in a raging nor'easter off Gloucester sailing as a cabin boy on his father's ship. And so he died with the clear conscience of a soldier who had just tried to do his duty, even though he failed.

36

As men live and die so towns live and die, and their lingering deaths have the same tawdry emptiness. Hamburg's population dwindled to five hundred, and the white men from Augusta would come over when they wanted to stage a gamecock fight once in a while in some derelict lot, and workmen from Augusta came over and dug up clay to make bricks, leaving behind empty craters of contempt. And someone would put a torch to a building from time to time for the fun of it, until it looked to a passing visitor like the vengeance visited upon Sodom and Gomorrah.

Louis Schiller came back and hung on, and enough water under the bridge had passed by 1893 that he and Tommy Butler were arrested together in Hamburg on the charge of selling whiskey on a Sunday. They hauled Schiller off to Aiken and gave him fifteen dollars or fifteen days; Tommy Butler seems to have gotten off.

At the turn of the century a new town called North Augusta was founded up the river a mile on the bluff, and in the winters rich Northerners came down to play polo and golf and shoot wild turkey, and business flourished, and churches and a fine high school were built.

In 1928 the old Sibley Building burned to the ground, and the North Augusta firemen came and watched it burn and the newspaper reported with a straight face that they hadn't had any water nearby to douse the flames, but they did work to make sure that the wooden trestle of the railroad nearby didn't catch fire.

In 1929 two huge floods swept down the Savannah River, and the last physical remains of Hamburg were swept away with them.

One day, fifty-one years after the year of liberation when the freedmen of Charleston had honored the Martyrs of the Race Course, there was another grand celebration on the streets of a South Carolina town, and schoolchildren again assembled and sang, and prayers were again read and orations again delivered, and again there was a march to unveil a memorial to the dead.

The state of South Carolina had provided some of the money to erect the monument, but private donations were raised, too, and the Hon. B. R. Tillman had contributed twenty-five dollars, and Mr. Henry Getzen had too.

And on that day a thousand people came and cheered and shouted the rebel yell as the Honorable D. S. Henderson retold the stirring story of how young McKie Meriwether had "perished for the cause of liberty" in "The Battle of Hamburg."

It was not a massacre in the brutal sense of that word, declaimed the speaker; "it was a rebellion against wrong, an armed rebuke to tyranny and oppression."

Ignorance and vice had reigned in those dark days. The Supreme Court of the state had been given over to "a superannuated Jew, a shrewd carpet-bagger and an ignorant black negro." A Negro militia terrorized decent white people. Military satraps ruled the state at the point of a bayonet.

But there in Hamburg, "the very citadel of negro Republicanism," the flame had been lit, and ignited "the white man's Revolution" of 1876.

And then, at the top of a picture-perfect square at the top of the prosperous main street of North Augusta, some pretty schoolgirls in pretty dresses unveiled the obelisk, revealing carved inscriptions to "the memory of the young hero of the Hamburg riot," who gave his life that the "civic and social institutions which the men and women of his race had struggled through the centuries to establish in South Carolina" might be passed on unimpaired, and the "supremacy" of "Anglo Saxon civilization" assured.

As for Hamburg, it vanished even from the maps. In the 1950s a dam was built upriver, and the floods that had periodically swept over the empty flats of grass and weeds and brambles where a town had once stood came no more. In 1988 the dam was renamed the Strom Thurmond Dam, in honor of another Edgefield hero; as a boy, Strom had been taught by Benjamin R. Tillman himself to shake hands with a firm grip, had followed Pitchfork Ben's footsteps to become the state's Democratic governor and U.S. senator. Then in midcareer Strom had switched parties and become a Republican, as in time did most other Southern white conservatives once the Democratic party became the champion of voting rights for African Americans in the 1960s, and the Grand Old Party saw more opportunity in appealing to disaffected white supremacists than in recovering its heritage as the party of Adelbert Ames, and Prince Rivers, and James Longstreet, and Albert T. Morgan that it had once been so long ago.

In 1998 an enterprising North Augustan built a golf course on the derelict land by the now tranquil river, and a row of what the real estate agents called "executive homes" went up right by the river's edge, with a pretty view. The bulldozers that cleared the home sites hit a few old bricks buried in the silt and clay and pushed them into a pile, and that was all there was to show that people had ever lived there before; except for the ghosts of old streets still to be seen, or perhaps merely imagined, where the new houses ended; a few mown avenues still improbably wide, streets of a town that was no more and a city that never had been.

Men die, and towns die, and cruelest of all, memories die. And when North Augusta celebrated its centennial in 2006, Hamburg was nowhere to be heard of, though the McKie Meriwether monument was duly catalogued in an inventory of local historical sites the town compiled for the occasion. They described it as a monument "to the only resident of Hamburg to be killed in the Hamburg riot of 1876."

Notes

ABBREVIATIONS

AA Adelbert Ames, Ames Family Papers, Sophia Smith Collection, Smith College
DSCL Duke University Special Collections Library
KKC U.S. Congress, *Ku Klux Conspiracy*
M1875 44th Cong., 1st Sess., *Mississippi in 1875*
MDAH Mississippi Department of Archives and History
NA National Archives
MFP 44th Cong., 1st Sess., *Message from the President*
MGP Mississippi Governor (1874–1876: Ames): Correspondence and Papers, Mississippi Department of Archives and History
POY Post of Yorkville, S.C., Record Group 393, Part V, National Archives
RG Record Group
SC1876 44th Cong., 2nd Sess., *South Carolina in 1876*
SCDAH South Carolina Department of Archives and History
SCL South Caroliniana Library, University of South Carolina
SSC Sophia Smith Collection, Smith College
VSCL University of Virginia Special Collections Library

PROLOGUE

1 "man who was in the house": *KKC,* XI, 271.
1 "good, respectable Democrat": Puckett, "Reconstruction in Monroe County," 116.
1 "not a hair of your head": *KKC,* XI, 271.
1 "gentlemanly fellows": *KKC,* XI, 275.
2 "radical ways": *KKC,* XI, 272.
2 "all wanted to get a chance at me": *KKC,* XI, 273.
2 recovered the bloody nightshirt: Puckett, "Reconstruction in Monroe County," 188*n*10; Horn, *Invisible Empire,* 151; Trelease, *White Terror,* 294.

4   impassioned speech about the Ku Klux: *Congressional Globe,* 42nd Cong., 1st Sess., 446, 449 (April 4, 1871).

4   "holy relic": "Sumner and Brooks," *New York Times,* July 19, 1874, p. 2.

4   Duchess of Argyle: "Another Secession Blast," *New York Times,* July 24, 1860, p. 4.

4   John Brown: "Sumner and Brooks," *New York Times,* July 19, 1874, p. 2.

4   "All the abject whines": "Walker Wanted to Govern Kansas," *New York Times,* November 18, 1856, p. 3.

5   "The only article the North can retain": Ibid.

5   lacked the Anglo-Saxon virtues: Chamberlain, "Reconstruction and the Negro," 172.

6   "The most horrible tales": A South Carolinian, "South Carolina Morals," 471.

6   "We had to shoot negroes": *Struggles of 1876,* 14.

6   "It had been the settled purpose": Ibid., 17.

7   "was little more than a ratification": Simkins, "Election of 1876," 343.

7   "A superior race": *Respectful Remonstrance,* 12.

7   "No free people, ever": *Proceedings of the Tax-payers' Convention,* 71.

7   "This is a white man's government": South Carolina, *Journal of the Convention,* 14; see also, e.g., Zuczek, *State of Rebellion,* 160; *M1875,* II, Documentary Evidence, 162.

9   "In all except the actual results": Current, *Terrible Carpetbaggers,* 376.

CHAPTER 1

13   Sleeping Beauty's castle: Rosen, *Confederate Charleston,* 142.

15   "the most exquisite happiness": A South Carolinian, "South Carolina Society," 684.

15   a celebration of patriotic joy: "Department of the South. Affairs in Charleston. The Jubilee among the Freedmen," *New York Times,* April 4, 1865, p. 9.

18   On the first was written, "No. 1": Redpath, "May-Day in Charleston."

18   ditches the prisoners had hacked: Redpath, "May-Day in Charleston Again."

18   MARTYRS OF THE RACE COURSE: Blight, *Race and Reunion,* 69.

19   not a speck of bare earth: Ibid., 70.

CHAPTER 2

19   "We are well aware": Aptheker, "Negro Conventions," 93–95.

21   "It is understood that a number of negroes": *Charleston Courier,* September 26, 1865, p. 2, quoted in Underwood, "Founding Fathers," 4–5, and Aptheker, "Negro Conventions," 95n8.

21　"laid on the table": Aptheker, "Negro Conventions," 95.
21　delegates to the convention: Ibid., 91–92.
21　"natural ruling element": Williamson, *After Slavery*, 71.
21　"write occasionally": Zuczek, *State of Rebellion*, 12.
22　"this is a white man's government": South Carolina, *Journal of the Convention*, 11–12, 14.
22　"The African has been, in all ages": *Charleston Daily Courier*, October 1, 1866, quoted in Holt, *Black Over White*, 25.

CHAPTER 3

23　"With great diffidence and some hesitation": Edmund Rhett to Armistead Burt, October 13, 1865, Armistead Burt Papers, DSCL.
26　"In obedience to verbal instruction": A. Ames to Lieutenant Clous, April 4, 1866, M619, roll 512, frames 583–89, Letters Received, RG 94, NA.

CHAPTER 4

28　"selected for his work": Dennett, *The South As It Is*, vii.
29　"G—— M—— has a wife": Ibid., 24.
29　"right good snack": Ibid., 36.
30　"Well, Oscar, reckon we'd better": Ibid., 38.
30　"B.C., Captain Wofford's Georgians": Ibid., 94.
30　"Mister, whar be ye frum?": Ibid., 145.
31　"Never heed": Ibid., 62.
31　"the preacher's hoss": Ibid., 118.
31　"Damned Yankee wagon": Ibid., 229.
31　"You're sitting up late": Ibid., 226.
33　"When the city was evacuated": Ibid., 14–15.
33　"Fare you well chile": Ibid., 17.
34　"No, sir, never": Ibid., 19–20.

CHAPTER 5

35　"In the country parts of Virginia": Dennett, *The South As It Is*, 67.
35　"can't get white men enough": Ibid., 39–40.
35　"tolerably well": Ibid., 48.
36　"I believe you never did, colonel": Ibid., 78–79.
36　"No money wages": Ibid., 82–83.
37　"Having tried the new labor system": Ibid., 84.
37　"See those damned niggers!": Ibid, 364–65.
37　"Under an agreement between me and James": Ibid., 97.
38　"You mark me": Ibid., 56.
39　"He knew I was a Yankee": Ibid., 174.

CHAPTER 6

40   "Mister Smith": Dennett, *The South As It Is,* 52.
40   "By colored man, John": Ibid., 125.
41   "We have been informed": Ibid., 344.
42   "I'll get it out of him": Ibid., 249.
43   "I'm told the nigger soldiers": Ibid., 193–96.
44   "The people were sorry for nothing": Ibid., 361–62.
45   "You must understand": Ibid., 348–49.
46   "For some time to come": Ibid., 362.
46   "I think that the Negroes unprotected": Ibid., 369.
47   "Let the Negro vote": Ibid., 41.

CHAPTER 7

51   Prince Rivers had been a coachman: Higginson, *Army Life,* 57.
52   tears were everywhere: Ibid., 40–41.
52   "There is not a white officer": Ibid., 57–58.
52   "The hour is at hand": Ibid., 292–93.
53   one of the roughest counties: *KKC,* III, 73.
53   "*disposition* is such": Kantrowitz, *Ben Tillman,* 23.
53   "false philanthropy": *A Defence of Southern Slavery.*
54   One Hundred and Twenty Negroes: Goodell, *American Slave Code,* 54–55.
55   "This taking Augusta will repent": Taylor, "Hamburg," 21.
55   "one of the dullest places": J. L. Knight to James Evans, April 27, 1851, SCL.
56   "the most lonely, desolate": Chapman, *History of Edgefield,* 20.
56   population swelled to eleven hundred: Hamburg, S.C., M593, roll 1494, pp. 248–61, Ninth Census of the United States, RG 29, NA.
56   "It is almost a daily occurrence": John Williams to Brigadier General C. H. Howard, December 4, 1865, M619, roll 505, Letters Received, RG 94, NA.
56   "bushwhackers": Captain Henry A. Shorey to assistant adjutant general, March 19, 1866, M619, roll 512, frames 518–32, ibid.
56   A band of a hundred men: "Washington News. What a Gallant Soldier Saw in South Carolina," *New York Times,* April 9, 1866, p. 5.
56   "14 or 15 Yanks": Burton, "Afro-American Town Life," 163.
57   Among their numbers were: Vandervelde, *Aiken County,* 367–72; *SC1876,* I, 47, 73–74, 709; II, 602.
57   routine matters of small crime: Trial Justice P. R. Rivers, Bundle 83, Miscellaneous Papers, Court of General Sessions (Aiken County): Indictments, SCDAH.
57   "We the undersigned citizens": Petition of Citizens of Edgefield County, November 22, 1869, Governor Scott: Letters Received and Sent, SCDAH.

58   The town's charter: "An Act to Repeal the Charter of the Town of Ham-
     burg," No. 47, General Assembly: Acts, Bills & Joint Resolutions, 1868,
     SCDAH; South Carolina, *Acts and Joint Resolutions,* Regular Session
     1870–71, 549–52.

CHAPTER 8

59   "Sketches of the Delegates": *Edgefield Advertiser,* February 12, 1868, p. 1.
61   "THE RESPECTFUL REMONSTRANCE": *Respectful Remonstrance,*
     12.
62   "Another Poland.": *Edgefield Advertiser,* May 27, 1868, p. 4.
63   "[Prince Rivers is] so black": Quoted in "Wayside Gleanings," *Augusta
     Chronicle,* October 13, 1931.
63   "Distinguished Official Visitor": *Augusta Chronicle,* June 16, 1872.
64   "Poor old Hamburg!": Quoted in "Wayside Gleanings," *Augusta Chroni-
     cle,* October 13, 1931.

CHAPTER 9

64   Adelbert Ames was born: Ames, *Adelbert Ames,* 3–4, 23.
64   "A seaport town like that": Ames, ed., *Chronicles,* I, 28.
65   "about as close an approximation": Current, *Terrible Carpetbaggers,* 113.
65   "This is a hell of a regiment!": Pullen, *20th Maine,* 17–18, 50.
65   "I will move over your line": Ibid., 66; Ames, ed., *Chronicles,* I, 16; Buice,
     "Military Career of Ames," 240–41.
65   "He seemed to have a life": Ames, *Adelbert Ames,* 188–90.
66   "*position* and *pay*": Ames, ed., *Chronicles,* I, 32.
66   "very shadowy": Ibid., I, 28–29.
66   "The climate is finer here": Ames, *Adelbert Ames,* 224–25.
67   noted his disappointments: Entries for November 1, November 5, Novem-
     ber 20, December 16, March 26, Diaries of Trip to Europe 1866–67, AA.
68   "seems happy and contented": Ibid., entry for November 13.
69   assigned to travel through Mississippi: Report, May 10, 1867, Profes-
     sional Correspondence, Reconstruction, AA.
70   "Under the pressure of federal bayonets": Wharton, *Negro in Mississippi,*
     84–89; Aptheker, "Mississippi Reconstruction," 167.
70   "for the purpose of making such arrangements": The complete exchange
     of letters is reprinted in Ames, *Adelbert Ames,* 271–73.
72   The First Act of Our New Despot: Garner, *Reconstruction in Missis-
     sippi,* 215.
72   dismissed all ex-Confederate officials: Ibid., 230–31.
73   Ames at once issued a military order: General Orders No. 32, April 27,
     1869, Headquarters 4th Military District, Professional Correspondence,
     Reconstruction, AA.
73   fourteen hundred U.S. troops: 40th Cong., 3rd Sess., *Condition of Affairs*

in Mississippi, 135; "Extracts from Returns of the Fourth Military District (Department of Mississippi) from June 1869, to December 1869, inclusive," Professional Correspondence, Reconstruction, AA.

73   "has been confined almost exclusively": Ames, ed., *Chronicles*, I, 37.
73   "Three hundred and twenty two men": Current, *Terrible Carpetbaggers*, 175.
73   "The contest is not between": Ibid., 174–75.

CHAPTER 10

74   "Boys, you'll rue the day": Morgan, *Yazoo*, 18.
74   Morgan and his brother: Current, *Terrible Carpetbaggers*, 37–38.
74   "Physically, I had all my life": Morgan, *Yazoo*, 79, 141.
74–75   begun the war as . . . private: *M1875*, II, 1729.
75   "Go South, young man": Morgan, *Yazoo*, 25.
75   "No Yankee radical": Ibid., 21–22.
77   "Good-morning, Bristol": Ibid., 30–32.
77   "that gal, Sal, by God": Ibid., 33–34.
78   "hey, you, boy": Ibid., 46–47.
79   "the nigrah character": Ibid., 77–78.
81   "Colonel, it 'peers to me": Ibid., 85–87.
81   he must publish a "card": Ibid., 91–96.
82   "nigger school marm": Ibid., 113.

CHAPTER 11

83   "coining money": Current, *Terrible Carpetbaggers*, 78; Morgan, *Yazoo*, 112.
83   "for the purpose of defrauding him": Morgan, *Yazoo*, 123; *M1875*, II, 1730.
84   "Hurrah for Colonel White": *M1875*, II, 1730–31; Morgan, *Yazoo*, 128.
84   "Nothin', marsa": Morgan, *Yazoo*, 118–21.
85   his colored friends rallied to him: Ibid., 134, 138, 152.
86   "Halloa, polecat!": Ibid., 157.
86   "radical black and tan convention": Ibid., 165.
86   "the Yankee Stronghold": Ibid., 160–66, 168, 179.
86   passed the time studying law: *M1875*, II, 1763.
86   "Say, got any money left over": Morgan, *Yazoo*, 214.
87   "Why, sir, that so-called constitution": Ibid., 211–12.
88   "We are always glad to have": Ibid., 346–47.
88   Her name was Carolyn Victoria Highgate: Ibid., 344–46, xix, li*n*3.
88   "Truly these are grand times!": A. T. Morgan to Ames, January 28, 1870, Professional Correspondence, Reconstruction, AA.
90   "The Colored People": *Hinds County Gazette*, August 18, 1870, p. 3.
91   "The world will condemn *me*": Sterling, ed., *We Are Your Sisters*, 303–4.
91   "content to stop with slandering me": "Letter from Senator Morgan," *Weekly Mississippi Pilot*, November 26, 1870, p. 1.
91   "Mrs. Senator Morgan": Morgan, *Yazoo*, 354–56.

CHAPTER 12

92   "Mississippi Democratic Platform": Clipping in Scrapbooks, AA.
93   "A GOOD RESOLUTION": Quoted in Morgan, *Yazoo*, 202–3.
94   "IT IS OVER": *Meridian Mercury*, July 7, 1868, clipping in Scrapbooks, AA.
96   "SONG": *Yazoo Banner*, May 1868, quoted in Morgan, *Yazoo*, 184–85.

CHAPTER 13

97   "I, Adelbert Ames": *Congressional Globe*, 41st Cong., 2nd Sess., III, 2125 (March 22, 1870).
97   "tyrant": Ibid., III, 2168–69, 2126–28, 2134 (March 22, 1870); III, 2307 (March 31, 1870).
98   "John got a paper": Ames, ed., *Chronicles*, I, 42.
98   Blanche Butler: Ames, *Adelbert Ames*, 314.
99   "I hope you are discontented too": Ames, ed., *Chronicles*, I, 116, 118, 178.
99   "I will close my first letter": Ibid., I, 117–18, 172, 180.
100 "Lonesome weather": Ibid., I, 192, 197.
100 "there will be time enough": Ibid., I, 202, 195.
100 "Men always seem to have the advantage": Entry for December 19, 1870, Blanche Butler Ames: Diary, 1870, pp. 29–30, Ames Family Papers, SSC.
100 "My breakfast": Ibid., entry for Wednesday, November 1870, pp. 15–23.
102 "From this circumstance I was tempted": A. T. Morgan to Ames, February 18, 1871, Professional Correspondence, Reconstruction, AA.
103 "If any effort should be made": Ibid., March 16, 1871.
104 "Gen'l Ames is in great tribulation": Ames, ed., *Chronicles*, I, 237.
105 "In 1869 I had to stand": *Congressional Globe*, 42nd Cong., 1st Sess., I, 571 (April 11, 1871).
105 "force political equality": *Congressional Globe*, 41st Cong., 2nd Sess., III, 2308 (March 31, 1870).

CHAPTER 14

109 "the head, face, and spectacles": *New York Daily Tribune*, November 13, 1871, quoted in Trelease, *White Terror*, 369–70.
109 "coffee-cooler": Johnson, *Custer, Reno, Merrill*, 2.
109 "when corrected in the usual and proper manner": Merrill, Lewis: Court Martial as United States Military Academy Cadet, 1855, Hugh Lenox Scott Family Papers, Southwest Collection, Texas Tech University.
110 "I cannot point to one": Merrill to Lieut. Col. F. A. Dick, December 15, 1862, ibid., Series I, XXII, Part I, 833–34.
110 he convened a military commission: U.S. War Department, *War of the Rebellion*, Series I, XIII, 660–61.
111 "I want to inquire": McNeil, "Retaliation in Missouri," 476.

111   Merrill learned to use spies: U.S. War Department, *War of the Rebellion*, Series I, XLI, Part III, 555, 582.
111   "public mule": Johnson, *Custer, Reno, Merrill*, 3.
112   "producing and publicly exhibiting": Ibid., 6.
113   "this was an illegal and improper": Merrill to Adjutant General, January 17, 1871, Personnel File of Lewis Merrill, RG 94, NA.
113   "official repute against malignant attack": Ibid., January 27, 1871.
113   "A very small amount of common courtesy": Merrill to G. A. Custer, April 26, 1871, ibid.
114   the exercise of "moral influence": *KKC*, V, 1464.
114   "When you get to South Carolina": *KKC*, V, 1482.
115   "about two o'clock": Post, "'Carpetbagger' in South Carolina," 42–43.
115   missed a minor battle: *KKC*, V, 1470–71.
116   endless minutiae and drudgery: Merrill to Chief Commissary of Subsistence, April 21, 1871; Merrill to Assistant Adjutant General, April 21, 1871; "Descriptive Report of the Post of Yorkville S.C.," September 16, 1871, Letters Sent, Entry 1, POY.
117   "You son of a bitch": General and Special Order Books, Entry 6, POY.
117   "there is no likelihood of any disturbances": "Public Meetings," *Yorkville Enquirer*, March 30, 1871, reprinted in *KKC*, V, 1541.
118   "force, if persisted in": "Public Meeting of the Whites," *Yorkville Enquirer*, April 6, 1871, reprinted in *KKC*, V, 1541–43.
118   the major went out for himself: *KKC*, V, 1465–68.

CHAPTER 15

119   "I have the honor to submit": Merrill to Assistant Adjutant General, May 4, 1871, Letters Sent, Entry 1, POY.
122   "We are going on to kill Williams": *KKC*, V, 1719.
123   "Jim Williams on his big muster": *KKC*, V, 1713.
123   "it is idle to attempt arrests": Merrill to Assistant Adjutant General, May 19, 1871, Letters Sent, Entry 1, POY.
123   "It requires great patience": Ibid.
123   "some means could be devised": *KKC*, V, 1497–99.
124   "prevent further acts of violence": *KKC*, V, 1499–1500.
124   "no great faith in pledges": Merrill to Assistant Adjutant General, May 19, 1871, Letters Sent, Entry 1, POY.
125   "Maj. Merrill had telegraphed for authority": Merrill, Endorsement on Letter of Department Commander, June 9, 1871, ibid.
126   "Choctaw": Akerman to Genl. Alfred H. Terry, November 18, 1871, Letterbooks, 1871–1876, Amos T. Akerman Papers, VSCL.
126   He had another informant: Merrill to Assistant Adjutant General, June 11, 1871, and September 17, 1871, Letters Sent, Entry 1, POY; *KKC*, V, 1481.

CHAPTER 16

127   "I have the honor to forward": Terry to Adjutant General, June 11, 1871, M666, roll 17, Letters Received, RG 94, NA.

128   Mephistopholean figure: Trelease, *White Terror*, 375.

128   "Ass Wallace": West, *Reconstruction Ku Klux*, 85.

128   "sub-outrage committee": *Yorkville Enquirer*, July 27 and August 3, 1871.

129   "Yankees," "damned Yankees": *KKC*, V, 1530.

129   "Are you the Hon. Mr. Wallace": "The Barry-Wallace Difficulty," *Yorkville Enquirer*, August 3, 1871, p. 2.

129   "Buttermilk Wallace": West, *Reconstruction Ku Klux*, 86.

130   *Answer.* I am now of opinion: *KKC*, V, 1482.

131   the testimony of Elias Hill: *KKC*, V, 1406–8, 1477.

132   *Answer.* Yes, sir; that is the fact: *KKC*, V, 1410.

132   *Question.* You do not feel very kindly: *KKC*, V, 1412–13.

133   "so broad a farce": *KKC*, V, 1601.

133   "Do not you think it would be inexpedient": *KKC*, V, 1610.

133   "I made extensive inquiry": Merrill to Assistant Adjutant General, September 17, 1871, Letters Sent, Entry 1, POY.

134   "each wishing to control the building": Ibid.

134   "willfully deceived": *KKC*, V, 1600.

134   "Information was furnished": *KKC*, V, 1612.

135   "diligent search": Johnson, *Custer, Reno, Merrill*, 11.

135   an additional company of infantry: 42nd Cong., 3rd Sess., *Report of Secretary of War*, I, 91.

135   Amos T. Akerman: McFeely, "Amos T. Akerman," 395–400.

135   Merrill sent squadrons of cavalry: "Arrests of Citizens," *Yorkville Enquirer*, October 26, 1871, p. 2.

CHAPTER 17

136   "I stayed at Yorkville over two weeks": Akerman to Genl. Alfred H. Terry, November 18, 1871, Letterbooks, 1871–1876, Amos T. Akerman Papers, VSCL.

137   "I shall be hung!": *New York Tribune*, November 23, 1871, quoted in West, *Reconstruction Ku Klux*, 92–93.

137   Hundreds of men who hadn't been arrested: Report of Major Lewis Merrill, January 8, 1872, reprinted in *KKC*, V, 1602–4.

138   "Bring him here at once!": Post, "'Carpetbagger' in South Carolina," 45–48.

139   He telegraphed his adjutant: Merrill to Lt. J. A. Aspinwall, December 8, 1871, Telegrams Received, Entry 5, POY.

140   "Well, gentlemen": newspaper clippings from *Southern Presbyterian*, "Journal of a Reputed Ku-Klux Prisoner," 1872, John Adams Leland Papers, SCL.

140   "as bequeathed to us in its purity": *KKC*, V, 1686.

140   "damn you, we'll make a democrat": *KKC*, V, 1747.

140   "of too obscene a nature": *KKC*, V, 1861–62.
140   "gentlemen of wealth and refinement": Williams, *Great Ku Klux Trials*, 89.
141   "Some of your comrades": *KKC*, V, 1983.
141   MR. CORBIN. If your honors please: Post, "'Carpetbagger' in South Carolina," 66.
142   "on the brain": McFeely, "Amos T. Akerman," 410.
142   "I thank you for your kind remarks": Akerman to Major Merrill, January 8, 1872, Letterbooks, 1871–1876, Amos T. Akerman Papers, VSCL.
142   "I have no doubt": Report of Major Lewis Merrill, September 23, 1872, reprinted in 42nd Cong., 3rd Sess., *Report of Secretary of War*, I, 85–91.
143   "Dog Merrill": Dawson, *Army Generals and Reconstruction*, 185.
144   "I beg to invite the attention": Merrill to Attorney General, September 30, 1872, Letters Sent, Entry 1, POY.
145   In spring of 1873 the pardons began: Trelease, *White Terror*, 415–17.
145   "flagrant cases of murder": Zuczek, *State of Rebellion*, 129.
145   "general prostration of the nervous system": Service record, Personnel File of Lewis Merrill, RG 94, NA.

CHAPTER 18

149   "too much trouble": Piston, *Lee's Tarnished Lieutenant*, 96.
149   At the Second Battle of Manassas: Gallagher, *Lee and His Generals*, 152–56.
150   "The enemy is there": McPherson, *Battle Cry of Freedom*, 656.
150   "old granny": Piston, *Lee's Tarnished Lieutenant*, 125.
151   sent their tattered battle flag: Pullen, *20th Maine*, 179.
151   "The fifteen thousand men": Longstreet, *Manassas to Appomattox*, 386–87.
151   "It is all wrong": Piston, *Lee's Tarnished Lieutenant*, 60.
151   "shall I advance?": Longstreet, *Manassas to Appomattox*, 392.
152   "That old man": Piston, *Lee's Tarnished Lieutenant*, 62.
152   "If General Lee doesn't know": Ibid., 91–92.
152   "most trusted lieutenant": Ibid., 96–99.
152   soon making fifteen thousand: Ibid., 120.
152   "plain honest convictions": *New Orleans Times*, March 19, 1867, quoted in Richter, "James Longstreet," 217.
153   "hazards of revolution": *New Orleans Times*, April 7, 1867, reprinted in "Reconstruction," *New York Times*, April 13, 1867, p. 5.
153   "It will ruin you, son": Piston, *Lee's Tarnished Lieutenant*, 105.
153   "unnatural condition": "Letter from Gen. Longstreet," *New Orleans Times*, June 8, 1867, clipping in James Longstreet Papers, DSCL.
154   "that a brilliant reputation in war": *New Orleans Picayune*, June 9, 1867, quoted in Richter, "James Longstreet," 224.
154   "theology or his loyalty": Quoted in Piston, *Lee's Tarnished Lieutenant*, 111.

154 "It is evident to my mind": Longstreet to My Dear General, June 8, 1867, James Longstreet Papers, DSCL.

155 "avoided all discussion": Robert E. Lee to Longstreet, October 29, 1867, reprinted in Jones, *Personal Reminiscences*, 227–28.

155 "sacred memory": Piston, *Lee's Tarnished Lieutenant*, 121.

155 "sinks into utter insignificance": Pendleton, "Personal Recollections," 608–9.

156 "The delay thus occasioned": Ibid., 625–27.

157 "School-boys may be misled": Piston, *Lee's Tarnished Lieutenant*, 123–24.

157 "Lee was never really beaten": Connelly and Bellows, *God and General Longstreet*, 33.

CHAPTER 19

158 CITIZENS OF NEW ORLEANS: Landry, *Battle of Liberty Place*, 83–84.

159 "immediate abdication": Ibid., 91.

159 "Hang Kellogg!": Ibid., 92.

160 "for the purpose of driving the usurpers": Singletary, *Negro Militia and Reconstruction*, 77.

160 cut the fire alarm and police telegraph: S. B. Packard to Attorney-General Williams, September 14, 1874, reprinted in 43rd Cong., 2nd Sess., *Message of the President*, 13.

160 governor then told his militia commander: Longstreet's Report, reprinted in Landry, *Battle of Liberty Place*, 125–26.

160 "Parisian fashion": Landry, *Battle of Liberty Place*, 94.

161 rebel yell: Singletary, *Negro Militia and Reconstruction*, 78.

161 restrained his men from firing particularly at General Longstreet: Piston, *Lee's Tarnished Lieutenant*, 123.

162 General Orders No. 2: Landry, *Battle of Liberty Place*, 131.

162 "Editor New Orleans Bulletin": Ibid., 111.

163 "a quiet elderly gentleman": *New Orleans Republican*, September 18, 1874, quoted in Dawson, *Army Generals and Reconstruction*, 176.

164 "Nearly every parish": Dawson, *Army Generals and Reconstruction*, 177.

CHAPTER 20

165 "There has been some red-handed work": Quoted in 43rd Cong., 2nd Sess., *Message of the President*, 32.

165 "We ask for no assistance": Quoted in ibid., 31.

166 "The white people intend": Quoted in ibid., 32.

166 "The people have determined": Ibid.

166 "We know the results of the election": Quoted in 43rd Cong., 2nd Sess., *Letter from Secretary of War*, 19–20.

167 "If a single hostile gun": Quoted in 43rd Cong., 2nd Sess., *Message of the President*, 33.

CHAPTER 21

168 "The following, received last night": Merrill to Assistant Adjutant General, October 26, 1874, reprinted in 43rd Cong., 2nd Sess., *Letter from Secretary of War*, 3–4.

169 "I have the honor now to add": Report of Lewis Merrill, October 27, 1874, ibid., 7–11.

171 "This may account for what Mrs. Dewees stated": Report of Lieutenant Donald McIntosh, November 14, 1874, ibid., 12–15.

172 "bedraggling his uniform": *Shreveport Times*, October 27, 1874, quoted in Dawson, *Army Generals and Reconstruction*, 187.

172 "political bummer": *New Orleans Bulletin*, October 27, 1874, quoted in ibid.

173 "That you are further instructed": Major Merrill to Captain Head, Telegram No. 2, November 6, 1874, reprinted in 43rd Cong., 2nd Sess., *Letter from Secretary of War*, 32.

173 "Who accompanies Lieutenant Hodgson?": Captain Head to Major Merrill, Telegram No. 5, November 6, 1874, ibid., 33.

173 "Go yourself at once": Major Merrill to Captain Head, Telegram No. 6, November 6, 1874, ibid.

173 "Employ competent legal advice": Major Merrill to Frank Morey, Telegram No. 9, November 6, 1874; and Major Merrill to Lieut. B. H. Hodgson—sent to care of sheriff at Vienna, Telegram No. 10, November 6, 1874, ibid., 34.

174 "No violence at all": Captain Head to Major Merrill, Telegram No, 14, November 6, 1874—11:30 p.m., ibid.

174 *Q*. What is status of case: Conversation at telegraph-office between Major Merrill and Mr. Hardy, Telegram No, 31, November 8, 1874—Sunday, ibid., 38.

175 "reversed sentence and discharged Hodgson": Captain Head to Major Merrill, Telegram No. 48, November 9, 1874, ibid., 43.

175 "Without delay, give me a distinct": Major Merrill to Captain Head, Telegram No. 51, November 10, 1874, ibid.

175 "They give Hodgson till to-morrow": W. R. Hardy, attorney, to Major Merrill, Telegram No. 58, November 10, 1874—6 p.m., ibid., 44.

175 "If it be possible to induce": Major Merrill to Captain Head, Telegram No. 61, November 10, 1874, ibid., 45.

175 "Further communication with you": Hardy to Major Merrill, Telegram No. 88, November 13, 1874, ibid., 50.

176 Morrow talked to the white people: report of Lieutenant Colonel Henry A. Morrow, December 24, 1874, ibid., 70–74.

176 more than two hundred colored men: 43rd Cong., 2nd Sess., *Condition of the South*, 189.

176 "so far as the private citizen, Lewis Merrill": Ibid., 181.

CHAPTER 22

179   "It causes two different": Ames, ed., *Chronicles*, I, 410.
179   "Do you know, my Love": Ibid., I, 317.
179   "Perhaps by this time": Ibid., I, 612.
179   "Facts I have": Ibid., I, 341–42.
180   "Is not that so?": Ibid., I, 324.
180   "Youse de man!": Ibid., I, 503.
180   "thought the day of judgment": Ibid., I, 382.
180   "Hit 'em again!": Ibid., I, 334.
180   "Gen. Ames has been misrepresented": Ibid., I, 611.
180   "What a fine child!": Ibid., I, 455–56.
180   By himself again in Mississippi: Ibid., I, 383, 410, 419, 610–11.
181   "a sort of brevet brigadier Senator": *Congressional Globe*, 42nd Cong., 2nd Sess., Appendix, 403 (May 20, 1872).
181   "He can do no harm": Ames, ed., *Chronicles*, I, 560.
182   "This is not living": Ibid., I, 568.
182   "When you run for Governor": Ibid., I, 486.
182   "My pleasantest hours": Ibid., I, 606–7.
182   "reluctant driver": Ibid., I, 627.
182   "My majority about thirty thousand": Ibid., I, 631.
182   "Never mind, my boy": Ibid., I, 630.

CHAPTER 23

183   they found the county was broke: Morgan, *Yazoo*, 404–16; *M1875*, II, 1740–41.
184   "Not more than a handful": A. T. Morgan to Ames, December 9, 1873, Professional Correspondence, Reconstruction, AA.
185   Morgan opened the desk drawer: Morgan to A. Ames, January 11, 1874, MGP.
185   Hilliard fell to the floor: Morgan, *Yazoo*, 382–91; *M1875*, II, 1734–39.
186   "My colored friends are true": Morgan to A. Ames, January 11, 1874, MGP.
186   "I have no doubt": Morgan to Ames, January 13, 1874, MGP.
186   The first attempt to move him: Testimony of A. T. Morgan in Mississippi, *Impeachment of Adelbert Ames*, 96.

CHAPTER 24

188   "great barn of a house": Ames, ed., *Chronicles*, I, 642.
188   "lard is not the staff of life": Ibid., I, 643–44.
188   "The great question which disturbs": Ibid., I, 651.
188   "Yours is a difficult part": Ibid., I, 654.
188   "If you always remember": Ibid., I, 661.
189   governor's inaugural message: reprinted in ibid., I, 635–40.

189   the one large, formal reception: Ibid., I, 668–70.
190   "What about rations": Telegram, A. T. Morgan to Ames, May 11, 1874, MGP.
190   "Senate Committee reported": Telegram, H. R. Pease to Ames, May 5, 1874, MGP.
190   "Shipped 10,000 rations": Ames to Morgan, May 13, 1874, MGP.
191   "I do not imagine it will": Ames, ed., Chronicles, I, 695.
191   "I cannot say that the house": Ibid., I, 702.
191   "Your letter enclosing note": Ibid., II, 11.
191   "played croquet in Vicksburg": Adelbert Ames to Blanche Ames, November 14, 1874, Personal Correspondence, AA.
192   "If I know myself": Ames, ed., Chronicles, II, 63.
192   "remorselessly drank all my whiskey": Ibid., I, 695.
192   "stagnation": Ibid., II, 62.
192   500 armed white men: 43rd Cong., 2nd Sess., Vicksburgh Troubles, I–XVII.
193   "If it can be done": Morgan to Governor, Ames Manuscripts, MDAH.
193   "Do you want any men?": 43rd Cong., 2nd Sess., Vicksburgh Troubles, IX.
194   "I have tonight assumed control": Telegram, P. H. Sheridan to Ames, January 5, 1875, MGP.
194   "Our brothers in your section": Quoted in M1875, II, Documentary Evidence, 26.

CHAPTER 25

194   "This is a very hot day": Ames, ed., Chronicles, II, 156–57.
195   "I had a call from a lady": Ibid, II, 159–60.
196   "I had finished my letter to you": Ibid., II, 163–64.
197   "Domestic violence, in its most aggravated form": Telegram, Ames to U. S. Grant, September 7, 1875, MGP.
198   "Eight days have now passed": M1875, II, Documentary Evidence, 97–98.
200   "Today I issued a proclamation": Ames, ed., Chronicles, II, 166–67.
200   "I shall write you only a short letter": Ibid., II, 164.

CHAPTER 26

201   "Now, therefore, I, A.A.": Quoted in Wharton, Negro in Mississippi, 193.
201   "What impudence": Quoted in Aptheker, "Mississippi Reconstruction," 179.
201   "Ames is organizing a war": Quoted in Garner, Reconstruction in Mississippi, 383.
202   "Appeal after appeal": Quoted in M1875, II, Documentary Evidence, 163.
202   "Below we give a list": Quoted in 44th Cong., 2nd Sess., Mississippi, Testimony, 1004.

202   "VOTE THE NEGRO DOWN": Quoted in *M1875*, II, Documentary Evidence, 162.

203   "Much as we deplore bloodshed": Quoted in *M1875*, II, Documentary Evidence, 165.

203   "The same tactics that saved Vicksburg": Quoted in Wharton, *Negro in Mississippi*, 190.

203   "CARRY THE ELECTION": Quoted in 44th Cong., 2nd Sess., *Mississippi, Testimony*, 319.

203   "Try the rope": Quoted in *M1875*, II, Documentary Evidence, 165.

CHAPTER 27

204   Morgan slipped out of his place: Morgan, *Yazoo*, 475–77; *M1875*, II, 1758.

204   Human Hornet: Morgan, *Yazoo*, 179.

204   a small, wiry, nervous man: *M1875*, II, 1756; Morgan, *Yazoo*, 179.

204   "the rope-bearer": Wharton, *Negro in Mississippi*, 191.

204   "Dixon's Scouts": *M1875*, II, 1652.

204   "There ain't one of them fit": *M1875*, II, 1755–56.

204   Dixon pulled out his pistol: *M1875*, II, 1760–61.

205   "Peace prevails": *M1875*, I, 382.

205   "The whole public are tired out": Edwards Pierrepont to Governor Ames, September 14, 1875, MGP.

205   "Let the odium": Ames to Attorney-General Pierrepont, September 11, 1875, MGP.

205   messages poured into: *M1875*, I, 9–10, 44; II, Documentary Evidence, 22–23, 43, 49, 61–62, 77, 87, 105–6; Telegram, John Brown to Adelbert Ames, October 7, 1875, MGP.

205   Fifty men, armed with needle guns: *M1875*, II, Documentary Evidence, 84.

206   fired into the governor's mansion: *M1875*, I, 15–16; II, 1805.

206   Senator Alcorn personally showed up: *M1875*, I, 28.

206   "Profound peace": *M1875*, I, 385.

206   Morgan called off the expedition: *M1875*, II, 1782–83, 1803.

206   Caldwell's militiamen: Mississippi, *Impeachment of Adelbert Ames*, 131–32; Aptheker, "Mississippi Reconstruction," 181; Morgan, *Yazoo*, 481; Ames, ed., *Chronicles*, II, 215–17.

206   "I beg you most fully": Houston Burris to Ames, November 1, 1875, MGP.

206   "The democrats was in Macon town": *M1875*, II, Documentary Evidence, 73.

207   "We as republicans of state of Mississippi": William Canly to Governor Ames, October 9, 1875, MGP.

207   "It is impossible to have a fair election": Geo. K. Chase to Edwards Pierrepont, October 27, 1875, MGP.

207   "No matter if they are going to carry": *M1875*, II, 1807.

207   the 215 United States troops: 44th Cong., 1st Sess., *Distribution of Troops*, 2.

207   "prevent bloodshed": Ames, ed., *Chronicles*, II, 248.
207   "Through the terror caused": Ibid., II, 216–17.
208   "This morning I received the babies' photographs": Adelbert Ames to Blanche Ames, October 29, 1875, Personal Correspondence, AA.
208   "bravado": *M1875*, I, 11.
208   TO THE BRAVEST OF THE BRAVE: Morgan, *Yazoo*, 486.
208   the Democrats gained a majority: Wharton, *Negro in Mississippi*, 197.
208   they impeached the lieutenant governor: reprinted in Ames, ed., *Chronicles*, II, 312–50.
209   Blanche proposed that he offer to resign: Ibid., II, 355.

CHAPTER 28

209   In Washington, D. C., he eked out a living: *M1875*, II, 1762.
210   "I would like to make a statement": *M1875*, II, 1777–78.
212   "He omitted to inform the committee": *M1875*, I, lxi.
212   a colored man named W. H. Bell: *M1875*, I, 507–17.
213   "Not one of you shall cast your vote": *M1875*, II, 1027–30.
213   "massing and taking possession": *M1875*, II, 1097, 1101, 1107.
213   "just for rejoicing": *M1875*, II, 1054, 1064, 1079.
214   "Yes, sir; the niggers": *M1875*, II, 1805.
214   "Of course I shall give importance": Adelbert Ames to Blanche Ames, November 18, 1876, Personal Correspondence, AA.
214   gave an interview to a newspaperman: "Mississippi Democrats," *New York Times*, May 2, 1876, p. 1.
216   heard, too, from the widow of Senator Caldwell: *M1875*, I, 435–40.

CHAPTER 29

221   "I cannot tell you exactly how": "Copy of General Ferguson's Mississippi Letter," Martin Witherspoon Gary Papers, SCL. The quoted Latin proverb is the equivalent of "an iron fist in a velvet glove."
223   "Plan of Campaign": Notebook, n.d., Martin Witherspoon Gary Papers, SCL.
223   "ready to strike for white supremacy": Quoted in Zuczek, *State of Rebellion*, 145.
224   And there were the Tillman brothers: "My Childhood Days," Benjamin Ryan Tillman Papers, SCL.
224   Sweetwater Sabre Club: *Struggles of 1876*, 43.
225   "one ounce of fear": Ibid., 28.
225   "nothing but bloodshed": Ibid., 17.
225   "terrorizing the negroes": Ibid., 28.
225   young white rowdies: Testimony of Samuel J. Lee in South Carolina, *Evidence Taken by the Committee*, 707; deposition of Paris Williams, July 17, 1876, in *MFP*, 23.

226   "my father's street": Testimony of T. J. Butler in *SC1876*, I, 309.

226   "he has good reason to fear": Peace Recognizance, November 19, 1874, Trial Justice P. R. Rivers, Bundle 83, Miscellaneous Papers, Court of General Sessions (Aiken County): Indictments, SCDAH.

226   Company A of the Eighteenth Regiment: Testimony of R. B. Elliott in *SC1876*, II, 448–49.

227   gathered . . . to hear a reading of the Declaration of Independence: Testimony of Louis Schiller, *SC1876*, I, 145.

227   "Mr. Getzen, I do not know": Testimony of Dock Adams, *SC1876*, I, 35–36.

227   "It is the first time that he ever was": Testimony of John Williams, *SC1876*, I, 708.

228   The white men . . . reached for their pistols: *Struggles of 1876*, 16.

CHAPTER 30

228   "Where is Rivers?": Testimony of William Nelson in *SC1876*, II, 603.

229   some of them had pistols: Testimony of T. J. Butler and Henry Getzen, *SC1876*, II, 317, 332; deposition of William Nelson in *MFP*, 21.

229   "I have come here as counsel": Testimony of M. C. Butler in *SC1876*, II, 240.

229   "I am not Mr. Rivers's office boy": Testimony of William Nelson, *SC1876*, II, 603.

229   "take your feet off": Deposition of William Nelson, July 13, 1876, in *MFP*, 20.

230   "I reckon not": Testimony of William Nelson in *SC1876*, II, 604.

230   "see what would turn up": *Struggles of 1876*, 17.

230   Butler sent word back: Testimony of D. L. Adams in *SC1876*, I, 58; Report of Attorney General William Stone to Gov. D. H. Chamberlain, July 12, 1876, in *MFP*, 7–10; testimony of P. R. Rivers, ibid., 10–11; deposition of Augustus Robertson, ibid., 24–27; "Address to the People of the United States" by Robt. B. Elliott et al. July 12, 1876, ibid., 50–51.

230   "parleying any longer": Testimony of Samuel B. Spencer in *SC1876*, I, 710.

232   "Damn the governor": *SC1876*, I, 713.

232   "All men having carbines": *Struggles of 1876*, 18.

233   three rounds apiece: Testimony of D. L. Adams in *SC1876*, I, 50.

233   "Go to Augusta": Deposition of D. L. Adams in *MFP*, 18.

233   "There is some damned nigger": Depositions of D. L. Adams, William Nelson, Willis Redrick, Butler Edwards in *MFP*, 18, 21, 29, 31; testimony of William Nelson in *SC1876*, II, 604.

234   "Keep that till morning": Deposition of John Fryer in *MFP*, 28.

234   "He'll chief no more": Deposition of Judge Blunt, *MFP*, 12.

234   "By God, he is looking at the moon": Testimony of Samuel B. Spencer in *SC1876*, I, 712.

235   "meanest characters": *Struggles of 1876*, 23–24.

235   "Mr. Getzen, do what you can": Deposition of John Fryer in *MFP*, 28.
235   "Turn around you yellow": Deposition of Pompey Curry, *MFP*, 13.
235   "By God, if you do that": Deposition of Butler Edwards, *MFP*, 32.
235   "All you niggers": deposition of Willis Redrick, *MFP*, 30.
236   FIVE DOLLAR FINE: *Struggles of 1876*, 26.
236   "young Meriwether": Ibid., 24–25.
236   "By God, we've killed": Testimony of Samuel B. Spencer in *SC1876*, I, 712.
237   "We've put a quietus": Ibid.
237   "By God, we'll carry": Testimony of D. L. Adams in *SC1876*, I, 72.
237   "This is the beginning": Ibid.

CHAPTER 31

237   "low Jew": *Struggles of 1876*, 23.
237   Schiller had been through several battles: Compiled military service record
       of Louis Schiller, Co. C, 1 South Carolina Cav. (Confederate), RG 109,
       NA.
238   hid out in Davis Lepfeld's house: Testimony of Louis Schiller in *SC1876*,
       I, 150–53.
238   Nelson had pushed aside the boards: Deposition of William Nelson in
       MFP, 21–22; testimony of William Nelson in *SC1876*, II, 605.
239   Dock Adams made it from his hiding place: Testimony of D. L. Adams
       in *SC1876*, I, 46–47.
239   "In those Southern States": *Congressional Record*, 44th Cong., 1st Sess.,
       4709 (July 18, 1876).
241   "so-called attorney general": M. C. Butler to the Editors, *Journal of Com-
       merce*, July 16, 1876, reprinted in *MFP*, 36.
241   "Some parties unknown to me": Statement of M. C. Butler to Editors,
       Columbia Register, in *MFP*, 35.
241   "a class of people": Testimony of M. C. Butler in *SC1876*, II, 244.
241   "a copper-colored negro": *MFP*, 37.
241   "This collision was the culmination": *MFP*, 35.
242   "Allow me to call your attention": "The Hamburg (S.C.) Massacre," *New
       York Times*, July 19, 1876, p. 4.
242   Rivers . . . issued arrest warrants: "The Hamburg Matter," *Augusta
       Chronicle and Sentinel*, August 2, 1876.
242   "The Hamburg 'bloody-shirt'": *Aiken Courier-Journal*, July 29, 1876, p. 5.
243   "like a wise and prudent man": *Struggles of 1876*, 33.
243   move for a habeas corpus hearing: Writ of Habeas Corpus, *The State vs.
       R J Butler, Thos Butler, Henry Getzen, A P Butler et al*, Filed 10 August
       1876, Bundle 89, Court of General Sessions (Aiken County): Indict-
       ments, SCDAH.
243   "bloody shirts": Ibid., 34–36.
244   "well-conditioned, mettlesome steeds": "The Hamburg Riot Cases,"
       Aiken Courier-Journal, August 12, 1876, p. 1.

244 "to kill out the whites": "The Truth About Hamburg," *Charleston News and Courier*, August 12, 1876, p. 1; "The Hamburg Cases," ibid., August 11, 1876, p. 1; "Suspiciously Broad Denials," *New York Times*, August 14, 1876, p. 2.

244 "and let these men get out of town": *Struggles of 1876*, 38; Order for Bail, The State against R J Butler, Thomas Butler, Henry Getzen et al., 10 August 1876, Court of General Sessions (Aiken County): Criminal Journals, SCDAH; Recognizance to Appear, The State Against Benj R Tillman, August 10, 1876, Bundle 89, Court of General Sessions (Aiken County): Indictments, ibid.

245 *Charleston News and Courier:* Reprinted in *SC1876*, III, 603–14.

245 Gary's challenge to the editor to a duel: Kantrowitz, *Ben Tillman*, 71.

245 "passion-stirring event at Hamburg": "Straight-Out Fight Gets Under Way," clipping of August 15, 1926, in Scrapbook, Alfred B. Williams Papers, SCL.

245 "Edgefield Plan": Simkins and Woody, *South Carolina During Reconstruction*, 500.

245 "not to desert their old general": A South Carolinian, "South Carolina Society," 673.

245 "division of time": Testimony of Governor D. H. Chamberlain in *SC1876*, II, 9–10; Speech of M. W. Gary, reprinted in ibid., III, 627–31; Simkins, "Election of 1876," 337.

245 The Rubicon Passed at Hamburg: "The State Convention," *Aiken Courier-Journal*, August 12, 1876, p. 1.

246 a continuation of the cases in Aiken: William Stone to D. H. Chamberlain. September 6, 1876, Governor Chamberlain: Letters Received, SCDAH.

246 "The recent occurrence at this place": Gardner to D. H. Chamberlain, August 25, 1876, Governor Chamberlain: Letters Received, SCDAH.

246 "Distinguished arrivals": *Aiken Courier-Journal*, August 17, 1876.

246 "grossly misrepresented": "A Southern Tildenite," *New York Times*, September 24, 1876, p. 7.

247 thousand federal troops: 44th Cong., 2nd Sess., *Report of Secretary of War*, I, 61–62, 68.

247 twenty thousand rifle club members: "List of Rifle Clubs in South Carolina," reprinted in *SC1876*, III, 499–509; Allen, *Governor Chamberlain's Administration*, 409–10.

247 This is Not a Rifle Club: "Troops in the South," *New York Times*, October 20, 1876, p. 5; "Oct '76 Critical for Carolina," clipping of December 12, 1926, in Scrapbook, Alfred B. Williams Papers, SCL.

247 torchlight procession: *A Boy's Recollections*, 12–13; Simkins, "Election of 1876," 335; Simkins and Woody, *South Carolina During Reconstruction*, 499.

CHAPTER 32

248 "Captain, I did not want": *Struggles of 1876*, 62.

248 Ben Tillman was at his post: Kantrowitz, *Ben Tillman*, 76; Simkins, "Election of 1876," 343.

248 **troops had not been able to do much:** Testimony of Capt. E. R. Kellogg in *SC1876*, II, 396; affidavit of Jesse Jones, November 9, 1876, Martin Witherspoon Gary Papers, DSCL.

248 **the Democrats' vote had exceeded by 3,000:** *SC1876*, I, i.

249 **"You will find inclosed":** Rivers to Chamberlain, January 22, 1877, Governor Chamberlain: Letters Received, SCDAH.

250 **"I am directed by His Excellency":** Chamberlain to P. R. Rivers, January 30, 1877, Governor Chamberlain: Letterbooks, SCDAH.

250 **"I see that the President":** Rivers to Chamberlain, April 6, 1877, Governor Chamberlain: Letters Received, SCDAH.

250 **"As to the effect of withdrawing the troops":** Chamberlain to Rivers, April 9, 1877, Governor Chamberlain: Letterbooks, SCDAH.

250–51 **the Democrats in the legislature expelled:** Gergel, "Wade Hampton," 9.

251 **On June 1 Hampton dismissed Rivers:** South Carolina, *Report of Joint Investigating Committee*, 17–18.

251 **revoked the town charter of Hamburg:** "An act to repeal an act entitled, 'An act to charter the Town of Hamburg approved February 28th 1871,'" No. 289, June 9, 1877, Acts of the General Assembly, SCDAH.

251 **"adroit and skillful maneuvering":** "History of a Crime," *Augusta Chronicle*, February 11, 1879, p. 1.

252 **Rivers was convicted:** Grand jury indictment, November 4, 1878, Attorney General's Office: Unarranged Records, 1878–79, SCDAH; State vs. S. J. Lee et al., September 6, 1878 and State vs. John Woolley et al., February 8 and 10, 1879, Court of General Sessions (Aiken County): Criminal Journal, ibid.; State vs. S. J. Lee et al., May 1885, Court of General Sessions (Orange County): Criminal Journal, ibid.

252 **"it would look very badly":** M. C. Butler to Dawson, April 20, 1879, Francis Warrington Dawson Papers, DSCL.

252 **quietly arranged two days later:** Le Roy Youmans to L. Northrop, April 22, 1879, ibid.

253 **"would not stand test":** Williamson, *After Slavery*, 414–15.

253 **all voters needed to reregister in May:** Tindall, "Campaign for Disfranchisement," 213–15.

253 **Sambo dialect:** "Cumberland Church Controversy," *Aiken Journal and Review*, July 1, 1885, reprinted in Vandervelde, *Aiken County*, 445–55.

253 **"little unpleasantness":** "A Point on the Hamburg Riots," *Augusta Chronicle*, July 22, 1885.

254 **Rivers died two years later:** "General Prince Rivers," *Aiken Review*, April 13, 1887, quoted in Vendervelde, *Aiken County*, 442–43.

CHAPTER 33

257 **Lamar fired him:** Morgan, *Yazoo*, xlvii; Lynch, *Reminiscences*, 314–19; Current, *Terrible Carpetbaggers*, 409–10.

257 **"a murderer, a gambler, a bully":** "Proceedings of the Democratic Mass

Meeting Held in Yazoo City, Miss., August 15 '79," reprinted in Morgan, *Yazoo*, 491.

257 "as a bribe to have the ballot-boxes": Morgan, *Yazoo*, 493.

258 "*no* man is fit to govern": Ibid., xlix.

258 "Bert, how can there be": Current, *Terrible Carpetbaggers*, 411.

258 "This is an unusual case": Ibid., 412.

259 "the happiest man on the top o'Earth": Morgan, *Yazoo*, xlix.

259 "left their work less than half done": Morgan to William Lloyd Garrison II, March 25, 1907, Garrison Family Papers, SSC.

260 "Would you have me marry": Morgan, *Yazoo*, 511–12.

260–61 Armes . . . paid a call on Colonel Custer: Johnson, *Custer, Reno, Merrill*, 11–12.

261 Merrill wrote a furious rejoinder: "Major Merrill's Defense," *New York Times*, April 28, 1876, p. 5.

261 "Maj Merrill was never a gentleman": M. A. Reno to G. A. Armes, November 25, 1885, Personnel File of Lewis Merrill, RG 94, NA.

261 "there is a little strategy": Armes to Secretary of War, November 17, 1885, ibid.

262 "Deference to the authority": Merrill to Adjutant General, September 10, 1885, ibid.

262 got the president to withdraw the nomination: "Major Merrill's Southern Foes," *New York Times*, February 18, 1886, p. 1.

262 "legal rights": Merrill to the President, June 9, 1886, Personnel File of Lewis Merrill, RG 94, NA.

262 to get out of paying: Hatfield & Sons to Merrill, September 1885, ibid.; report of Major George B. Davis, December 6, 1894, ibid.

263 "They were cheering you": Piston, *Lee's Tarnished Lieutenant*, 163.

263 "renegade": Ibid., 148.

263 "Everywhere except in the South": Ibid., 166.

264 "My arm is paralyzed": Ibid., 153.

CHAPTER 34

264 "military dude factory": Katrowitz, *Ben Tillman*, 118–19.

264 "a solid front to all comers": Ibid., 125.

266 "tasted blood": Ibid., 259.

266 "warmed into life again": *Speech of Tillman: Suffrage*, 4, 22–24.

267 "no conception of the word": Kantrowitz, *Ben Tillman*, 220.

267 "Sir, it is no secret": Wharton, *Negro in Mississippi*, 206.

268 "The old men of the present generation": Ibid., 207.

268 "My 'understanding' ": Kantrowitz, *Ben Tillman*, 226.

268 crimes . . . would lead to permanent disfranchisement: Tindall, "Question of Race," 287.

268 "Within thirty years": Tourgée, "South as Field for Fiction," 404–5.

269 "The dashing Confederate cavalier": Ibid., 408.

269 "were merely players": Tourgée, "Renaissance of Nationalism," 6.

269 "oratorical nonsense": Blight, *Race and Reunion*, 297–99.
270 "the most sacred rights": McPherson, "Southern Textbook Crusade," 67–68, 72.
270 "self-protection against outrages": Ibid., 69.
271 "From early colonial times": *A Mississippi View*, 4–8, 20–21.
272 "is only a shadow": Tourgée, "South as Field for Fiction," 409.

CHAPTER 35

273 "You have been extremely unfortunate": Ames to Benjamin Andrews, May 24, 1895, Ames Manuscripts, MDAH.
274 "give the statement of each side": Andrews to Ames, October 20, 1895, ibid.
274 "The northern men in Mississippi": Ames to Andrews, February 29, 1896, ibid.
275 Another young historian: James W. Garner to Ames, December 4, 1899, Professional Correspondence, James W. Garner, AA.
275 "it seemed to me I had a Mission": Ames to Jas. W. Garner, January 17, 1900, Garner Manuscripts, MDAH.
276 "dangerous experiment": Garner, *Reconstruction in Mississippi*, 353.
276 "frightful experiment": Chamberlain, "Reconstruction in South Carolina," 475–76, 481, 484.
276 "as illogical as they are immoral": Chamberlain, "Reconstruction and the Negro," 172.
277 the Democratic state treasurer: Lynch, *Facts of Reconstruction*, 165–68.
277 "I have read with much interest": Ames to Lynch, April 15, 1914, Professional Correspondence, John R. Lynch, AA.
278 "In reply to your courteous note": Ames to Rowland, March 20, 1929, Ames Manuscripts, MDAH.

CHAPTER 36

279 Sodom and Gomorrah: McElwin, *Travels in the South*, 13.
279 hauled Schiller off to Aiken: Louis Schiller, June 21, 1893, Bundle 76, Court of General Sessions (Aiken County): Indictments, SCDAH.
279 Sibley Building burned: "Historic Old Building in Hamburg Destroyed by Fire; Scene of Riot 50 Years Ago," *Augusta Chronicle*, January 22, 1928.
280 unveil a memorial to the dead: "To Unveil Shaft to M'kie Meriwether," *Augusta Chronicle*, February 15, 1916; "Monument to be Unveiled at 3 p.m.," ibid., February 16, 1916; "Unveil Shaft to M'kie Meriwether," ibid., February 17, 1916.
280 "perished for the cause of liberty": *White Man's Revolution*, 1–4.
281 "to the only resident of Hamburg": North Augusta, *2005 Comprehensive Plan*, ch.7, p. 9.

References

MANUSCRIPT COLLECTIONS

Duke University Special Collections Library, Durham, N.C. (DSCL)
   Armistead Burt
   Francis Warrington Dawson
   Martin Witherspoon Gary
   James Longstreet
Mississippi Department of Archives and History, Jackson, Miss. (MDAH)
   Manuscripts
      Ames (Adelbert)
      Garner (James W.)
   State Government Records
      Mississippi Governor (1874–1876: Ames): Correspondence and Papers
National Archives Building, Washington, D.C. (NA)
   RG 29, Bureau of the Census, 1790–1996
      Ninth Census of the United States, 1870, Microcopy 593
   RG 94, Adjutant General's Office, 1780s–1917
      Letters Received by the Office of the Adjutant General
         Microcopy 619, 1861–1870
         Microcopy 666, 1871–1880
      Personnel File of Lewis Merrill (M103 CB1863), Letters Received by
         the Commission Branch, Microcopy 1064, roll 38
   RG 109, War Department Collection of Confederate Records
      Compiled Service Records of Confederate Soldiers
   RG 393, United States Army Continental Commands, 1821–1920 (Part V,
      Military Installations)
      Post of Yorkville, S.C. (532)
Sophia Smith Collection, Smith College, Northampton, Mass. (SSC)
   Ames Family
   Garrison Family
South Carolina Department of Archives and History, Columbia, S.C. (SCDAH)
   Attorney General's Office

Court of General Sessions (Aiken County)
Court of General Sessions (Orange County)
General Assembly
Gov. Daniel H. Chamberlain
Gov. Wade Hampton
Gov. Robert K. Scott
South Caroliniana Library, University of South Carolina, Columbia, S.C. (SCL)
Martin Witherspoon Gary
John Adams Leland
Benjamin Ryan Tillman
Alfred B. Williams
Southwest Collection, Texas Tech University, Lubbock, Tex.
Hugh Lenox Scott Family
University of Virginia Special Collections Library, Charlottesville, Va. (VSCL)
Amos T. Akerman

GOVERNMENT PUBLICATIONS

Mississippi. Legislature. House. *Testimony in the Impeachment of Adelbert Ames as Governor of Mississippi.* Jackson, Miss.: Power & Barksdale, 1877.
North Augusta. *City of North Augusta 2005 Comprehensive Plan.* December 19, 2005.
South Carolina. General Assembly. *Acts and Joint Resolutions of the General Assembly.* Columbia, S.C.
————. *Evidence Taken by the Committee of Investigation of the Third Congressional District . . . 1868–'69.* Columbia, S.C.: J. W. Denny, printer to the state, 1870.
————. *Journal of the Convention of the People of South Carolina, held in Columbia, S.C., September 1865.* Columbia, S.C.: J. A. Selby, printer to the convention, 1865.
————. *Report of the Joint Investigating Committee on Public Frauds and Election of Hon. J. J. Patterson to the United States Senate. Miscellaneous Reports.* Columbia, S.C.: Calvo & Patton, State Printers, 1878.
U. S. Congress. Joint Select Committee to Inquire into the Condition of Affairs in the Late Insurrectionary States. *The Ku Klux Conspiracy. Testimony Taken by the Joint Select Committee to Inquire into the Condition of Affairs in the Late Insurrectionary States.* Washington, D.C.: GPO, 1872. Reprint. New York: AMS Press, 1968.
————. U.S. Congressional Serial Set.
40th Congress, 3rd Session
Condition of Affairs in Mississippi. Evidence taken by the Committee on Reconstruction. House Misc. Doc. No. 53.
42nd Congress, 3rd Session
Report of the Secretary of War. House Ex. Doc. No. 1, Pt. 2.

43rd Congress, 2nd Session

Message of the President of the United States communicating . . . information in relation to an alleged interference in the organization of the General Assembly of the State of Louisiana. Senate Ex. Doc. No. 13.

Letter from the Secretary of War transmitting . . . copies of correspondence relative to certain disorders in the State of Louisiana. Senate Ex. Doc. No. 17.

Condition of the South. House Report No. 261.

Vicksburgh Troubles. House Report No. 265.

44th Congress, 1st Session

Message from the President of the United States communicating . . . information in relation to the slaughter of American citizens at Hamburgh, S.C. Senate Ex. Doc. No. 85.

Mississippi in 1875. Report of the Select Committee to Inquire into the Mississippi Election of 1875, with the Testimony and Documentary Evidence. Senate Report No. 527.

Distribution of United States Troops. Letter from the Chief Clerk of the War Department transmitting a statement showing the distribution of United States troops in the States of Alabama, Mississippi, Arkansas, and Louisiana on December 1, 1875. House Ex. Doc. No. 47.

44th Congress, 2nd Session

Mississippi. Testimony as to the Denial of Elective Franchise in Mississippi at the Elections of 1875 and 1876. Senate Misc. Doc. No. 45.

South Carolina in 1876. Testimony as to the Denial of the Elective Franchise in South Carolina at the Elections of 1875 and 1876. Senate Misc. Doc. No. 48.

Report of the Secretary of War. House Ex. Doc. No. 1, Pt. 2.

U.S. War Department. *The War of the Rebellion: a compilation of the official records of the Union and Confederate armies.* Washington, D.C.: GPO, 1880–1900.

PAMPHLETS AND SPEECHES

Unless otherwise noted, the following publications (which include a number of rare and hard to find items) are in the South Caroliniana Library, University of South Carolina.

A Boy's Recollections of the Red Shirt Campaign of 1876 in South Carolina. Paper read before the Kosmos Club of Columbia, S.C., by W. W. Ball, January 21, 1911.

A Defence of Southern Slavery Against the Attacks of Henry Clay and Alx'r Campbell. By a Southern Clergyman [Brookes, Iveson L.]. Hamburg, S.C.: Robinson and Carlisle, 1851. VSCL.

A Mississippi View of Race Relations in the South by Dunbar Rowland, read before the alumni association of the University of Mississippi, June 3rd, 1902. MDAH.

Proceedings of the Tax-payers' Convention of South Carolina, held at Columbia, beginning February 17, and ending February 20, 1874... Charleston, S.C.: News and Courier Job Presses, 1874.

The respectful remonstrance, on behalf of the white people of South Carolina, against the constitution of the late Convention of that state, now submitted to Congress for ratification. Columbia, S.C.: Phoenix Book and Job Power Press, 1868.

Speech of Hon. B. R. Tillman in the Constitutional Convention of South Carolina, on Thursday, October 31st, 1895: Suffrage. Columbia, S.C.: Charles A. Calvo, Jr., State printer, 1895.

The Struggles of 1876. Address delivered at the Red Shirt Reunion, Anderson, S.C., August 25th, 1909, by Senator B. R. Tillman.

The White Man's Revolution in South Carolina. Address delivered by D. S. Henderson at the unveiling of the M'Kie Merriwether Monument, North Augusta, South Carolina, February 16th, 1916.

NEWSPAPERS

Aiken (S.C.) Courier-Journal
Augusta (Ga.) Chronicle
Charleston (S.C.) News and Courier
Edgefield (S.C.) Advertiser
Hinds County (Miss.) Gazette
New York Times
Weekly Mississippi Pilot
Yorkville (S.C.) Enquirer

MEMOIRS AND CONTEMPORARY VIEWS

Allen, Walter. *Governor Chamberlain's Administration in South Carolina: A Chapter of Reconstruction in the Southern States.* 1888. Reprint. New York: Negro Universities Press, 1969.

Ames, Blanche Butler, ed. *Chronicles from the Nineteenth Century: Family Letters of Blanche Butler and Adelbert Ames.* 1957.

Chamberlain, Daniel H. "Reconstruction and the Negro." *North American Review* 128 (1879): 161–73.

———. "Reconstruction in South Carolina." *The Atlantic Monthly*, April 1901, 473–84.

Dennett, John Richard. *The South As It Is, 1865–1866.* Reprint. New York: Compass Books, 1967.

Goodell, William. *The American Slave Code in Theory and Practice.* New York: American and Foreign Anti-Slavery Society, 1853.

Higginson, Thomas Wentworth. *Army Life in a Black Regiment.* 1869. Reprint. Boston: Beacon Press, 1962.

Jones, J. William. *Personal Reminiscences of General Robert E. Lee.* 1875. Reprint. Richmond, Va.: United States Historical Society Press, 1989.

Longstreet, James. *From Manassas to Appomattox: Memoirs of the Civil War in America.* Philadelphia: Lippincott, 1896.

Lynch, John R. *The Facts of Reconstruction.* 1913. Reprint. Indianapolis: Bobbs-Merrill, 1970.

———. *Reminiscences of an Active Life.* Chicago: University of Chicago Press, 1970.

McElwin, Henry. *Travels in the South.* 1886.

McNeil, John. "Retaliation in Missouri." *Century Magazine* 38 (1889): 475–76.

Morgan, Albert T. *Yazoo; or, On the Picket Line of Freedom in the South: A Personal Narrative.* 1884. Reprint. Columbia: University of South Carolina Press, 2000.

Pendleton, W. N. "Personal Recollections of General Lee." *Southern Magazine* 15 (1874): 603–36.

Post, Louis F. "A 'Carpetbagger' in South Carolina." *Journal of Negro History* 10 (1925): 10–79.

Redpath, James ["Uncle James"]. "Eye and Ear Notes: May-Day in Charleston, S.C." *The Youth's Companion,* June 1, 1865, 86.

———. "Eye and Ear Notes: May-Day in Charleston Again." *The Youth's Companion,* June 8, 1865, 90.

A South Carolinian [Belton O'Neall Townsend]. "South Carolina Morals." *The Atlantic Monthly,* April 1877, 467–75.

——— "South Carolina Society." *The Atlantic Monthly,* June 1877, 670–84.

Sterling, Dorothy, ed. *We Are Your Sisters: Black Women in the Nineteenth Century.* New York: Norton, 1984.

Tourgée, Albion W. "The Renaissance of Nationalism." *North American Review* 144 (1887): 1–11.

———. "The South as a Field for Fiction." *Forum* (New York) 6 (1888): 404–13.

SECONDARY SOURCES: BOOKS AND ARTICLES

Ames, Blanche Ames. *Adelbert Ames: Broken Oaths and Reconstruction in Mississippi.* New York: Argosy-Antiquarian, 1964.

Aptheker, Herbert. "South Carolina Negro Conventions, 1865." *Journal of Negro History* 31 (1946): 91–97.

———. "Mississippi Reconstruction and the Negro Leader Charles Caldwell." In *To Be Free: Pioneering Studies in Afro-American History.* 1948. Reprint. New York: Citadel Press, 1991.

Blight, David W. *Race and Reunion: The Civil War in American Memory.* Cambridge: Harvard University Press, 2001.

Buice, A. David. "The Military Career of Adelbert Ames." *Southern Quarterly* 2 (1964): 236–46.

Burton, Orville Vernon. "The Rise and Fall of Afro-American Town Life." In *Toward a New South*, edited by Orville Vernon Burton and Robert C. McMath. Westport, Conn.: Greenwood Press, 1988.

Chapman, John Abney. *History of Edgefield County from the Earliest Settlement to 1897*. Newberry, S.C., 1897.

Connelly, Thomas L., and Barbara L. Bellows. *God and General Longstreet: The Lost Cause and the Southern Mind*. Baton Rouge: Louisiana State University Press, 1982.

Current, Richard N. *Those Terrible Carpetbaggers: A Reinterpretation*. New York: Oxford University Press, 1988.

Dawson, Joseph G. *Army Generals and Reconstruction: Louisiana, 1862–1877*. Baton Rouge: Louisiana State University Press, 1982.

Foner, Eric. *Reconstruction: America's Unfinished Revolution, 1863–1877*. New York: Harper & Row, 1988.

———. *Freedom's Lawmakers: A Directory of Black Officeholders during Reconstruction*. New York: Oxford University Press, 1993.

Gallagher, Gary. *Lee and His Generals in War and Memory*. Baton Rouge: Louisiana State University Press, 1998.

Garner, James W. *Reconstruction in Mississippi*. 1901. Reprint. Baton Rouge: Louisiana State University Press, 1969.

Gergel, Richard Mark. "Wade Hampton and the Rise of One-Party Racial Orthodoxy in South Carolina." *Proceedings of the South Carolina Historical Association* 1977, 5–16.

Holt, Thomas. *Black Over White: Negro Political Leadership in South Carolina during Reconstruction*. Urbana: University of Illinois Press, 1977.

Horn, Stanley F. *Invisible Empire: The Story of the Ku Klux Klan, 1866–1871*. Boston: Houghton Mifflin, 1939.

Johnson, Barry C. *Custer, Reno, Merrill and the Lauffer Case: Some Warfare in "The Fighting Seventh."* London: The English Westerners' Society, 1971.

Kantrowitz, Stephen. *Ben Tillman & the Reconstruction of White Supremacy*. Chapel Hill: University of North Carolina Press, 2000.

Landry, Stuart O. *The Battle of Liberty Place and the Overthrow of Carpet-Bag Rule in New Orleans*. New Orleans: Pelican Publication Company, 1955.

McFeely, William S. "Amos T. Akerman: The Lawyer and Racial Justice." In *Region, Race, and Reconstruction: Essays in Honor of C. Vann Woodward*. New York: Oxford University Press, 1982.

McPherson, James M. *Battle Cry of Freedom*. New York: Oxford University Press, 1988.

———. "Long-Legged Yankee Lies: The Southern Textbook Crusade." In *The Memory of the Civil War in American Culture*, edited by Alice Fahs and Joan Waugh. Chapel Hill: University of North Carolina Press, 2004.

Piston, William Garret. *Lee's Tarnished Lieutenant: James Longstreet and His Place in Southern History*. Athens: University of Georgia Press, 1987.

Puckett, R. P. "Reconstruction in Monroe County." *Publications of the Mississippi Historical Society* 11 (1910): 103–61.

Pullen, John J. *The 20th Maine.* New York: Fawcett, 1962.

Richter, William L. "James Longstreet: From Rebel to Scalawag." *Louisiana History* 11 (1970): 215–30.

Rosen, Robert N. *Confederate Charleston: An Illustrated History of the City and the People during the Civil War.* Columbia: University of South Carolina Press, 1994.

Simkins, Francis B. "The Election of 1876 in South Carolina." Parts 1, 2. *South Atlantic Quarterly* 21 (1922): 225–40, 335–51.

Simkins, Francis B., and Robert H. Woody. *South Carolina During Reconstruction.* Chapel Hill: University of North Carolina Press, 1932.

Singletary, Otis. *Negro Militia and Reconstruction.* 1957. Reprint. New York: McGraw-Hill, 1963.

Taylor, Rosser H. "Hamburg: An Experiment in Town Promotion." *North Carolina Historical Review* 11 (January 1934): 20–38.

Tindall, George B. "The Campaign for the Disfranchisement of Negroes in South Carolina." *Journal of Southern History* 15 (1949): 212–34.

———. "The Question of Race in the South Carolina Constitutional Convention of 1895." *Journal of Negro History* 37 (1952): 277–303.

Trelease, Allen W. *White Terror: The Ku Klux Klan Conspiracy and Southern Reconstruction.* Baton Rouge: Louisiana State University Press, 1971.

Underwood, James Lowell. "African American Founding Fathers: The Making of the South Carolina Constitution of 1868." In *At Freedom's Door: African American Founding Fathers and Lawyers in Reconstruction South Carolina,* edited by James Lowell Underwood and W. Lewis Burke, Jr. Columbia: University of South Carolina Press, 2000.

Vandervelde, Isabel. *Aiken County: The Only South Carolina County Founded During Reconstruction.* Spartanburg, S.C.: The Reprint Co., 1999.

West, Jerry L. *The Reconstruction Ku Klux Klan in York County, South Carolina, 1865–1877.* Jefferson, N.C.: McFarland, 2002.

Wharton, Vernon Lane. *The Negro in Mississippi, 1865–1890.* 1947. Reprint. New York: Harper & Row, 1965.

Williams, Lou Falkner. *The Great South Carolina Ku Klux Klan Trials, 1871–1872.* Athens: University of Georgia Press, 1996.

Williamson, Joel. *After Slavery: The Negro in South Carolina During Reconstruction, 1861–1877.* Chapel Hill: University of North Carolina Press, 1965.

Zuczek, Richard. *State of Rebellion: Reconstruction in South Carolina.* Columbia: University of South Carolina Press, 1996.

Index